GW00371194

MICHELIN GUIDE

TOKYO YOKOHAMA SHONAN 2012

RESTAURANTS & HOTELS

DEAR READER

We are delighted to present the 2012 edition of the MICHELIN Guide Tokyo Yokohama and Shonan.

With this guide we celebrate our 5th anniversary in Japan. Our first guide to Tokyo featured 150 establishments – in this edition that figure has almost doubled as we continue to include only establishments that we consider worthy of at least one star. Tokyo remains the city with the most Michelin stars in the world.

The success of our previous guides made quite an impact. The quality of the restaurants in the Kanto region is constantly improving and we have continued to seek out those establishments offering the finest cooking.

We are pleased to announce that we have expanded our coverage of the region and now include Shonan for the first time, making this one of the most exciting gastronomic areas in the world.

We have highlighted those restaurants that are new to the guide (NEW) as well as those that have been newly promoted (). Our inspectors have also taken budgetary factors into account and so look out for the symbol which points out those establishments in which one can eat for 5,000 yen or less.

As part of our meticulous and confidential evaluation process, Michelin inspectors make many anonymous visits in order to fully reflect the richness and diversity of the hotel and restaurant scene. The inspectors are the eyes and ears of our readers and thus their anonymity is key to ensuring that they receive the same treatment as any other guest.

This guide is renewed and revised each year and we are committed to providing the most up to date information to ensure the success

of your dining experience. This is why only this year's edition of the guide is worthy of your complete trust.

The decision to award a star is a collective one, based on the consensus of all the inspectors who have visited that establishment. When awarding stars, we consider a number of factors, including the quality of the ingredients, the technical skill and flair that has gone into their preparation, the clarity of flavours and the balance of the menu. Just as important is the ability to produce excellent cooking time and again. We make as many visits as we need to be sure of the quality and consistency of each establishment.

Our company's founders, Édouard and André Michelin, published the first MICHELIN Guide in France in 1900, to provide motorists with practical information about where to service and repair their cars, find accommodation or enjoy a good meal.
The star rating system for outstanding cooking was introduced in 1926. Today, these awards are the benchmark of reliability and excellence in over twenty European countries, the USA, Japan, Hong Kong and Macau.

We are always very interested to hear what you, our readers, think. Your opinions and suggestions matter greatly to us and help shape the guide, so please get in touch.

Email us at nmt.michelinguide@jp.michelin.com

We wish you the very best in your hotel, ryokan and dining experiences in Tokyo, Yokohama and Shonan.

Bon appétit!

THE MICHELIN GUIDE'S COMMITMENTS

"This volume was created at the turn of the century and will last at least as long".

This foreword to the very first edition of the MICHELIN Guide, written in 1900, has become famous over the years and the guide has lived up to the prediction. It is read across the world and the key to its popularity is the consistency of its commitment to its readers, which is based on the following promises:

Anonymous inspections:

Our inspectors make regular and anonymous visits to restaurants and hotels to gauge the quality of products and services offered to an ordinary customer. They settle their own bill and may then introduce themselves and ask for more information about the establishment. Our readers' comments are also a valuable source of information, which we can then follow up with another visit of our own.

Independence:

Our choice of establishments is a completely independent one, made for the benefit of our readers alone. The decisions to be taken are discussed around the table by the inspectors and the editor. Inclusion in the guide is completely free of charge.

Selection and choice:
Our guide offers a selection of the best restaurants and hotels. This is only possible because all the inspectors rigorously apply the same methods.

Annual updates:
All the practical information, the classifications and awards are revised and updated every single year to give the most reliable information possible.

Consistency:
The criteria for the classifications are the same in every country covered by the MICHELIN Guide.

...And our aim:
To do everything possible to make travel, holidays and eating out a pleasure, as part of Michelin's ongoing commitment to improving travel and mobility.

CONTENTS

THE MICHELIN GUIDE OVER THE YEARS

Today the MICHELIN Guide and its famous red cover are known around the world. But who really knows the story behind this «travellers' bible» that has served people in many countries for many years? After winning over Europe and the United States, Bibendum – «The Michelin Man» – is now in Asia, and will relate the fantastic adventure that started in France, a long time ago...

The first steps

Everything began one fine day in 1900, when André and Édouard Michelin published a guide to be offered free of charge to motorists. It included information to help these pioneers (barely 3,500 automobiles were on the road) to travel around France: garages, town plans, sights to see, lodgings and restaurants, and so forth. The guide was an instant success and became the indispensable companion of all drivers and travellers, bar none.

On the strength of this success and driven on by the development of the motor car, *the Manufacture française* extended the scope of «the little book with the Ared cover» to other European countries beginning in 1904, and a few years later (1908) published an adaptation of the *Guide France* in English.

A star is born

As of 1920, the guide was no longer free, but marketed for sale. Little by little, the practical information gave way to a wider selection of hotels and restaurants. The mysterious, daunting «Michelin inspector» was not in the picture at first. Rather, it was touring clubs and readers that contributed to the discerning selection of establishments.

The goal of officially identifying places «where one dines well» was materialized in 1926 by the *Étoile de Bonne Table* – the first Michelin star – soon to be followed by two and three-star establishments (1931 for the provinces and 1933 for Paris). The guide thus clearly focused on gastronomy and the quest for good restaurants became its real driving force.

In step with the times

During the Second World War, the guide did not appear. The post-war edition of 1945 did not use star ratings, which were applied again as of 1951, when conditions were more settled. Ever more successful, the guide was to cover all of Western Europe as of the 1960s. In 1982, *Main Cities of Europe* was published in English, marking Michelin's decidedly European dimension.

100 years young...

2000 was a winning year for Michelin: the guide celebrated its 100th anniversary and The Michelin Man was voted best corporate logo of the century!

More dynamic than ever, the «little red guide» took on new challenges and set off for the United States. The MICHELIN Guide New York not only lived up to expectations, but the first edition was awarded the prize for «Best Restaurant Guide in the World».

The newest challenge: discovering the best restaurants in Asia. In autumn 2007, MICHELIN Tokyo Guide was published with a great response. Tokyo is well known as one of the world's famous capitals of fine cuisine.

Twenty countries covered in Europe, three guides to US cities, one guide to Hong Kong and Macau and three guides to Japan (Kyoto Osaka Kobe Nara, Tokyo Yokohama Shonan and Bonnes Petites Tables) : in the third millennium, the MICHELIN Guide confirms its international credentials. Just a glint in the eyes of the founders more than a century ago, The Michelin Man is now an international star to be proud of, carrying the Michelin tradition into the 21st century.

HOW TO USE THIS GUIDE – RESTAURANT

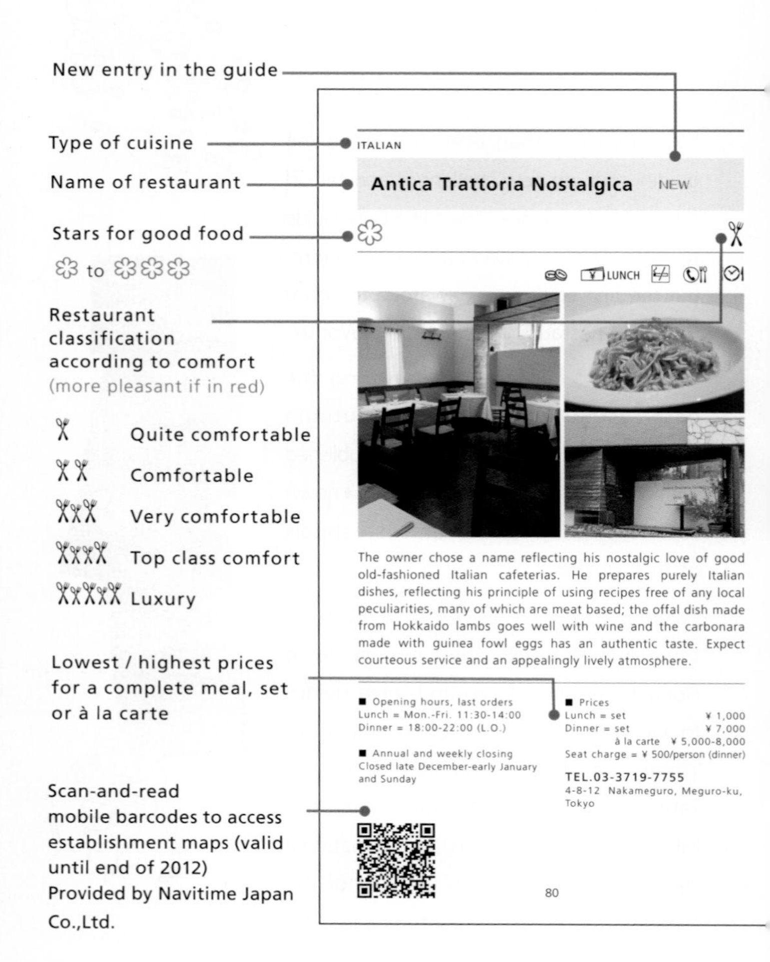
New entry in the guide
Type of cuisine
Name of restaurant
Stars for good food
to
Restaurant classification according to comfort
(more pleasant if in red)
Quite comfortable
Comfortable
Very comfortable
Top class comfort
Luxury
Lowest / highest prices for a complete meal, set or à la carte
Scan-and-read mobile barcodes to access establishment maps (valid until end of 2012)
Provided by Navitime Japan Co.,Ltd.
ITALIAN
Antica Trattoria Nostalgica NEW
LUNCH
The owner chose a name reflecting his nostalgic love of good old-fashioned Italian cafeterias. He prepares purely Italian dishes, reflecting his principle of using recipes free of any local peculiarities, many of which are meat based; the offal dish made from Hokkaido lambs goes well with wine and the carbonara made with guinea fowl eggs has an authentic taste. Expect courteous service and an appealingly lively atmosphere.
■ Opening hours, last orders
Lunch = Mon.-Fri. 11:30-14:00
Dinner = 18:00-22:00 (L.O.)
■ Annual and weekly closing
Closed late December-early January and Sunday
■ Prices
Lunch = set ¥ 1,000
Dinner = set ¥ 7,000
à la carte ¥ 5,000-8,000
Seat charge = ¥ 500/person (dinner)
TEL.03-3719-7755
4-8-12 Nakameguro, Meguro-ku, Tokyo
80

JAPANESE

Hifumian
一二三庵

The building dates from the late Taisho period and was home to a *Noh* performer. There are just two rooms: Western-style on the 1st floor, Japanese-style on the 2nd. Takamitsu Aihara opened Hifumian after training in Osaka, Kobe and Tokyo. The lightly roasted sea bass with *misansho* pepper and white *miso* is highly recommended. Just two groups, by reservation only, are served at each meal and only set courses are offered.

■ Opening hours, last orders
Lunch = 12:00-15:00 L.O.14:00
Dinner = 18:00-23:00 L.O.20:00

■ Annual and weekly closing
Closed Golden week, mid-August and late December-early January

■ Price
Lunch = set ¥ 10,500-15,750
Dinner = set ¥ 15,750-21,000
Service charge = 10%

TEL. 03-5832-8677
4-2-18 Sendagi, Bunkyo-ku, Tokyo
www.hifumi-an.com

131

Restaurant promoted from 1 to 2 stars or 2 to 3 stars

Restaurant symbols

- lunch and/or dinner for ¥ 5,000 and less
- Cash only
- LUNCH Cash only at lunch
- Wheelchair access
- Garden
- Shoes must be removed
- Terrace dining
- No smoking area
- Completely no smoking restaurant
- Interesting view
- Car park
- 25 Private room with maximum capacity
- Counter restaurant
- Reservations required
- Reservations not accepted
- Open Sunday
- Late dining
- Interesting wine list
- Interesting sake list

HOW TO USE THIS GUIDE – RYOKAN

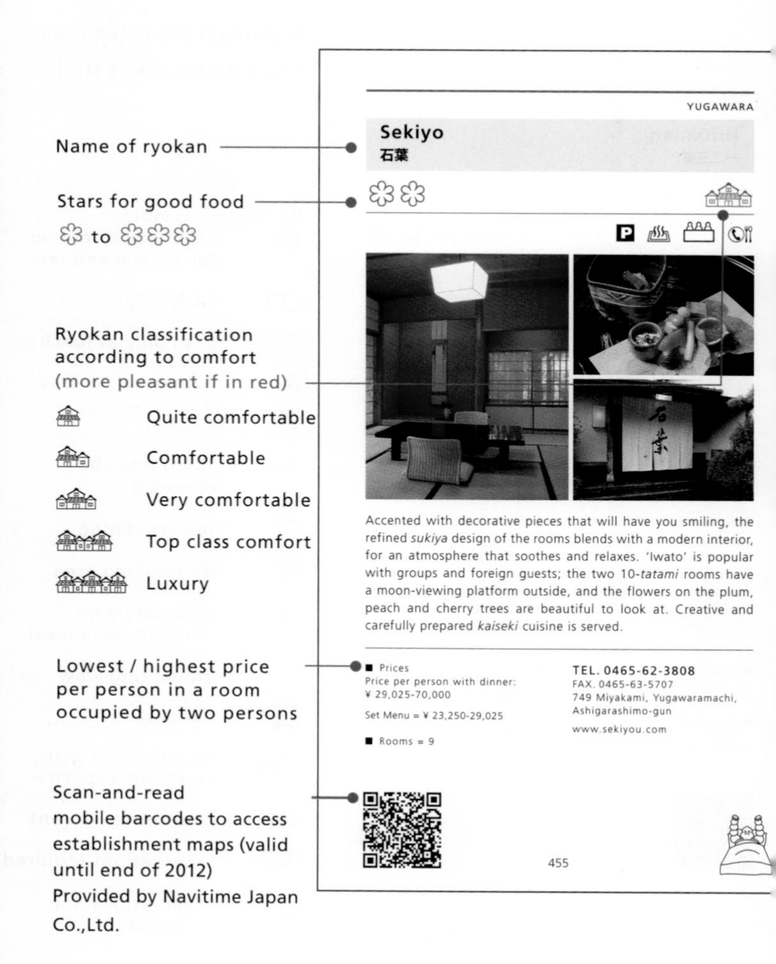

Name of ryokan
Stars for good food
to
Ryokan classification according to comfort (more pleasant if in red)
Quite comfortable
Comfortable
Very comfortable
Top class comfort
Luxury
Lowest / highest price per person in a room occupied by two persons
Scan-and-read mobile barcodes to access establishment maps (valid until end of 2012) Provided by Navitime Japan Co.,Ltd.
YUGAWARA
Sekiyo
石葉
P
Accented with decorative pieces that will have you smiling, the refined sukiya design of the rooms blends with a modern interior, for an atmosphere that soothes and relaxes. 'Iwato' is popular with groups and foreign guests; the two 10-tatami rooms have a moon-viewing platform outside, and the flowers on the plum, peach and cherry trees are beautiful to look at. Creative and carefully prepared kaiseki cuisine is served.
■ Prices
Price per person with dinner: ¥ 29,025-70,000
Set Menu = ¥ 23,250-29,025
■ Rooms = 9
TEL. 0465-62-3808
FAX. 0465-63-5707
749 Miyakami, Yugawaramachi, Ashigarashimo-gun
www.sekiyou.com
455

New entry in the guide

KAMAKURA

Kaihin-so NEW
かいひん荘

Ryokan symbols

The western-style part of this beachfront inn, built in 1924 as a private residence, is a registered cultural property. On the 1st floor is the lobby and salon, and on the 2nd floor are 2 western-style rooms, 'Ran-no-ma' being the most popular. All rooms in the new building are Japanese-style, with alcoves; the 15-*tatami* 'Takenoma' looks out on the garden. A book by former Prime Minister Eisaku Sato is placed at the entrance.

■ Prices
Price per person with dinner:
¥ 18,900-36,750

Set Menu = ¥ 6,000-15,000

■ Rooms = 14

TEL. 0467-22-0960
FAX. 0467-25-6324
4-8-14 Yuigahama, Kamakura City
www.kaihinso.jp

452

- Cash only
- Garden
- Quiet ryokan
- With a view
- Car park
- Non smoking room
- Outdoor swimming pool
- Onsen
- Private bath
- Shared bath
- Reservations required
- Interesting wine list
- Interesting sake list

HOW TO USE THIS GUIDE – HOTEL

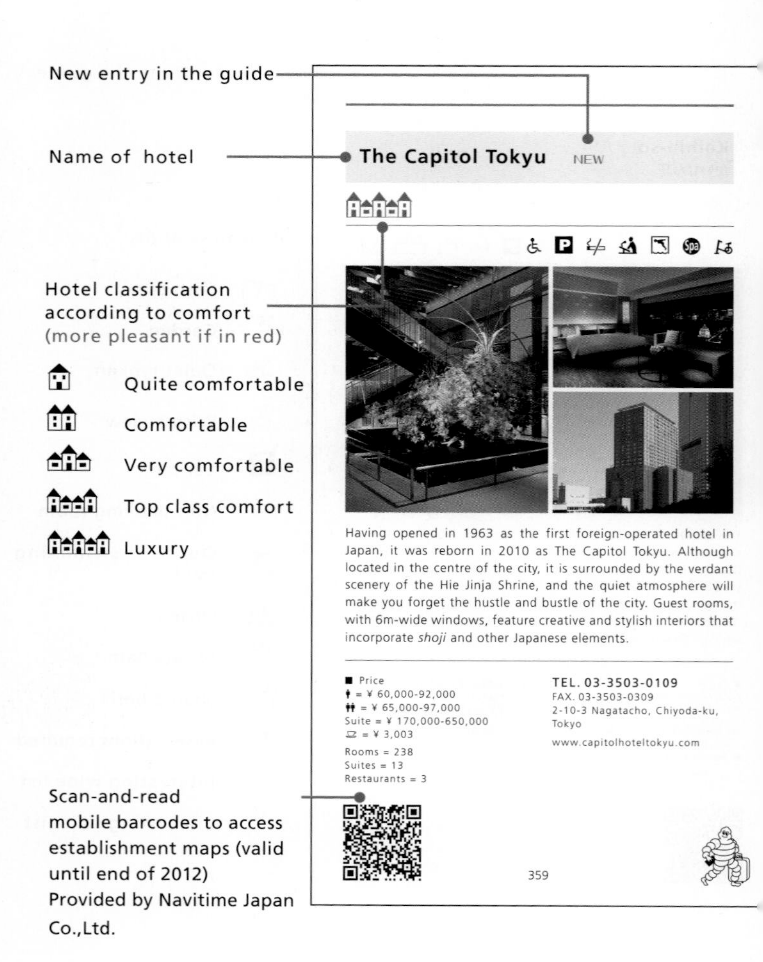
New entry in the guide
Name of hotel
Hotel classification
according to comfort
(more pleasant if in red)
Quite comfortable
Comfortable
Very comfortable
Top class comfort
Luxury
The Capitol Tokyu
NEW
Having opened in 1963 as the first foreign-operated hotel in Japan, it was reborn in 2010 as The Capitol Tokyu. Although located in the centre of the city, it is surrounded by the verdant scenery of the Hie Jinja Shrine, and the quiet atmosphere will make you forget the hustle and bustle of the city. Guest rooms, with 6m-wide windows, feature creative and stylish interiors that incorporate shoji and other Japanese elements.
Price
= ¥ 60,000-92,000
= ¥ 65,000-97,000
Suite = ¥ 170,000-650,000
= ¥ 3,003
Rooms = 238
Suites = 13
Restaurants = 3
TEL. 03-3503-0109
FAX. 03-3503-0309
2-10-3 Nagatacho, Chiyoda-ku, Tokyo
www.capitolhoteltokyu.com
359
Scan-and-read
mobile barcodes to access
establishment maps (valid
until end of 2012)
Provided by Navitime Japan
Co.,Ltd.

ANA Intercontinental

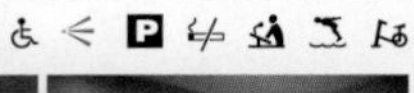

Opened in 1986, at the same time as Akasaka Ark Hills. Rooms are on the 7-35th floors; the front lobby is on the 2nd. Standard rooms are between 28 - 32m² and have a comfortable, chic feel. Those staying on the Club Intercontinental Floor have access to the lounge, which is the biggest in Japan. The three sides of the triangular-shaped hotel provide views of the Imperial Palace Outer Garden, Tokyo Tower and Roppongi Hills.

■ Price
single = ¥ 38,850-51,450
double = ¥ 38,850-51,450
Suite = ¥ 78,750-252,000
breakfast = ¥ 2,300
Service charge = 10%
Rooms = 801
Suites = 43
Restaurants = 7

TEL. 03–3505–1111
FAX. 03–3505–1155
1-12-33 Akasaka, Minato-ku, Tokyo
www.anaintercontinental-tokyo.jp

326

Hotel symbols

- Wheelchair access
- Garden
- Interesting view from bedrooms
- Car park
- No smoking bedrooms
- Conference rooms
- Indoor swimming pool
- Outdoor swimming pool
- Spa
- Fitness

The Michelin Adventure

It all started with rubber balls! This was the product made by a small company based in Clermont-Ferrand that André and Edouard Michelin inherited, back in 1880. The brothers quickly saw the potential for a new means of transport and their first success was the invention of detachable pneumatic tyres for bicycles. However, the automobile was to provide the greatest scope for their creative talents. Throughout the 20th century, Michelin never ceased developing and creating ever more reliable and high-performance tyres, not only for vehicles ranging from trucks to F1 but also for underground transit systems and aeroplanes.

From early on, Michelin provided its customers with tools and services to facilitate mobility and make travelling a more pleasurable and more frequent experience. As early as 1900, the Michelin Guide supplied motorists with a host of useful information related to vehicle maintenance, accommodation and restaurants, and was to become a benchmark for good food. At the same time, the Travel Information Bureau offered travellers personalised tips and itineraries.

The publication of the first collection of roadmaps, in 1910, was an instant hit! In 1926, the first regional guide to France was published, devoted to the principal sites of Brittany, and before long each region of France had its own Green Guide. The collection was later extended to more far-flung destinations, including New York in 1968 and Taiwan in 2011.

In the 21st century, with the growth of digital technology, the challenge for Michelin maps and guides is to continue to develop alongside the company's tyre activities. Now, as before,Michelin is committed to improving the mobility of travellers.

MICHELIN TODAY

WORLD NUMBER ONE TYRE MANUFACTURER

- 70 production sites in 18 countries
- 111,000 employees from all cultures and on every continent
- 6,000 people employed in research and development

Moving
for a world

Moving forward means developing tyres with better road grip and shorter braking distances, whatever the state of the road.

CORRECT TYRE PRESSURE

RIGHT PRESSURE

- Safety
- Longevity
- Optimum fuel consumption

-0,5 bar

- Durability reduced by 20% (- 8,000 km)

-1 bar

- Risk of blowouts
- Increased fuel consumption
- Longer braking distances on wet surfaces

forward together
where mobility is safer

It also involves helping motorists take care of their safety and their tyres. To do so, Michelin organises "Fill Up With Air" campaigns all over the world to remind us that correct tyre pressure is vital.

WEAR

DETECTING TYRE WEAR

The legal minimum depth of tyre tread is 1.6mm.

Tyre manufacturers equip their tyres with tread wear indicators, which are small blocks of rubber moulded into the base of the main grooves at a depth of 1.6mm.

Tyres are the only point of contact between vehicle and road.

The photo below shows the actual contact zone.

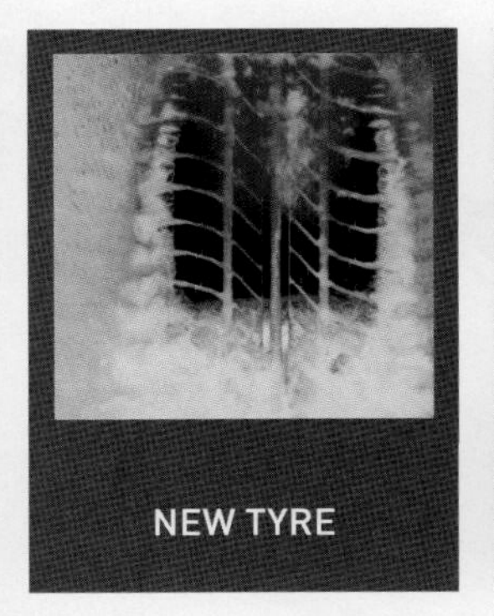

NEW TYRE

WORN TYRE
(1,6mm tread)

If the tread depth is less than 1.6mm, tyres are considered to be worn and dangerous on wet surfaces.

Moving forward means sustainable mobility

INNOVATION AND THE ENVIRONMENT

By 2050, Michelin aims to cut the quantity of raw materials used in its tyre manufacturing process by half and to have developed renewable energy in its facilities. The design of MICHELIN tyres has already saved billions of litres of fuel and, by extension, billions of tonnes of CO2.

Similarly, Michelin prints its maps and guides on paper produced from sustainably managed forests and is diversifying its publishing media by offering digital solutions to make travelling easier, more fuel efficient and more enjoyable!

The group's whole-hearted commitment to eco-design on a daily basis is demonstrated by ISO 14001 certification.

Like you, Michelin is committed to preserving our planet.

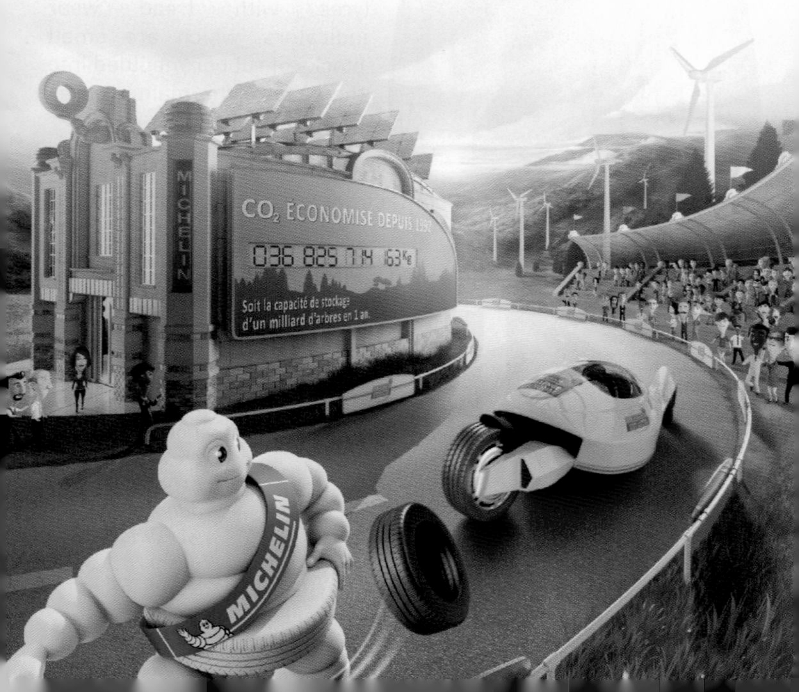

Chat with Bibendum

Go to
www.michelin.com/corporate/fr
Find out more about Michelin's
history and the latest news.

QUIZ

Michelin develops tyres for all types of vehicles. See if you can match the right tyre with the right vehicle…

Solution : A-6 / B-4 / C-2 / D-1 / E-3 / F-7 / G-5

TOKYO

RESTAURANTS & HOTELS

RESTAURANTS

STARRED RESTAURANTS

All the restaurants within the Tokyo Yokohama Shonan Guide have one, two or three Michelin Stars and are our way of highlighting restaurants that offer particularly good food.

When awarding stars there are a number of factors we consider: the quality and freshness of the ingredients, the technical skill and flair that goes into their preparation, the clarity of the flavours, the value for money and, ultimately, the taste. Of equal importance is the ability to produce excellent food not once but time and time again. Our inspectors make as many visits as necessary so that you can be sure of this quality and consistency.

A two or three star restaurant has to offer something very special in its cooking that separates it from the rest. Three stars – our highest award – are given to the very best. Cuisines in any style of restaurant and of any nationality are eligible for a star. The decoration, service and comfort levels have no bearing on the award.

Exceptional cuisine, worth a special journey.

One always eats here extremely well, sometimes superbly. Distinctive dishes are precisely executed, using superlative ingredients.

Araki		XX	Japanese Sushi	83
Azabu Yukimura		XX	Japanese	89
Esaki		XX	Japanese contemporary	113
Hamadaya		XXXX	Japanese	126
Ishikawa		XX	Japanese	151
Joël Robuchon		XXXXX	French contemporary	155
Kanda		XX	Japanese	160
Koju		X	Japanese	171
Quintessence		XXX	French contemporary	229
Ryugin	↗	XXX	Japanese contemporary	241
7chome Kyoboshi		X	Japanese Tempura	257
Sukiyabashi Jiro Honten		X	Japanese Sushi	264
Sushi Mizutani		X	Japanese Sushi	274
Sushi Saito		X	Japanese Sushi	276
Sushi Yoshitake	NEW	X	Japanese Sushi	278
Usukifugu Yamadaya		XXX	Japanese Fugu	305

NEW : new entry in the guide
↗ : restaurant promoted from 1 to 2 stars or 2 to 3 stars

Excellent cuisine, worth a detour.

Skillfully and carefully crafted dishes of outstanding quality.

Aimée Vibert		XXXX	French	75
Ajiman		X	Japanese Fugu	76
Beige Alain Ducasse		XXXX	French contemporary	92
Chugoku Hanten Fureika		XX	Chinese	100
Crescent		XXXX	French	102
Cuisine[s] Michel Troisgros		XXXX	French contemporary	103
Daigo		XXXX	Japanese Shojin	104
Den		XX	Japanese contemporary	105
Édition Koji Shimomura	NEW	XXX	French contemporary	108
Fugu Fukuji		X	Japanese Fugu	117
Fukudaya		XXXXX	Japanese	119
Fukuju		X	Japanese	120
Ginza Okuda	NEW	XXX	Japanese	121
Ginza Toyoda		XX	Japanese	122
Hatsunezushi		XX	Japanese Sushi	130
Hifumian		XX	Japanese	131
Hishinuma		XX	Japanese	135
Horikane		X	Japanese	138
Ichimonji		XX	Japanese	145
Ichirin		XX	Japanese	146
Kadowaki		X	Japanese	157
Kikuchi		X	Japanese	163
Kikunoi		XXXX	Japanese	164
KM	NEW	XX	French	167
Kodama		XX	Japanese contemporary	168

A very good restaurant in its category.

A place offering cuisine prepared to a consistently high standard.

RESTAURANTS BY AREA

Arakawa-ku

Obana		✿	X	Japanese Unagi	219

Bunkyo-ku

Echikatsu		✿	XXX	Japanese Sukiyaki	107
Hashimoto	NEW	✿	X	Japanese Unagi	128
Hifumian	➚	✿✿	XX	Japanese	131
Ishibashi		✿	XX	Japanese Unagi	150
Kurogi		✿	X	Japanese	174
Shinsuke		✿	X	Japanese Izakaya	259

Chiyoda-ku

Aimée Vibert		✿✿	XXXX	French	75
Akimoto		✿	X	Japanese Unagi	79
Au Goût du Jour Nouvelle Ère		✿	XX	French contemporary	87
Den	➚	✿✿	XX	Japanese contemporary	105
Fukudaya		✿✿	XXXXX	Japanese	119
Grill Ukai		✿	XXX	European	125
Ishibashi		✿	XXX	Japanese Sukiyaki	149
La Tour d'Argent		✿	XXXXX	French	183
Les Saisons		✿	XXXXX	French	195
Monnalisa Marunouchi		✿	XXX	French	207
Nadaman Honten Sazanka-so		✿✿	XXXX	Japanese	213
Ranjatai		✿	X	Japanese Yakitori	231
Shofukuro		✿	XX	Japanese	260
Yamanochaya		✿	XX	Japanese Unagi	308

Chuo-ku

Ajisen		✿	X	Japanese Izakaya	77

NEW : new entry in the guide
➚ : restaurant promoted from 1 to 2 stars or 2 to 3 stars

Koto-ku

Meguro-ku

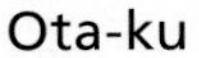

Ota-ku

Setagaya-ku

Shibuya-ku

Shinagawa-ku

Ise		✿	X	Japanese Tempura	148
Makimura		✿✿	XX	Japanese	198
Ohara's		✿	XXX	French	221
Takahashi		✿	X	Japanese Yakitori	282
Torishiki		✿	X	Japanese Yakitori	293
Yoshicho		✿	X	Japanese Yakitori	315

Shinjuku-ku

Cuisine[s] Michel Troisgros		✿✿	XXXX	French contemporary	103
Ichimonji		✿✿	XX	Japanese	145
Ishikawa		✿✿✿	XX	Japanese	151
Kitajima-tei	NEW	✿	XX	French	166
Kohaku	NEW	✿✿	XX	Japanese contemporary	170
Komuro		✿✿	X	Japanese	172
Kyoraku-tei		✿	X	Japanese Soba	176
L'Anneau d'Or		✿	XX	French	178
Le Mange-Tout		✿✿	XX	French	190
Lugdunum Bouchon Lyonnais		✿	X	French	196
Masumi		✿	X	Japanese	200
Matsunomi	NEW	✿	XX	Korean	201
Nakajima		✿	X	Japanese	215
Ogasawara Hakushaku-tei		✿	XXXX	Spanish contemporary	220
Ren		✿✿	X	Japanese	233
Suzunari	NEW	✿	X	Japanese	280
Takumi Tatsuhiro	NEW	✿	X	Japanese Sushi	284
Uotoku		✿	XXX	Japanese	304
Yamasaki		✿	X	Japanese	309
Yoneyama		✿	X	Japanese	313
Yorozuya Okagesan		✿	X	Japanese Izakaya	314
Yotsuya Uemura	NEW	✿	X	Japanese	319

Suginami-ku

Soba Miwa	NEW	✿	X	Japanese Soba	263

Sumida-ku

Edosoba Hosokawa		✿	X	Japanese Soba	109
Toriki		✿	X	Japanese Yakitori	292
Yokoyama		✿	X	Japanese Tempura	311

Taito-ku

Emori		✿	X	Japanese	110
Hommage	NEW	✿	XX	French	137
Ikku	NEW	✿	X	Japanese	147
Sushi Isshin Asakusa		✿	X	Japanese Sushi	270

Toshima-ku

Nabeya		✿	XX	Japanese	212

RESTAURANTS BY CUISINE TYPE

JAPANESE

Restaurant		Stars	Comfort	Area	Page
Akasaka Tan-tei	NEW	✿	XX	Minato-ku	78
Azabu Yukimura		✿✿✿	XX	Minato-ku	89
Basara		✿	XX	Minato-ku	91
Chiso Sottaku		✿	X	Chuo-ku	99
Emori		✿	X	Taito-ku	110
Fukudaya		✿✿	XXXXX	Chiyoda-ku	119
Fukuju		✿✿	X	Chuo-ku	120
Ginza Okuda	NEW	✿✿	XXX	Chuo-ku	121
Ginza Toyoda		✿✿	XX	Chuo-ku	122
Hamadaya		✿✿✿	XXXX	Chuo-ku	126
Hifumian	↗	✿✿	XX	Bunkyo-ku	131
Higuchi		✿	X	Shibuya-ku	132
Hirosaku		✿	X	Minato-ku	134
Hishinuma		✿✿	XX	Minato-ku	135
Horikane		✿✿	X	Minato-ku	138
Hosokawa		✿	X	Minato-ku	139
Hyo-tei	NEW	✿	XX	Setagaya-ku	140
Ibuki	NEW	✿	X	Chuo-ku	141
Ichie		✿	X	Shibuya-ku	143
Ichimonji		✿✿	XX	Shinjuku-ku	145
Ichirin	↗	✿✿	XX	Shibuya-ku	146
Ikku	NEW	✿	X	Taito-ku	147
Ishikawa		✿✿✿	XX	Shinjuku-ku	151
Jushu	NEW	✿	X	Minato-ku	156
Kadowaki		✿✿	X	Minato-ku	157

NEW : new entry in the guide
↗ : restaurant promoted from 1 to 2 stars or 2 to 3 stars

JAPANESE IZAKAYA

JAPANESE KUSHIAGE

JAPANESE ODEN

JAPANESE SHOJIN

JAPANESE SOBA

JAPANESE SUKIYAKI

Yoshihashi		✿	XX	Minato-ku	317

JAPANESE SUSHI

Araki		✿✿✿	XX	Chuo-ku	83
Harutaka		✿	X	Chuo-ku	127
Hatsunezushi		✿✿	XX	Ota-ku	130
Kuwano		✿	X	Chuo-ku	175
Otaninosushi	NEW	✿	X	Minato-ku	224
Sawada		✿✿	X	Chuo-ku	249
Sukiyabashi Jiro Honten		✿✿✿	X	Chuo-ku	264
Sukiyabashi Jiro Roppongi		✿✿	X	Minato-ku	265
Sushi Aoki Ginza		✿	X	Chuo-ku	266
Sushi Fukumoto		✿	X	Setagaya-ku	267
Sushiichi		✿	XX	Chuo-ku	268
Sushi Imamura		✿	X	Minato-ku	269
Sushi Isshin Asakusa		✿	X	Taito-ku	270
Sushi Isshin Ginza		✿	X	Chuo-ku	271
Sushi Iwa		✿	X	Chuo-ku	272
Sushi Kanesaka		✿✿	X	Chuo-ku	273
Sushi Mizutani		✿✿✿	X	Chuo-ku	274
Sushi Nakamura		✿	X	Minato-ku	275
Sushi Saito		✿✿✿	X	Minato-ku	276
Sushi Shin		✿	X	Minato-ku	277
Sushi Yoshitake	NEW	✿✿✿	X	Chuo-ku	278
Taku		✿✿	XX	Minato-ku	283
Takumi Tatsuhiro	NEW	✿	X	Shinjuku-ku	284
Umi		✿✿	X	Minato-ku	303

JAPANESE TEMPURA

Asagi		✿	X	Chuo-ku	86
Fukamachi		✿	X	Chuo-ku	118
Hatanaka		✿	X	Minato-ku	129

Takahashi	✿	X	Shinagawa-ku	282
Toriki	✿	X	Sumida-ku	292
Torishiki	✿	X	Shinagawa-ku	293
Yoshicho	✿	X	Shinagawa-ku	315

CHINESE

China Blue	✿	XXX	Minato-ku	98
Chugoku Hanten Fureika	✿✿	XX	Minato-ku	100
Masa's Kitchen 47	✿	XX	Shibuya-ku	199
Momonoki	✿	X	Minato-ku	205
Reikasai	✿	XX	Minato-ku	232
Ryuan	✿	XX	Minato-ku	240
Sense	✿	XXX	Chuo-ku	256

EUROPEAN

Grill Ukai	✿	XXX	Chiyoda-ku	125

FRENCH

Abasque	✿	X	Shibuya-ku	74
Aimée Vibert	✿✿	XXXX	Chiyoda-ku	75
Bon Chemin	NEW ✿	XX	Meguro-ku	94
Chez Matsuo	✿	XXX	Shibuya-ku	97
Côte d'Or	NEW ✿	XXX	Minato-ku	101
Crescent	✿✿	XXXX	Minato-ku	102
Gordon Ramsay	✿	XXX	Minato-ku	123
Hiramatsu	✿	XXXX	Minato-ku	133
Hommage	NEW ✿	XX	Taito-ku	137
Kitajima-tei	NEW ✿	XX	Shinjuku-ku	166
KM	NEW ✿✿	XX	Chuo-ku	167
L'Anneau d'Or	✿	XX	Shinjuku-ku	178
La Tour	✿	XXX	Chuo-ku	182
La Tour d'Argent	✿	XXXXX	Chiyoda-ku	183
Lauburu	✿	X	Minato-ku	184

FRENCH CONTEMPORARY

SPANISH CONTEMPORARY

Restaurant		Stars	Comfort	Ward	Page
Ogasawara Hakushaku-tei		✪	XXXX	Shinjuku-ku	220
Sant Pau		✪	XXXX	Chuo-ku	247
Zurriola	NEW	✪	XXX	Minato-ku	320

STEAKHOUSE

Restaurant		Stars	Comfort	Ward	Page
Aragawa		✪	XXX	Minato-ku	82
Dons de la Nature		✪	XXX	Chuo-ku	106
Gorio		✪	XX	Chuo-ku	124

RESTAURANTS SERVING LUNCH AND/ OR DINNER FOR ¥ 5,000 AND LESS

Restaurant		Stars	Comfort	Service	Page
Abasque		✿	✗	lunch & dinner	74
Ajisen		✿	✗	dinner	77
Akasaka Tan-tei	NEW	✿	✗✗	lunch	78
Akimoto		✿	✗	lunch & dinner	79
Antica Trattoria Nostalgica	NEW	✿	✗	lunch & dinner	80
Ànu Retrouvez-vous		✿	✗✗	lunch	81
Au Goût du Jour Nouvelle Ère		✿	✗✗	lunch	87
Basara		✿	✗✗	lunch & dinner	91
Beige Alain Ducasse	⤴	✿✿	✗✗✗✗	lunch	92
Bon Chemin	NEW	✿	✗✗	lunch	94
Bulgari Il Ristorante	NEW	✿	✗✗✗	lunch	95
China Blue		✿	✗✗✗	lunch	98
Chugoku Hanten Fureika		✿✿	✗✗	lunch	100
Édition Koji Shimomura	NEW	✿✿	✗✗✗	lunch (weekday)	108
Edosoba Hosokawa		✿	✗	lunch & dinner	109
Émun		✿	✗✗	lunch	111
Equilibrio	NEW	✿	✗✗✗	lunch	112
Faro		✿	✗✗✗	lunch	114
Feu	NEW	✿	✗✗	lunch	115
Florilège		✿	✗✗	lunch	116
Grill Ukai		✿	✗✗✗	lunch	125
Hashimoto	NEW	✿	✗	lunch & dinner	128
Hishinuma		✿✿	✗✗	lunch	135
Hommage	NEW	✿	✗✗	lunch	137
Hosokawa		✿	✗	dinner	139
Ibuki	NEW	✿	✗	lunch	141
Ichirin	⤴	✿✿	✗✗	lunch	146
Ikku	NEW	✿	✗	lunch	147

NEW : new entry in the guide
⤴ : restaurant promoted from 1 to 2 stars or 2 to 3 stars

PARTICULARLY PLEASANT RESTAURANTS

NEW : new entry in the guide
↗ : restaurant promoted from 1 to 2 stars or 2 to 3 stars

La Bombance		✿	XX	Japanese contemporary	177
L'Atelier de Joël Robuchon		✿✿	XX	French contemporary	181
La Tour d'Argent		✿	XXXXX	French	183
L'Effervescence	NEW	✿	XXX	French contemporary	188
Les Rosiers Eguzkilore	NEW	✿	XX	French	194
Lugdunum Bouchon Lyonnais		✿	X	French	196
Makimura		✿✿	XX	Japanese	198
Mikawa Zezankyo		✿	XX	Japanese Tempura	202
Nadaman Honten Sazanka-so		✿✿	XXXX	Japanese	213
Nico		✿	X	Japanese	216
Otaninosushi	NEW	✿	X	Japanese Sushi	224
Pachon		✿	XXX	French	226
Pierre Gagnaire		✿✿	XXXX	French contemporary	228
Quintessence		✿✿✿	XXX	French contemporary	229
Reikasai		✿	XX	Chinese	232
Ren		✿✿	X	Japanese	233
Ristorante Aso		✿	XXXX	Italian contemporary	236
Ryugin		✿✿✿	XXX	Japanese contemporary	241
Sant Pau		✿	XXXX	Spanish contemporary	247
Seisoka		✿✿	XXX	Japanese	252
Sense		✿	XXX	Chinese	256
Shofukuro		✿	XX	Japanese	260
Signature		✿	XXXX	French contemporary	262
Sushiichi		✿	XX	Japanese Sushi	268
Sushi Imamura		✿	X	Japanese Sushi	269
Sushi Mizutani		✿✿✿	X	Japanese Sushi	274
Sushi Yoshitake	NEW	✿✿✿	X	Japanese Sushi	278
Takumi Tatsuhiro	NEW	✿	X	Japanese Sushi	284
Uchitsu		✿	X	Japanese Tempura	298
Ukai-tei Ginza		✿	XXX	Japanese Teppanyaki	301
Ukai-tei Omotesando		✿	XXXX	Japanese Teppanyaki	302
Umi		✿✿	X	Japanese Sushi	303
Usukifugu Yamadaya		✿✿✿	XXX	Japanese Fugu	305
Waketokuyama		✿✿	XX	Japanese	306

RESTAURANTS OPEN ON SUNDAY

Restaurant		Stars	Comfort	Cuisine	Page
Abasque		✪	X	French	74
Aimée Vibert		✪✪	XXXX	French	75
Ànu Retrouvez-vous		✪	XX	French contemporary	81
Araki		✪✪✪	XX	Japanese Sushi	83
Argento Aso		✪	XXXX	Italian contemporary	84
Au Goût du Jour Nouvelle Ère		✪	XX	French contemporary	87
Azabu Rokkaku		✪	X	Japanese Izakaya	88
Azabu Yukimura		✪✪✪	XX	Japanese	89
Beige Alain Ducasse	↗	✪✪	XXXX	French contemporary	92
Bon Chemin	NEW	✪	XX	French	94
Bulgari Il Ristorante	NEW	✪	XXX	Italian contemporary	95
Casa Vinitalia		✪	XXX	Italian	96
Chez Matsuo		✪	XXX	French	97
China Blue		✪	XXX	Chinese	98
Chugoku Hanten Fureika		✪✪	XX	Chinese	100
Côte d'Or	NEW	✪	XXX	French	101
Cuisine[s] Michel Troisgros		✪✪	XXXX	French contemporary	103
Daigo		✪✪	XXXX	Japanese Shojin	104
Edosoba Hosokawa		✪	X	Japanese Soba	109
Emori		✪	X	Japanese	110
Émun		✪	XX	French contemporary	111
Equilibrio	NEW	✪	XXX	Fusion	112
Florilège		✪	XX	French contemporary	116
Grill Ukai		✪	XXX	European	125
Hashimoto	NEW	✪	X	Japanese Unagi	128
Hatanaka		✪	X	Japanese Tempura	129
Hifumian	↗	✪✪	XX	Japanese	131
Hiramatsu		✪	XXXX	French	133

NEW : new entry in the guide
↗ : restaurant promoted from 1 to 2 stars or 2 to 3 stars

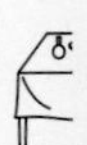

LATE DINING

Restaurant		Stars	Comfort	Hours	Page
Abasque		✿	X	L.O.22:00	74
Ajiman		✿✿	X	L.O.22:00	76
Ajisen		✿	X	L.O.22:20	77
Antica Trattoria Nostalgica	NEW	✿	X	L.O.22:00	80
Aragawa		✿	XXX	L.O.22:00	82
Azabu Rokkaku		✿	X	L.O.23:30	88
Casa Vinitalia		✿	XXX	L.O.1:00 (Sun. 20:30)	96
Chugoku Hanten Fureika		✿✿	XX	L.O.22:00	100
Den	↗	✿✿	XX	L.O.22:30	105
Emori		✿	X	L.O.23:00	110
Gorio		✿	XX	L.O.22:00	124
Harutaka		✿	X	Closing 24:00 (Sat. 22:30)	127
Hishinuma		✿✿	XX	L.O.22:00	135
Hosokawa		✿	X	Closing 23:00	139
Ibuki	NEW	✿	X	L.O.22:00	141
Icaro		✿	X	Closing 1:00 (Sat. 24:00)	142
Ichigo		✿	XX	L.O.23:30	144
Ishikawa		✿✿✿	XX	L.O.22:00	151
Jushu	NEW	✿	X	Closing 24:00	156
Kadowaki		✿✿	X	L.O.23:00 (Sat. 22:00)	157
Kagura		✿	XX	L.O.22:00	158
Kanda		✿✿✿	XX	L.O.22:00	160
Kasane	NEW	✿	X	L.O.22:00	161
Kisaku		✿	X	L.O.22:00	165
Kohaku	NEW	✿✿	XX	L.O.22:30	170

NEW : new entry in the guide
↗ : restaurant promoted from 1 to 2 stars or 2 to 3 stars

RESTAURANTS WITH PRIVATE ROOMS

				capacity	
Aimée Vibert		✿✿	XXXX	4	75
Ajiman		✿✿	X	12	76
Akasaka Tan-tei	NEW	✿	XX	14	78
Akimoto		✿	X	20	79
Ànu Retrouvez-vous		✿	XX	8	81
Aragawa		✿	XXX	6	82
Argento Aso		✿	XXXX	10	84
Banrekiryukodo		✿	XXX	10	90
Basara		✿	XX	18	91
Bulgari Il Ristorante	NEW	✿	XXX	8	95
Chez Matsuo		✿	XXX	16	97
China Blue		✿	XXX	10	98
Chugoku Hanten Fureika		✿✿	XX	100	100
Crescent		✿✿	XXXX	24	102
Cuisine[s] Michel Troisgros		✿✿	XXXX	12	103
Daigo		✿✿	XXXX	48	104
Den	⤴	✿✿	XX	6	105
Echikatsu		✿	XXX	85	107
Édition Koji Shimomura	NEW	✿✿	XXX	6	108
Esaki		✿✿✿	XX	10	113
Fugu Fukuji		✿✿	X	15	117
Fukudaya		✿✿	XXXXX	40	119
Fukuju		✿✿	X	8	120
Ginza Okuda	NEW	✿✿	XXX	6	121
Grill Ukai		✿	XXX	10	125
Hamadaya		✿✿✿	XXXX	60	126

NEW : new entry in the guide
⤴ : restaurant promoted from 1 to 2 stars or 2 to 3 stars

				capacity	
Harutaka		✿	✕	4	127
Hashimoto	NEW	✿	✕	25	128
Hifumian		✿✿	✕✕	6	131
Higuchi		✿	✕	2	132
Hiramatsu		✿	✕✕✕✕	14	133
Hirosaku		✿	✕	4	134
Hiyama		✿	✕✕✕	50	136
Horikane		✿✿	✕	16	138
Hyo-tei	NEW	✿	✕✕	14	140
Ichimonji		✿✿	✕✕	14	145
Ichirin		✿✿	✕✕	8	146
Ise		✿	✕	8	148
Ishibashi (Japanese Sukiyaki)		✿	✕✕✕	30	149
Ishibashi (Japanese Unagi)		✿	✕✕	20	150
Ishikawa		✿✿✿	✕✕	6	151
Itosho		✿	✕✕	25	152
Izumi		✿	✕✕✕	12	153
Jirocho	NEW	✿	✕✕	18	154
Joël Robuchon		✿✿✿	✕✕✕✕✕	30	155
Kadowaki		✿✿	✕	6	157
Kagura		✿	✕✕	8	158
Kamiya Nogizaka		✿	✕✕	12	159
Kanda		✿✿✿	✕✕	6	160
Kasane	NEW	✿	✕	8	161
Katsuzen		✿	✕	4	162
Kikunoi		✿✿	✕✕✕✕	25	164
Kisaku		✿	✕	6	165
Kodama		✿✿	✕✕	8	168
Kogetsu		✿✿	✕	6	169
Koju		✿✿✿	✕	10	171
Komuro		✿✿	✕	4	172
Kurogi		✿	✕	15	174

				capacity	
La Bombance		✿	XX	8	177
La Tour		✿	XXX	12	182
La Tour d'Argent		✿	XXXXX	30	183
Le Bouchon	NEW	✿	XX	4	185
L'Effervescence	NEW	✿	XXX	10	188
Le Jeu de l'Assiette		✿	XX	8	189
L'Embellir		✿	XXX	10	191
Les Enfants Gâtés		✿	XXX	8	193
Les Saisons		✿	XXXXX	18	195
Makimura		✿✿	XX	8	198
Masa's Kitchen 47		✿	XX	6	199
Matsunomi	NEW	✿	XX	18	201
Mikawa Zezankyo		✿	XX	10	202
Mitsuta		✿	XX	14	204
Monnalisa Ebisu		✿	XXX	12	206
Monnalisa Marunouchi		✿	XXX	12	207
Moranbong	NEW	✿✿	XXX	16	208
Muroi		✿	X	8	210
Nabeya		✿	XX	20	212
Nadaman Honten Sazanka-so		✿✿	XXXX	16	213
Nakajima		✿	X	20	215
Nigyo	NEW	✿	X	16	217
Nodaiwa		✿	XX	25	218
Ogasawara Hakushaku-tei		✿	XXXX	20	220
Okina		✿	XX	8	222
Ozaki		✿	X	12	225
Pachon		✿	XXX	20	226
Pierre Gagnaire		✿✿	XXXX	6	228
Quintessence		✿✿✿	XXX	6	229
Reikasai		✿	XX	24	232
Restaurant-I		✿	XXX	20	234
Ristorante Aso		✿	XXXX	20	236

				capacity	
Ristorante La Primula		✿	XX	3	238
Ryugin		✿✿✿	XXX	4	241
Ryuzu	NEW	✿	XXX	10	242
Sakuragawa		✿	XX	20	243
Sankame		✿	X	6	246
Sant Pau		✿	XXXX	8	247
Sanyukyo		✿	XX	4	248
Seisoka		✿✿	XXX	10	252
Sekiho-tei		✿✿	XX	10	253
Sekine	NEW	✿	X	8	254
Sennohana	NEW	✿	XX	8	255
Sense		✿	XXX	18	256
Shigeyoshi		✿✿	X	10	258
Shofukuro		✿	XX	24	260
Signature		✿	XXXX	10	262
Sushi Aoki Ginza		✿	X	10	266
Sushi Fukumoto		✿	X	6	267
Sushi Shin		✿	X	4	277
Sushi Yoshitake	NEW	✿✿✿	X	4	278
Taku		✿✿	XX	6	283
Tateru Yoshino Ginza		✿	XXXX	4	285
Tateru Yoshino Shiba		✿✿	XXX	12	286
Tateru Yoshino Shiodome		✿	XXX	28	287
Tatsumura		✿	X	8	288
Tenmo		✿	X	8	289
Tomura		✿✿	XX	14	291
Totoya Uoshin		✿	XX	6	294
Tsujitome		✿✿	XXX	20	295
Tsukasa		✿	X	8	296
Tsukiji Yamamoto		✿✿	XXX	12	297
Uchitsu		✿	X	4	298
Uchiyama		✿	XX	16	299

				capacity	
Uemura Honten		✿	XXX	12	300
Ukai-tei Ginza		✿	XXX	9	301
Ukai-tei Omotesando		✿	XXXX	8	302
Uotoku		✿	XXX	25	304
Usukifugu Yamadaya		✿✿✿	XXX	13	305
Waketokuyama		✿✿	XX	8	306
Yamaji		✿	X	6	307
Yamanochaya		✿	XX	30	308
Yonemura		✿	XX	4	312
Yoshihashi		✿	XX	12	317
Zurriola	NEW	✿	XXX	8	320

FRENCH

Abasque

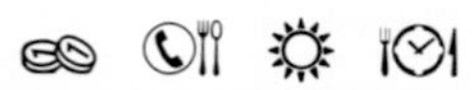

This is the place to enjoy Basque cuisine and wine, presented by the owner-sommelier and his chef, who trained in France, working as a team. The menu, featuring dishes characteristic of the Basque region on the Spanish-French border, changes with each season. Choose a main dish after first trying some tapas or, as we recommend, order the *dégustation* menu which includes specialities like cod *pil pil* and Basque-style pork roast.

■ Opening hours, last orders
Lunch = Wed.- Fri. 11:30-13:30 (L.O.)
Sun. and Public Holidays
12:00-14:00 (L.O.)
Dinner = 18:00-22:00 (L.O.)

■ Annual and weekly closing
Closed mid-August, late December-early January and Monday

■ Price
Lunch = set ¥ 1,260-2,100
set Sun. ¥ 3,675
Dinner = set ¥ 4,935-6,300
à la carte ¥ 5,000-7,000
Seat charge = ¥525/person (dinner)

TEL. 03–5468–8908
2-12-11 Shibuya, Shibuya-ku, Tokyo

www.esdesign.biz

FRENCH

Aimée Vibert

This restaurant near Kojimachi Station is housed in an Ile de France-style mansion and is named after the rose, also known as *Bouquet de la Mariée*. Traditional French cuisine is the draw: the hors d'oeuvre of crustacean gelée with sea urchin and cauliflower cream is an example. Dishes in which the meat is cooked in a cocotte provide wonderful balance as the accompanying vegetables become saturated with the flavour of the meat.

■ Opening hours, last orders
Lunch = 11:30-14:00 (L.O.)
Dinner = 18:00-21:00 (L.O.)

■ Annual and weekly closing
Closed mid-August, late December-early January and Tuesday

■ Price
Lunch = set ¥ 5,250-8,400
à la carte ¥ 10,000-19,000
Dinner = set ¥ 10,500-21,000
à la carte ¥ 10,000-19,000
Private room fee = ¥ 21,000
Service charge = 10%

TEL. 03–5216–8585
14-1 Nibancho, Chiyoda-ku, Tokyo

www.aimeevibert.com

Ajiman
味満ん

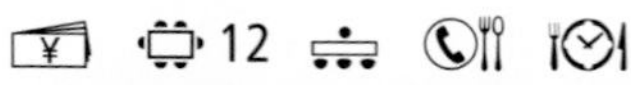

This cosy restaurant is run by owner-chef Sadao Matsubara and four family members. He only uses firm, flavoursome wild *shiro tora-fugu* and most diners opt for *omakase*. Other *fugu* dishes include grilled *shirako* full of aroma, *shioyaki*, *kara-age*, *shabu-shabu* and rich *zosui* with *shirako* to end with. While *fugu* is considered a winter dish, here it can be enjoyed up to May. The name's literal translation is 'filled with taste'.

■ Opening hours, last orders
Dinner = 18:00-24:00 L.O.22:00

■ Annual and weekly closing
Closed July, August, 31 December-4 January and Sunday from April-June

■ Price
Dinner = set ¥ 35,000-45,000
à la carte¥ 30,000-40,000

TEL. 03–3408–2910
3-8-8 Roppongi, Minato-ku, Tokyo

JAPANESE IZAKAYA

Ajisen
味泉

Shinichi Araki, who worked at the market in Tsukiji for 8 years, uses his trained eye to pick out quality seafood. Always packed in the evenings, the restaurant's specialities are homemade *satsuma age* and *nianago*. He is also proud of his sake selection, from prominent brands to obscure breweries. Dishes arrive quickly and in a random order so it's best to order as you go along. There is a 2½ hour limit on table usage.

■ Opening hours, last orders
Dinner = 17:30-23:00 L.O.22:20

■ Annual and weekly closing
Closed mid -August, late December-early January,Sunday, Monday and Public Holidays

■ Price
Dinner = set ¥4,500-6,000
à la carte ¥3,500-7,000

TEL. 03–3534–8483
1-18-10 Tsukishima, Chuo-ku, Tokyo

JAPANESE

Akasaka Tan-tei NEW
赤坂 潭亭

Using Okinawa produce, this restaurant serves traditional Ryukyu cuisine in a *kaiseki*-style arrangement. Reproducing the meals served in the court, an assortment of sashimi, including Okinawan tuna, is garnished with mustard. The speciality is *rafute* slow-stewed in *awamori* for a gelatinous texture; popular *soba* sauce has a full taste. All seats, besides those at the counter, are in private rooms, so it's ideal for entertaining.

■ Opening hours, last orders
Lunch = 12:00-15:00
Dinner = 18:00-21:00 (L.O.)

■ Annual and weekly closing
Closed late December-early January and Sunday

■ Prices
Lunch = set ¥ 1,950-8,000
Dinner = set ¥ 10,500-15,750
Private room fee = ¥ 2,000-6,000 (dinner)
Service charge = 10% (dinner)

TEL.03-3584-6646
6-16-11 Akasaka, Minato-ku, Tokyo

www.akasakatantei.com

Akimoto
秋本

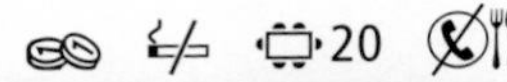

Take Exit 3 from Kojimachi Station and look for the sign with the hiragana 'う'. The *shirayaki* is almost too soft to pick up with chopsticks, with the outside browned to seal in flavour; the *unaju* is served in a Wajima lacquered box separating the rice and the *kabayaki*. The *unagi-maki*, covered in stock, has a slightly sweet taste. It gets crowded at lunch, so arrive early. The *tatami* room is available by reservation only.

■ Opening hours, last orders
Lunch = 11:30-14:30 L.O.14:00
Dinner = 17:00-20:30 L.O.20:00

■ Annual and weekly closing
Closed mid-August, late December-early January, Sunday, 2nd Saturday and Public Holidays

■ Prices
Lunch = à la carte ¥ 2,000-6,000
Dinner = set ¥ 9,000-13,500
à la carte ¥ 2,000-6,000
Private room fee = 15% (lunch 10%)
Service charge = 10% (dinner)

TEL.03–3261–6762
3-4 Kojimachi, Chiyoda-ku, Tokyo

ITALIAN

Antica Trattoria Nostalgica NEW

The owner chose a name reflecting his nostalgic love of good old-fashioned Italian cafeterias. He prepares purely Italian dishes, reflecting his principle of using recipes free of any local peculiarities, many of which are meat based; the offal dish made from Hokkaido lambs goes well with wine and the carbonara made with guinea fowl eggs has an authentic taste. Expect courteous service and an appealingly lively atmosphere.

■ Opening hours, last orders
Lunch = Mon.-Fri. 11:30-14:00
Dinner = 18:00-22:00 (L.O.)

■ Annual and weekly closing
Closed late December-early January and Sunday

■ Prices
Lunch = set ¥ 1,000
Dinner = set ¥ 7,000
à la carte ¥ 5,000-8,000
Seat charge = ¥ 500/person (dinner)

TEL.03-3719-7755
4-8-12 Nakameguro, Meguro-ku, Tokyo

FRENCH CONTEMPORARY

Ànu Retrouvez-vous

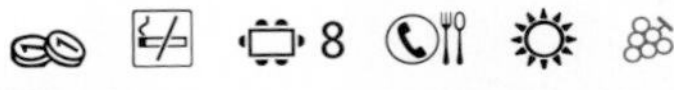

Shohei Shimono's philosophy is to pick the best ingredients and maximise their flavour. Vegetables are from farms in Nagano and Ishikawa; fish comes directly from his hometown of Hagi City, Yamaguchi. Placing importance on aroma and texture, the set menus consist of a large number of small plates. The speciality is duck *rôti*, and the champagne is reasonably priced. Make your reservations early as it is always crowded.

■ Opening hours, last orders
Lunch = 11:30-16:00 L.O.13:30
Dinner = 18:00-24:00 L.O.21:00

■ Annual and weekly closing
Closed late December-early January and Tuesday

■ Prices
Lunch = set ¥ 3,500-12,000
Dinner = set ¥ 8,000-18,000
à la carte ¥ 8,000-12,000
Service charge = 10%

TEL.03-5422-8851
5-19-4 Hiroo, Shibuya-ku, Tokyo
www.restaurant-anu.com

STEAKHOUSE

Aragawa
麤皮

Emphasis is on unchanging values and creating the same feel as the original restaurant which opened in 1967 and moved here in 2009. There are no menus - the maître d' offers a verbal explanation. Tajima-Sanda beef from Hyogo is used exclusively. The meat is seasoned only with salt and pepper; the steaks are broiled on a brick stove using Bincho charcoal. Sirloin is the main choice; if you prefer tenderloin check availability.

■ Opening hours, last orders
12:00-22:00 (L.O.)

■ Annual and weekly closing
Closed late December-early January, Sunday and Public Holidays

■ Price
Lunch = set ¥ 52,500
à la carte ¥40,000-80,000
Dinner = set ¥ 52,500
à la carte ¥40,000-80,000
Service charge = 12%

TEL. 03–3438–1867
3-23-11 Nishishinbashi, Minato-ku, Tokyo

JAPANESE SUSHI

Araki
あら輝

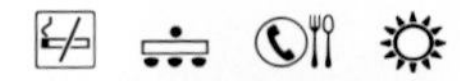

In 2010, this popular restaurant in Kaminoge opened a long-awaited branch in Ginza. Mitsuhiro Araki has an obsession with tuna. Letting the top quality tuna stand for a few days to bring out the flavour, he prepares five in a row of *akami*, *chu-toro* and *o-toro*; rice is salted and unsweetened to go with it. He is also a man of action, growing rice and going on fishing expeditions. His impulse for exploration knows no bounds.

■ Opening hours, last orders
Lunch = 12:00-14:00
Dinner = 18:00-20:30 (L.O.)

■ Annual and weekly closing
Closed early January, mid-August and Wednesday

■ Price
Lunch = set ¥ 21,000-26,250
Dinner = set ¥ 21,000-26,250

TEL. 03–3545–0199
5-14-14 Ginza, Chuo-ku, Tokyo

ITALIAN CONTEMPORARY

Argento Aso

Bright and sunny by day, romantic and softly lit by night, the restaurant is elegant and graceful. Lobster with white balsamic vinegar jelly, served as an hors d'oeuvre, and spaghetti alla pescatora, with the seafood served separately, are house specialities. Dishes come on glass, adding a touch of fun to the experience. The extensive wine list is big on Italian and French regions, but it also has a wide selection of Armagnac.

■ Opening hours, last orders
Lunch = 11:30-15:30 L.O.13:30
Dinner = 18:00-23:00 L.O.20:30

■ Annual and weekly closing
Closed 1 January

■ Price

Lunch =	set	¥ 5,250-7,350
	à la carte	¥11,500-15,000
Dinner =	set	¥ 9,450-15,750
	à la carte	¥11,500-15,000

Service charge = 13%

TEL. 03–5524–1270
Zoe Ginza 8F,
3-3-1 Ginza, Chuo-ku, Tokyo

www.hiramatsu.co.jp/restaurants/argento-aso

ITALIAN CONTEMPORARY

Aroma-Fresca

Relocated for a second time, the restaurant is now in Ginza making use of the luxurious top floor of a 12-storey building. The menu remains unchanged: dishes are light with delicate seasoning to fully bring out the freshness and natural flavours of the ingredients without overdoing the preparations. The service team also leave a favourable impression. After the meal, relax in the salon. The hard part is getting reservations.

■ Opening hours, last orders
Dinner = 17:30-23:00 L.O.20:30

■ Annual and weekly closing
Closed mid-August, late December-early January, Sunday and 1st Monday

■ Price
Dinner = set ¥ 16,000-20,000

TEL. 03–3535–6667
Ginza Trecious 12F,
2-6-5 Ginza, Chuo-ku, Tokyo

JAPANESE TEMPURA

Asagi
あさぎ

Owner-chef Hiroshi Asagi runs this modern tempura restaurant with his family. Using a large frying pot at the centre of the cooking counter, he delicately fries each ingredient using sesame oil. Bite into the shrimp *tempura* and it feels as if you are eating pure shrimp as his unique technique allows the seafood flavour to permeate the batter. He relocated from Sendagi district in 1999 and visits nearby Tsukiji market daily.

■ Opening hours, last orders
Lunch = Mon.-Fri. 12:00-13:00 (L.O.)
except Public Holidays
Dinner = 17:30-20:30 (L.O.)

■ Annual and weekly closing
Closed Golden week, mid-August, late December-early January, Sunday and Public Holiday Mondays

■ Price
Lunch = set ¥ 5,775-7,875
Dinner = set ¥ 12,000-15,000

TEL. 03–3289–8188
6-4-13 Ginza, Chuo-ku, Tokyo

FRENCH CONTEMPORARY

Au Goût du Jour Nouvelle Ère

The fresh produce is complemented here with light, fragrant sauces. The restaurant considers its cuisine to be of a 'new era', as its name suggests. The flavour-laden pork back ribs and shoulder loin, cooked for two days and served with a port sauce, is one recommendation. The chef was a former pâtissier so at dinner expect to see a variety of desserts. In winter, try apple chiboust with salted caramel ice cream.

■ Opening hours, last orders
Lunch = 11:00-13:30 (L.O.)
Dinner = 18:00-21:30 (L.O.)

■ Annual and weekly closing
Closed 1 January

■ Price

Lunch = set	¥ 3,800-10,000
Dinner = set	¥ 8,000-13,000

TEL. 03–5224–8070
Shin-Marunouchi Building 5F,
1-5-1 Marunouchi, Chiyoda-ku,
Tokyo

www.augoutdujour-group.com/no

Azabu Rokkaku
麻布 六角

If you're after a simply-adorned izakaya with a laid-back atmosphere then try Azabu Rokkaku. Since opening, this establishment has shunned advertising while quietly catering to its regulars. An assortment of starters, soups and appetisers are brought to your table, followed by the menu. First-timers should ask the chef for recommendations. Prices may be higher than a typical izakaya but here you can enjoy real artisanal cuisine.

■ Opening hours, last orders
Dinner = 18:00-23:30 (L.O.)

■ Annual and weekly closing
Closed Golden week, mid-August and late December-early January

■ Price
Dinner = à la carte ¥ 10,000-20,000
Service charge = 5%

TEL. 03–3401–8516
Yuken Azabu .10 Building 4F,
1-5-5 Azabujuban, Minato-ku,
Tokyo

JAPANESE

Azabu Yukimura
麻布 幸村

As there is no sign, look for the blue board with the address on the wall. Having worked for 25 years in Kyoto, Yukimura Jun bases his cooking on the city's culinary traditions. Deserving of mention are *shabu-shabu* with *hanasansho* in spring, and the *ayu* in summer; charcoal-grilled *matsutake* wrapped in *hamo* feature in autumn and snow crab in winter. The originality of the cuisine leaves a lasting impression.

■ Opening hours, last orders
Dinner = 17:30-20:00 (L.O.)

■ Annual and weekly closing
Closed Golden week, mid-August and late December-early January

■ Price
Dinner = set ¥ 23,100-31,500
Service charge = 10%

TEL. 03–5772–1610
Yuken Azabu.10 Building 3F,
1-5-5 Azabujuban, Minato-ku,
Tokyo

JAPANESE CONTEMPORARY

Banrekiryukodo
万歴龍呼堂

XXX

10

The restaurant features a simple, modern décor and its cavern-like basement has semi-private table seating. The menu changes monthly and features items like soup flavoured with the first tea of the season and smoke-scented broiled fish. Offering a new style of Japanese cuisine while respecting tradition, the set menus include meat dishes that go well with wine. Similar flair and individuality is reflected in the tableware.

■ Opening hours, last orders
Lunch = 11:30-13:30 (L.O.)
Dinner = 18:00-21:00 (L.O.)

■ Annual and weekly closing
Closed late December-early January and Sunday

■ Price
Lunch = set ¥ 6,300-12,600
Dinner = set ¥ 8,400-31,500
Service charge = 10%

TEL. 03-3505-5686
2-33-5 Higashiazabu, Minato-ku, Tokyo

www.banreki.com

Basara
ばさら

We recommend the *tomato sukiyaki* speciality, a healthy choice that is available all year round, prepared and served by the waiting staff. First the tomatoes go in, followed by the onions and then the beef; the sweet *warishita* draws out the flavours. To end the meal, the remaining *warishita* is used to dress tomatoes and *tagliatelle* for some Japanese-style Italian. Prices are reasonable. Also popular is the *lettuce shabu-shabu*.

■ Opening hours, last orders
Lunch = 11:30-15:00 L.O.14:00
Dinner = 17:30-23:00 L.O.21:00

■ Annual and weekly closing
Closed mid-August, late December-early January, Sunday and Public Holidays

■ Price
Lunch = set ¥ 900-12,000
à la carte ¥ 6,000-18,000
Dinner = set ¥ 5,000-12,000
à la carte ¥ 6,000-18,000
Private room fee = ¥ 8,000-20,000
Service charge = 10% (dinner)

TEL. 03–5444–6700
DNI Mita Building B1F,
3-43-16 Shiba, Minato-ku, Tokyo

FRENCH CONTEMPORARY

Beige Alain Ducasse

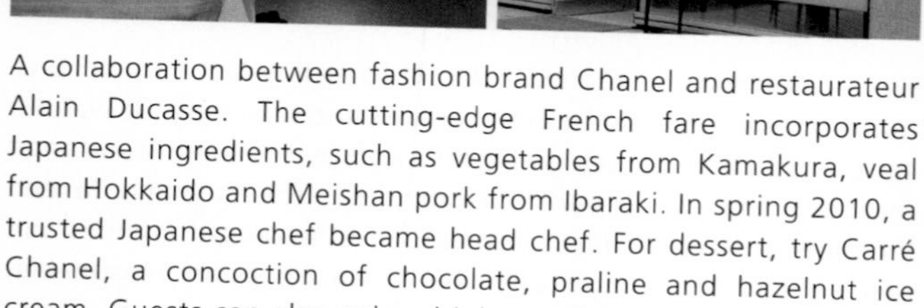

A collaboration between fashion brand Chanel and restaurateur Alain Ducasse. The cutting-edge French fare incorporates Japanese ingredients, such as vegetables from Kamakura, veal from Hokkaido and Meishan pork from Ibaraki. In spring 2010, a trusted Japanese chef became head chef. For dessert, try Carré Chanel, a concoction of chocolate, praline and hazelnut ice cream. Guests can also enjoy drinks on the rooftop terrace.

■ Opening hours, last orders
Lunch = 11:30-14:30 (L.O.)
Dinner = 18:00-20:30 (L.O.)

■ Annual and weekly closing
Closed mid-August, late December-early January, Monday and Tuesday

■ Price
Lunch = set ¥ 5,000-12,000
à la carte ¥ 15,500-17,000
Dinner = set ¥ 13,000-22,000
à la carte ¥ 14,500-17,000
Service charge = 10%

TEL. 03–5159–5500
Chanel Building 10F,
3-5-3 Ginza, Chuo-ku, Tokyo

www.beige-tokyo.com

JAPANESE YAKITORI

Bird Land

The chicken and eggs are from the okukuji breed, raised in Ibaraki. The menu includes *wasabi-yaki*, along with more original items like homemade patties and chicken breast with basil. The ingredients of the kebab vary but sometimes include chicken oysters - this was the first restaurant to serve them as part of the *yakitori*, at the suggestion of a customer. There are two starting times for dinner on Fridays and Saturdays.

■ Opening hours, last orders
Dinner = 17:00-22:00 L.O.21:30

■ Annual and weekly closing
Closed late December-early January, Sunday, Monday and Public Holidays

■ Price
Dinner = set ¥ 6,300-8,400
à la carte ¥ 6,000-10,000
Service charge = 10%

TEL. 03–5250–1081
Tsukamoto Sozan Building B1F,
4-2-15 Ginza, Chuo-ku, Tokyo

www.ginza-birdland.sakura.ne.jp

FRENCH

Bon Chemin NEW

Seeking universal tastes in his cooking, the owner-chef adds his own interpretation to classic Escoffier recipes and brings them in line with the times. For example, simmered just right, the beef cheeks in red wine are light and covered in a fragrant sauce. There is a wide selection of set menus for dinner, and the size of the portions can be adjusted. There are many wines from Burgundy, where his wife trained as a cook.

■ Opening hours, last orders
Lunch = 11:30-14:00 (L.O.)
Dinner = 18:00-21:30 (L.O.)

■ Annual and weekly closing
Closed late December-early January and Wednesday

■ Price
Lunch = set ¥ 1,890-6,825
Dinner = set ¥ 5,145-9,135
Service charge = 10%

TEL. 03-3791-3900
2-40-5 Gohongi, Meguro-ku, Tokyo

www.bonchemin.com

ITALIAN CONTEMPORARY

Bulgari Il Ristorante NEW

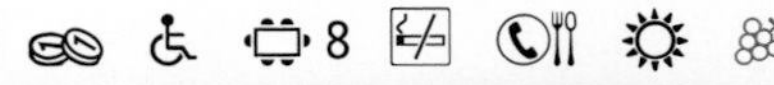

Sunlight pours into the dining room through the large window creating a relaxed, open feel. The cooking defies boundaries by giving a modern twist to traditional dishes. The theme of the set menu is a gastronomic journey, so expect some surprising combinations. The chef's particular speciality is pasta, so we recommend the tagliolini made with *uni* and carrot juice, which features a wondrous harmony between sauce and pasta.

■ Opening hours, last orders
Lunch = 11:30-14:30 (L.O.)
Dinner = Mon.-Sat. 18:00-21:30 (L.O.)

■ Price
Lunch = set ¥ 5,000-10,000
Dinner = set ¥ 15,000-22,000
à la carte ¥ 15,000-20,000
Service charge = 10%
Private room fee = ¥ 10,000 (lunch)
¥ 30,000 (dinner)

TEL. 03-6362-0555
Bulgari Ginza Tower 9F, 2-7-12
Ginza, Chuo-ku, Tokyo

www.bulgarihotels.com

ITALIAN

Casa Vinitalia

Sit on the terrace side for a feeling of spaciousness. Placing importance on freshness, the chef uses many domestically grown vegetables in dishes like vegetable *cocotte* and the colourful *bagna càuda* with about 20 different raw vegetables. We recommend the crab *riso pilaf*. There are also plenty of handmade pasta dishes. It is difficult to get reservations, but if you call at 2pm, there are sometimes openings for that evening.

■ Opening hours, last orders
Dinner = 17:30-1:00 (L.O.)
Sun. 14:30-20:30 (L.O.)

■ Annual and weekly closing
Closed mid-August, late December-early January and Monday

■ Price
Dinner = set ¥ 7,500
à la carte ¥ 6,000-10,500

TEL. 03–5439–4110
1-7-31 Minamiazabu, Minato-ku, Tokyo

FRENCH

Chez Matsuo

XXX

16

Chez Matsuo opened in 1980 as the city's first restaurant within a detached house. Just off the entrance is a salon-bar with a fireplace and furniture from the early 1900s; private rooms past the bar have wooden flooring and panelling. Preparations are simple and adapted to the ingredients; sauces tend to be light but side dishes, on the other hand, are more elaborate in nature and are coordinated with the main ingredient.

■ Opening hours, last orders
Lunch = 12:00-15:00 L.O.13:00
Dinner = 18:00-23:00 L.O.20:30

■ Annual and weekly closing
Closed late December-early January

■ Price
Lunch = set ¥ 8,400
Dinner = set ¥ 21,000-52,500
Private room fee = ¥ 31,500
Service charge = 10%

TEL. 03–3485–0566
1-23-15 Shoto, Shibuya-ku, Tokyo
www.chez-matsuo.co.jp

CHINESE

China Blue

Up on the 28th floor of the Conrad hotel, lights covered in blue cloth hang from the 8m high ceiling and the room provides views of Hamarikyu Onshi Teien Garden and the Tokyo Bay area. Of the three private rooms, the glass corner one is particularly popular. Dishes are served Western style and guests can enjoy not only traditional Cantonese cuisine but also contemporary creations accented with flavours of other Asian countries.

■ Opening hours, last orders
Lunch = 11:30-14:00 (L.O.)
Dinner = 17:30-21:00 (L.O.)

■ Price
Lunch = set ¥ 3,900-7,800
à la carte ¥ 6,000-13,500
Dinner = set ¥ 12,000-22,800
à la carte ¥ 6,000-13,500
Private room fee = ¥15,000-25,000

TEL. 03-6388-8000
Conrad Hotel 28F,
1-9-1 Higashishinbashi,
Minato-ku, Tokyo

www.conradtokyo.co.jp

Chiso Sottaku
馳走 啐啄

This small restaurant is found in Ginza 6-chome in a building right in front of the parking lot of the Kojun Building. Shigemitsu Nishizuka takes delight in the tea ceremony and adheres to the philosophy of cherishing every encounter. Dishes are well-balanced, such as the jellied spiny lobster and the large, tenderised abalone. There are three *omakase* menus at dinner; the priciest one requires pre-ordering the day before.

■ Opening hours, last orders
Lunch = Mon.-Fri. 12:00-13:00 (L.O.)
Dinner = 18:00-22:00 L.O.20:00

■ Annual and weekly closing
Closed mid-August, late December-early January, Sunday and Public Holidays

■ Price
Lunch = set ¥ 5,250-8,400
Dinner = set ¥ 10,500-18,900
Service charge = 10%

TEL. 03-3289-8010
Urano Building 2F,
6-7-7 Ginza, Chuo-ku, Tokyo

Chugoku Hanten Fureika

中国飯店 富麗華

The menu offers a large variety of Cantonese and Shanghainese dishes, which come not only on large plates but are also served in individual portions. Recommended is the roasted pork dish prepared by the specialist Grill and Roast food chef. Shanghai soup dumplings bursting with juicy meat are prepared from scratch. Live performances featuring classical Chinese instruments showcase the subtlety and depth of Chinese culture.

■ Opening hours, last orders
Lunch = 11:30-14:00 (L.O.)
Dinner = 17:30-22:00 (L.O.)

■ Annual and weekly closing
Closed 31 December-1 January

■ Price
Lunch = set ¥ 2,000-6,000
à la carte ¥ 6,000-12,000
Dinner = set ¥ 8,400-33,600
à la carte ¥ 6,000-12,000
Service charge = 10% (dinner)

TEL. 03–5561–7788
3-7-5 Higashiazabu, Minato-ku, Tokyo

www.chuugokuhanten.com/storefureika

FRENCH

Côte d'Or NEW
コートドール

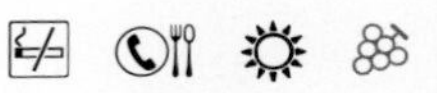

The owner-chef opened his restaurant in 1986, having worked with Bernard Pacaud in Paris. Eschewing excess, his deft touch creates exquisite dishes. Along with the standard red bell pepper mousse, sherry-flavoured ray fin and red wine simmered oxtail, are seasonal specialities such as shiso soup in summer. Staff offer consistently friendly service, and the comfortable dining room is suitable for dates and special occasions.

■ Opening hours, last orders
Lunch = 12:00-14:00 (L.O.)
Dinner = 18:00-20:30 (L.O.)

■ Annual and weekly closing
Closed mid-August, late December-early January, Monday and 2nd Tuesday

■ Prices
Lunch = set ¥ 5,250
à la carte ¥ 10,000-17,000
Dinner = set ¥ 15,750
à la carte ¥ 10,000-17,000
Service charge = 10%

TEL.03-3455-5145
Mita House 1F, 5-2-18 Mita, Minato-ku, Tokyo

Crescent

The house speciality, *compression de tomate*, consists of three layers: mousse, tartar and jelly. Lamb comes from Shiranuka in Hokkaido and various cuts are roasted on the bone and served on one plate with a typical seasonal sauce —salted lemon sauce in summer, for example, or truffle sauce in winter. Crescent offers four different *omakase* set menus. This restaurant is particularly suitable for those special occasions.

■ Opening hours, last orders
Dinner = 17:30-22:30 L.O.20:30

■ Annual and weekly closing
Closed mid-August, late December-early January, Sunday and Public Holidays

■ Price
Dinner = set ¥ 18,900-31,500
Service charge = 10%

TEL. 03–3436–3211
1-8-20 Shibakoen, Minato-ku, Tokyo

www.restaurantcrescent.com

FRENCH CONTEMPORARY

Cuisine[s] Michel Troisgros

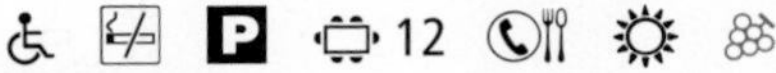
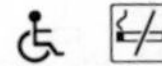   12   

Michel Troisgros is the third-generation owner-chef of Troisgros, a famed restaurant in Roanne, northwest of Lyons, and looks to Japanese cuisine as a source of inspiration. The chefs entrusted by him offer contemporary French cuisine with accents of citrus fruit, herbs and spices incorporating Japanese tastes. Aside from poultry, all ingredients are from Japan. Specialities include 'Cuisses de grenouilles sautées au tamarin'.

■ Opening hours, last orders
Lunch = 11:30-13:30 (L.O.)
Dinner = 18:00-20:30 (L.O.)

■ Annual and weekly closing
Closed Wednesday except December

■ Price

Lunch = set		¥ 5,300-10,500
	à la carte	¥ 12,500-17,500
Dinner = set		¥ 14,700-18,900
	à la carte	¥ 12,500-17,500

Service charge = 10%

TEL. 03–5321–3915
Hyatt Regency Hotel 1F,
2-7-2 Nishishinjuku, Shinjuku-ku,
Tokyo

www.troisgros.jp

JAPANESE SHOJIN

Daigo
醍醐

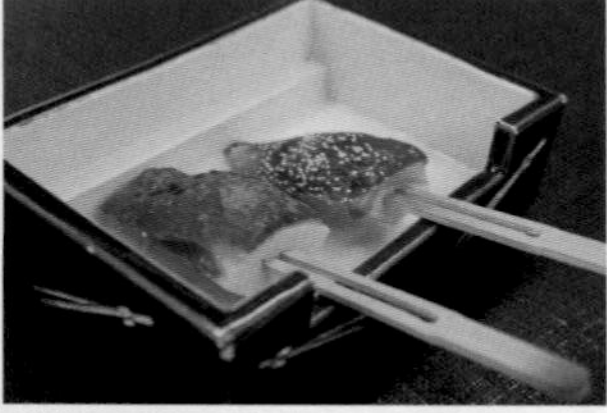

Shojin ryori is meat-free and based on the concept of appreciating simple food; various root vegetables are used as a starting point. Close attention is paid to seasonal ingredients and, in the *kaiseki* style, dishes arrive one at a time. Various flavoured broths are used: dried bonito, kelp and *shiitake*. The dining room exudes the refined *wabi-sabi* essence of Zen Buddhism, complemented by ikebana floral arrangements.

■ Opening hours, last orders
Lunch = 11:30-15:00 L.O.14:00
Dinner = 17:00-22:30 L.O.20:00

■ Annual and weekly closing
Closed early January

■ Price
Lunch = set ¥ 10,000-19,000
Dinner = set ¥ 15,000-19,000
Service charge = 15%

TEL. 03-3431-0811
Forest Tower 2F,
2-3-1 Atago, Minato-ku, Tokyo

www.atago-daigo.com

JAPANESE CONTEMPORARY

Den
傳

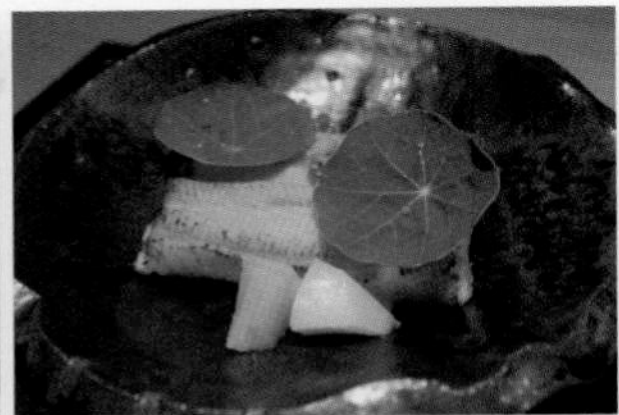

The young owner-chef here uses only domestic ingredients and places importance on natural flavours. The salad is prepared with morning-fresh vegetables garnished with chopped *kombu*; cold *yuba chawanmushi* is topped with béchamel sauce made from soy milk. While Western-style techniques are incorporated, the basis is Japanese cuisine. The serving dishes, made by a friend, highlight the food. Recommended for the health-conscious.

■ Opening hours, last orders
Dinner = 17:00-23:30 L.O.22:30

■ Annual and weekly closing
Closed mid-August, late December-early January, Sunday and Public Holidays

■ Price
Dinner = set ¥ 6,500-12,000
Private room fee = ¥ 4,000
Service charge = 10%

TEL. 03–3222–3978
2-2-32 Kandajinbocho,
Chiyoda-ku, Tokyo

STEAKHOUSE

Dons de la Nature

Yoshiji Otsuka is experienced in French cuisine and opened his restaurant after working at a steakhouse. Only Japanese black-haired heifers aged around 33 months are considered; the meat is aged and later smaller cuts are carved and swathed in cloth. Aged for another 7-10 days in a vacuum, an original salt blend and black pepper are then rubbed into it before grilling. Orders start at a minimum weight of 400 grams.

■ Opening hours, last orders
Dinner = 17:00-22:00 L.O.21:00

■ Annual and weekly closing
Closed mid-August, late December-early January, Sunday and Public Holidays

■ Price
Dinner = set ¥ 21,000
à la carte ¥ 21,000-34,000
Service charge = 10%

TEL. 03-3563-4129
Kawai Building B1F,
1-7-6 Ginza, Chuo-ku, Tokyo

www.dons-nature.jp

JAPANESE SUKIYAKI

Echikatsu

江知勝

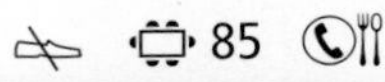

Echigo native Katsujiro founded this restaurant in the early 1870s, and it was a favourite of great writers of the day. The hallway, its wood tanned by time, gives you a feel of its history. Carp swim in the garden pond, and there are old-style tatami rooms from which you can hear the murmuring water. Most meat is marbled, but there is also less fatty thigh meat available. The proprietress prepares spicy Edo style *warishita*.

■ Opening hours, last orders
Dinner = 17:00-21:30 L.O.19:30

■ Annual and weekly closing
Closed mid-August, late December-early January, Saturday in August, Sunday and Public Holidays

■ Price
Dinner = set ¥ 7,350-11,550
Service charge = 10%

TEL. 03–3811–5293
2-31-23 Yushima, Bunkyo-ku, Tokyo

FRENCH CONTEMPORARY

Édition Koji Shimomura NEW

エディション・コウジ シモムラ

Koji Shimomura minimizes the use of oil and fat to prepare cuisine that is not too heavy. His specialities, which reflect his experience in France, include poached oysters with seawater jelly and seaweed, and crispy John Dory wrapped in kadaïf with broccoli sauce. His originality can be seen in the roasted Challandais duck breast, based on the philosophy of Bernard Loiseau. The low-priced lunch is only available on weekdays.

■ Opening hours, last orders
Lunch = 12:00-15:30 L.O.13:30
Dinner = 18:00-24:00 L.O.21:30

■ Annual and weekly closing
Closed late December-early January

■ Price
Lunch = set weekday ¥ 4,200-13,650
Sat., Sun. ¥ 6,300-13,650
Dinner = set ¥ 13,650-21,000
Private room fee = less than 5 persons ¥5,250-31,500
Service charge = 10%

TEL. 03-5549-4562
Roppongi T-Cube 1F,
3-1-1 Roppongi, Minato-ku,
Tokyo

www.koji-shimomura.jp

JAPANESE SOBA

Edosoba Hosokawa

江戸蕎麦 ほそ川

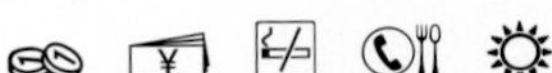

Owner-chef Takashi Hosokawa not only buys good buckwheat but also grows his own on his farm in Ibaraki. The thin noodles are made from 100% buckwheat flour. Enjoying popularity in August is the cold *kaki soba*, while in October and later it's its warm counterpart; *anago tempura* is a favourite appetiser. The interior is simple, with shared tables and one semi-private room. Bookings are not accepted at weekends or holidays; guests are asked not to bring small children.

■ Opening hours, last orders
Lunch = 11:45-15:00
Dinner = 17:30-21:00

■ Annual and weekly closing
Closed mid-August, early January, Monday and 3rd Tuesday

■ Price
Lunch = à la carte ¥ 3,000-6,000
Dinner = à la carte ¥ 3,000-6,000

TEL. 03–3626–1125
1-6-5 Kamezawa, Sumida-ku, Tokyo

www.edosoba-hosokawa.jp

Emori
江森

The menu on the wall has typical Kyoto items like whole roasted Kamo eggplant and marinated *tokishirazu* salmon. The simmered Daitokuji wheat gluten and the *yuba* made from Tanba black soybeans are rare items in the Kanto area. The *chawanmushi* with no filling is especially recommended. The highlight of the set menu is the hotpot made with freshwater clam stock. Owner-chef Hiroyuki Emori handles all the cooking himself.

■ Opening hours, last orders
Dinner = 18:00-24:00 L.O.23:00

■ Annual and weekly closing
Closed mid-August, late December-early January, Monday and 1st Tuesday

■ Price
Dinner = set ¥ 10,500

TEL. 03–3875–5785
3-9-10 Asakusa, Taito-ku, Tokyo

FRENCH CONTEMPORARY

Émun

Although compact, this glass-enclosed restaurant has a high ceiling and feels more spacious than it is. Only set menus are available, but there is a wide selection; they are mainly comprised of vegetables and fish accented with olive oil or herbs. The speciality is the *exposition des légumes* featuring several dozen instantaneously chilled vegetables, each prepared differently. The proprietress provides memorable service.

■ Opening hours, last orders
Lunch = 12:00-15:00 L.O.14:00
Dinner = 18:00-22:30 L.O.21:00

■ Annual and weekly closing
Closed late December-early January and Monday

■ Price
Lunch = set ¥ 3,150-6,300
Dinner = set ¥ 6,000-12,000
Service charge = 10% (dinner)

TEL. 03-6452-2525
Ebisu Hana Building 2F,
2-25-3 Ebisuminami, Shibuya-ku,
Tokyo

www.emu-francaise.jp

FUSION

Equilibrio NEW

The name refers to the bringing together of the best that the French and Italian worlds have to offer. The *omakase* set menu starts off with a foie gras and caramel cream puff. The idea of serving tomato and passion fruit pasta is original. Sometimes creativity is placed above taste, but customers will enjoy the modern dishes that transcend borders. If you can't decide between French and Italian, this is the place to go.

■ Opening hours, last orders
Lunch = 12:00-14:00 (L.O.)
Dinner = 18:00-21:00 (L.O.)

■ Annual and weekly closing
Closed late December-early January and Wednesday

■ Price
Lunch = set ¥ 5,000
Dinner = set ¥ 10,500
Service charge = 10% (dinner)

TEL. 03-3700-4647
Rise Plaza Mall 202, 1-15-6
Tamagawa, Setagaya-ku, Tokyo
www.equilibrio-rise.jp

JAPANESE CONTEMPORARY

Esaki
えさき

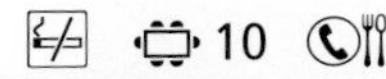
10

Shintaro Esaki's cuisine is inspiring and original; he conducts meticulous research on each product and his mastery of technique allows him to cross culinary boundaries. *Yurine manju senbei zutsumi* is a signature dish, which is replaced by *ayu* soup in summer. The same dishes are incorporated into both the lunch and dinner set menus; the prices of these differ according to the number of dishes but are both very appealing.

■ Opening hours, last orders
Lunch = Thu.-Sat. 12:00-14:00 L.O.13:30
Dinner = 18:00-23:00 L.O.21:30

■ Annual and weekly closing
Closed Golden week, mid-August, late December-early January, Sunday and Public Holidays

■ Price
Lunch = set ¥ 5,250
Dinner = set ¥ 8,400-13,650
Service charge = 10% (lunch 5%)

TEL. 03-3408-5056
Hills Aoyama B1F,
3-39-9 Jingumae, Shibuya-ku,
Tokyo

www.aoyamaesaki.net

ITALIAN

Faro

Traditional Italian recipes are executed with the *esprit* of French cuisine. Homemade spaghetti with snow crab comes with a complementary tomato reduction and is one highlight and, in winter, one can enjoy risotto with black truffles. As well as typical Italian desserts such as tiramisu and panna cotta, the kitchen offers savarin, opéra and other French favourites. The wine list is extensive and the service pleasant.

■ Opening hours, last orders
Lunch = 11:30-15:30 L.O.14:30
Dinner = 17:30-23:00 L.O.21:30

■ Annual and weekly closing
Closed late December-early January, Sunday and Public Holidays

■ Price

Lunch =	set weekday	¥ 2,800-8,000
	Sat.	¥ 3,800-8,000
	à la carte	¥ 7,000-21,000
Dinner =	set	¥ 6,800-15,000
	à la carte	¥ 7,000-21,000

Service charge = 10%

TEL. 03-3572-3911
Tokyo Ginza Shiseido Building 10F,
8-8-3 Ginza, Chuo-ku, Tokyo

http://faro.shiseido.co.jp

Feu NEW

The chef's philosophy is 'cooked yet fresh, modified yet natural'. Featuring a combination of ingredients with distinctive fragrances and textures, the intricately arranged 'Foie Gras Mont Blanc' embodies that very philosophy and was created as homage to Albert 1er, the restaurant which had the greatest influence on him during his six years spent training in France - he got the idea for the dish while climbing in Chamonix.

■ Opening hours, last orders
Lunch = 11:30-15:00 L.O.14:00
Dinner = 18:00-23:00 L.O.21:30

■ Annual and weekly closing
Closed mid-August, late December-early January, Sunday and 3rd Monday

■ Price
Lunch = set ¥ 3,150-9,450
à la carte ¥ 8,500-10,000
Dinner = set ¥ 8,400-15,750
à la carte ¥ 8,500-10,000
Service charge = 10%

TEL. 03-3479-0230
1-26-16 Minamiaoyama, Minato-ku, Tokyo

www.feu.co.jp

Florilège

Owner-chef Hiroyasu Kawate's approach to cuisine involves fusing elaborate classical elements, achieved through techniques handed down by master chefs, with a contemporary style in which dishes are meticulously arranged. He innovatively pairs roasted foie gras with a lightly salted meringue, yielding a heavy-light contrast of textures and flavours. Meat consists of two dishes, prepared to complement each particular cut.

■ Opening hours, last orders
Lunch = 12:00-13:30 (L.O.)
Dinner = 18:30-21:00 (L.O.)

■ Annual and weekly closing
Closed late December-early January, Wednesday and 1st Tuesday

■ Price
Lunch = set ¥ 4,200
Dinner = set ¥ 10,500
Service charge = 10%

TEL. 03–6440–0878
4-9-9 Minamiaoyama, Minato-ku, Tokyo

www.aoyama-florilege.jp

JAPANESE FUGU

Fugu Fukuji

ふぐ 福治

15

Takeshi Yasuge uses only wild tiger *fugu* from the Bungo Strait. For *sashimi*, the *fugu* is aged for several days to develop flavour and sliced thicker than usual. The *ponzu* sauce is made with *daidai* juice; the red chilli pepper used for the *momiji-oroshi* is ground with a stone mill to enhance its aroma. To finish, the chef or proprietress prepares *zosui* using eggs, *koto-negi* and soup from the hotpot with its bold *fugu* flavour.

■ Opening hours, last orders
Dinner = 17:00-23:00 L.O.21:30

■ Annual and weekly closing
Closed mid-August, late December-early January, Saturday, Sunday and Public Holidays from April-October

■ Price
Dinner = set ¥ 27,300-34,650
Service charge = 10%

TEL. 03-5148-2922
Koda Building 3F,
5-11-13 Ginza, Chuo-ku, Tokyo

www.fukuji.jp

JAPANESE TEMPURA

Fukamachi
深町

The owner-chef's *tempura* is thinly battered and lightly fried so as not to spoil the original taste of the ingredients. He uses two fryers set at two temperatures and high-quality white sesame oil for *tempura* soft on the palate. Vegetables are fried at a lower temperature to maintain their freshness and colour; seafood at a higher temperature to ensure a crisp tastiness. Enjoy *Edomae tempura* at this stylish restaurant.

■ Opening hours, last orders
Lunch = 11:30-14:00 L.O.13:30
Dinner = 17:00-22:00 L.O.21:00

■ Annual and weekly closing
Closed Golden week, mid-August, late December-early January, Monday, 1st and 3rd Sunday

■ Price
Lunch = set ¥ 6,300-8,400
à la carte ¥ 7,000-12,000
Dinner = set ¥ 10,500-15,750
à la carte ¥ 7,000-12,000

TEL. 03–5250–8777
2-5-2 Kyobashi, Chuo-ku, Tokyo

JAPANESE

Fukudaya
福田家

 40

Fukudaya is well known for its close relationship with Rosanjin Kitaoji, distinguished calligrapher, ceramicist and master chef. Now run by the 3rd-generation owner, the restaurant has seven bi-level dining rooms that are fine examples of traditional architecture. Antiques and garden views behind the *shoji* screens make you forget you're in the city. The traditionally prepared *kaiseki* dishes will satisfy your five senses.

■ Opening hours, last orders
Lunch = 11:30-14:30 L.O.13:00
Dinner = 17:00-22:00 L.O.20:00

■ Annual and weekly closing
Closed late December-early January,
Sunday and Public Holidays

■ Price
Lunch = set ¥ 21,000-26,250
Dinner = set ¥ 26,250-36,750
Private room fee = ¥ 5,250/person
Service charge = 20%

TEL. 03–3261–8577
6-12 Kioicho, Chiyoda-ku, Tokyo

Fukuju
福樹

8

The private dining space is in the style of a tea ceremony room where, if reserved, guests enjoy a tea ceremony and meal put together by the chef, a certified instructor. Dishes are prepared to retain flavour and aroma; the disk abalone from the Sanriku coast served in a soup with a freshwater clam base is well worth trying. Beautiful serving vessels, including some from the Edo Period, add to the appeal of each dish.

■ Opening hours, last orders
Lunch = 12:00-15:00 L.O.13:00
Dinner = 18:00-22:30 L.O.20:30

■ Annual and weekly closing
Closed mid-August, late December-early January, Sunday and Public Holidays

■ Price
Lunch = set ¥ 21,000-26,250
Dinner = set ¥ 21,000-52,500
Service charge = 10%

TEL. 03-3571-8596
Iseyoshi Building 5F,
8-8-19 Ginza, Chuo-ku, Tokyo

JAPANESE

Ginza Okuda NEW

銀座 奥田

Toru Okuda's energy knows no bounds; this, his third restaurant, bears his name and offers the same dishes and customer service as Koju. Although delicate and original, the dishes stay within the boundaries of Japanese cuisine. Summer specialities include abalone *somen* and seasonal vegetables in gelatine. At the end comes *soba*, prepared by a professional. At lunch, he's behind the counter, so those are the special seats.

■ Opening hours, last orders
Lunch = 12:00-13:00 (L.O.)
Dinner = 18:00-21:30 (L.O.)

■ Annual and weekly closing
Closed mid-August, late December-early January, Sunday and Public Holidays

■ Price
Lunch = set ¥ 10,500-21,000
Dinner = set ¥ 15,750-21,000
Service charge = 10%

TEL. 03-5537-3338
Carioka Building B1F, 5-4-8 Ginza, Chuo-ku, Tokyo

www.ginzaokuda.com

JAPANESE

Ginza Toyoda
銀座 とよだ

Seasonal ingredients are selected for their texture and flavour: in spring, thick bamboo shoots grilled over charcoal; in summer, sweetfish, dried and marinated with *shuto* before being grilled and served with *honesenbei*. In autumn it is kelp hotpot with pike conger and *matsutake;* grilled *matsubagani* crab is popular in the cold months. The owner-chef welcomes customers at the entrance and the waitress is pleasant.

■ Opening hours, last orders
Lunch = 11:30-14:30 L.O. 13:30
Dinner = 17:30-22:00 L.O. 20:30

■ Annual and weekly closing
Closed mid-August, late December-early January, Sunday and Public Holidays

■ Price
Lunch = set ¥ 5,250-10,500
Dinner = set ¥ 10,500-21,000
Service charge = 10%

TEL. 03–5568–5822
La Vialle Ginza Building 2F,
7-5-4 Ginza, Chuo-ku, Tokyo

FRENCH

Gordon Ramsay

Just past the chic entrance is an open kitchen; the chef's table here seats 6-8 people. The cooking style avoids placing too many ingredients on a single plate and accentuates them with side dishes and sauces. For example, *tortellini* of lobster features shellfish enveloped with thin pasta which is steamed and served with lemongrass sauce, basil and tomato chutney. The wine list includes well-known labels and a range of prices.

■ Opening hours, last orders
Dinner = 17:30-21:00 (L.O.)

■ Annual and weekly closing
Closed Sunday except before a Public Holiday, and Monday

■ Price
Dinner = set ¥ 11,500-22,000

TEL. 03–6388–8000
Conrad Hotel 28F,
1-9-1 Higashishinbashi,
Minato-ku, Tokyo

http://gordonramsay.jp

STEAKHOUSE

Gorio
哥利歐

This restaurant serves Tajima Sanda beef - choose from sirloin, filet, H-bone or rump, as the cut will determine the thickness. The only seasoning is salt and pepper. The meat is cooked on a skewer over a white charcoal grill, the dripping fat filling the air with a pleasant aroma. The name comes from *Le Père Goriot*, the novel by Balzac, a meat lover. A friendly veteran maître d' offers careful explanations of the meat.

■ Opening hours, last orders
12:00-23:00 L.O.22:00

■ Annual and weekly closing
Closed late December-early January and 2nd Sunday

■ Price
set ¥ 26,250
à la carte ¥ 30,000-50,000
Service charge = 10%

TEL. 03-3543-7214
8-18-3 Ginza, Chuo-ku, Tokyo

EUROPEAN

Grill Ukai

   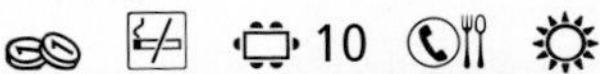 10 

The interior is an appealing cross between Japanese and Western sensibilities and the menu consists primarily of French cuisine, but the speciality is dishes grilled with infrared rays. As well as standard Ukai *kuroge wagyu* beef and Sanriku abalone, the wide range of items include Ezo pork, Kawamata Shamo chicken and *unagi*. To take in the atmosphere, a seat by the window is recommended; the courtyard is illuminated by night.

■ Opening hours, last orders
Lunch = 11:00-14:00 (L.O.)
Dinner = 17:30-21:00 (L.O.)

■ Annual and weekly closing
Closed 1 January

■ Price
Lunch = set ¥ 3,680-6,300
à la carte ¥ 6,500-21,000
Dinner = set ¥ 7,350-15,750
à la carte ¥ 6,500-21,000
Service charge = 10%

TEL. 03–5221–5252
Marunouchi Park Building 2F,
2-6-1 Marunouchi, Chiyoda-ku,
Tokyo

www.grill-ukai.jp

JAPANESE

Hamadaya

濱田家

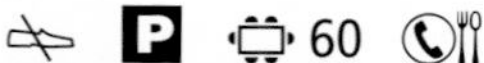

  60 

This prestigious restaurant is one of the few *sukiya*-style buildings remaining today. The head chef keeps to the traditions passed down from his predecessors: dishes are given subtle variations of flavour depending on the ingredients used and the order in which they are served. In *hamo* season, the *hamo* is covered with *kudzu* and rolled *yuba* is served in a soup using a light and tasty stock, while the hot pot of sliced Japanese beef and *sansho* are served *Edomae sukiyaki*.

■ Opening hours, last orders
Lunch = Wed., Thu. and Sat.
11:00-15:00 L.O.14:00
Dinner = 17:30-23:00 L.O.20:00

■ Annual and weekly closing
Closed mid-August, late December-early January, Sunday and Public Holidays

■ Price
Lunch = set ¥ 15,750-24,150
Dinner = set ¥ 26,250-52,500
Private room fee = ¥ 3,150/person (dinner)
Service charge = 20% (lunch 15%)

TEL. 03–3661–5940
3-13-5 Nihonbashiningyocho,
Chuo-ku, Tokyo

www.hamadaya.info

JAPANESE SUSHI

Harutaka
青空

Harutaka Takahashi's day begins with a trip to Tsukiji market, where he selects only ingredients he judges to be good. *Hatsu gatsuo* is seared over a straw fire in May; there is wild *madaka* abalone between April and June; *shako* is purchased alive and quickly steamed to ensure freshness. The temperature ensures each topping is kept at its best. The rice is a special blend combining sweet-tasting rice with a less sticky variety.

■ Opening hours, last orders
Dinner = 17:00-24:00
Saturday 17:00-22:30

■ Annual and weekly closing
Closed Golden week, mid-August, late December-early January, Sunday and Public Holidays

■ Price
Dinner = set ¥ 18,000-30,000

TEL. 03-3573-1144
Kawabata Building 3F,
8-5-8 Ginza, Chuo-ku, Tokyo

Hashimoto NEW
はし本

   25 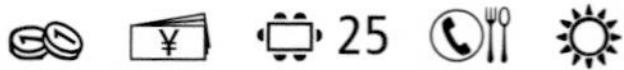  

Founded in 1835, the restaurant is run by the 6th generation owner-chef. The *unaju* consists of tasty, tender steamed *unagi* on rice, covered evenly in sauce. The recipe for the somewhat salty sauce has been passed down from generation to generation and the owner-chef says he looks for strong tasting *unagi* that will go well with the sauce. The *unaju* takes 20-30 minutes so enjoy snacks like *mukobone* and *hire* while you wait.

■ Opening hours, last orders
Lunch = 11:30-14:00 (L.O.)
Dinner = 16:30-20:00 L.O.19:30

■ Annual and weekly closing
Closed late December-early January and Thursday

■ Price
Lunch = à la carte ¥ 2,500-4,500
Dinner = à la carte ¥ 2,500-4,500
Private room fee = 10%

TEL. 03-3811-4850
2-5-7 Suido, Bunkyo-ku, Tokyo
www.unagi-hashimoto.jp

Hatanaka
畑中

Hiroyoshi Hatanaka set up his dream restaurant in Azabujuban in 1997, serving *tempura* using aromatic sesame oil. We recommend the combined seafood and vegetable set menu. The *makiebi* are cooked two different ways for contrasting sweetness and texture. The round aubergine slices, fried lightly golden and halved, are recommended with soy sauce. As the natural aroma of the ingredients is important, avoid wearing strong perfumes.

■ Opening hours, last orders
Dinner = 17:30-22:00 L.O.20:30

■ Annual and weekly closing
Closed mid-August, late December-early January and Wednesday

■ Price
Dinner = set ¥ 8,400-10,500
à la carte ¥ 8,000-12,000
Service charge = 5%

TEL. 03–3456–2406
2-21-10 Azabujuban, Minato-ku, Tokyo

Hatsunezushi
初音鮨

Owner-chef Katsu Nakaji serves only sushi - without appetisers. He prefers slightly firmer rice and flavours it with akazu; special care ensures the right temperature. Although he generally uses *Edomae* techniques, he also boldly tries new things like tiger prawn and crab sakamushi and boiling and hand-pressing natural sweetfish in June. The hospitable nature of the owner-chef's wife also leaves a favourable impression.

■ Opening hours, last orders
Lunch = Sat. 12:00-14:00
Dinner = 17:30-19:45 and 20:00-22:30

■ Annual and weekly closing
Closed Golden week, mid-August, late December-early January, Sunday and Public Holidays

■ Price
Lunch = set ¥ 15,750-21,000
Dinner = set ¥ 15,750-21,000

TEL. 03-3731-2403
5-20-2 Nishikamata, Ota-ku, Tokyo

JAPANESE

Hifumian

一二三庵

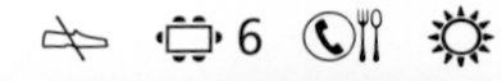

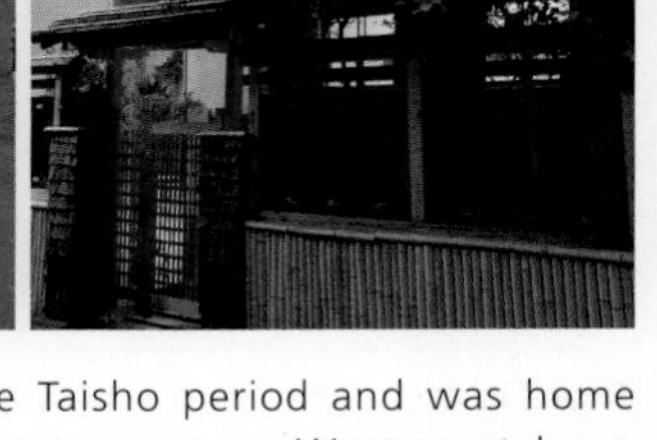

The building dates from the late Taisho period and was home to a *Noh* performer. There are just two rooms: Western-style on the 1st floor, Japanese-style on the 2nd. Takamitsu Aihara opened Hifumian after training in Osaka, Kobe and Tokyo. The lightly roasted sea bass with *misansho* pepper and white *miso* is highly recommended. Just two groups, by reservation only, are served at each meal and only set courses are offered.

■ Opening hours, last orders
Lunch = 12:00-15:00 L.O.14:00
Dinner = 18:00-23:00 L.O.20:00

■ Annual and weekly closing
Closed Golden week, mid-August and late December-early January

■ Price
Lunch = set ¥ 10,500-15,750
Dinner = set ¥ 15,750-21,000
Service charge = 10%

TEL. 03–5832–8677
4-2-18 Sendagi, Bunkyo-ku, Tokyo

www.hifumi-an.com

JAPANESE

Higuchi
樋口

There is a counter, two tables and a private room for up to four. Sea urchin jelly is a staple; the *hamo shabu-shabu*, using stock made with *hamo* bones, is a pleasant summer dish, while in autumn, *matsutake* is added. In winter, savoury egg custard with sea cucumber gut and mackerel sushi are recommended. The last course is either *jako meshi* or *tai meshi*. The chef works alone, so sit back and enjoy the leisurely pace.

■ Opening hours, last orders
Dinner = 18:00-21:00 (L.O.)

■ Annual and weekly closing
Closed Golden week, mid-August, late December-early January, Sunday and Public Holidays

■ Price
Dinner = set ¥ 12,600-18,900
Private room fee = ¥ 3,000
Service charge = 10%

TEL. 03-3402-7038
2-19-12 Jingumae, Shibuya-ku, Tokyo

FRENCH

Hiramatsu

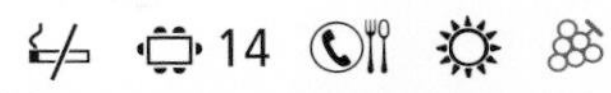

Hiroyuki Hiramatsu decided to pursue a culinary career after reading a book by 20C French chef Fernand Point. He now has several restaurants in Japan and has established a partnership with another French chef, Paul Bocuse. The dishes are a contemporary take on traditional French cuisine. Specialities include duck foie gras rolled in cabbage with truffle sauce and roast lamb slices and onion compote with truffle sauce.

■ Opening hours, last orders
Lunch = 12:00-13:30 (L.O.)
Dinner = 18:00-20:30 (L.O.)

■ Annual and weekly closing
Closed 1 January

■ Price
Lunch = set ¥ 6,300-8,400
à la carte ¥ 16,000-18,000
Dinner = set ¥ 9,500-15,000
à la carte ¥ 16,000-18,000
Service charge = 15%

TEL. 03–3444–3967
5-15-13 Minamiazabu, Minato-ku, Tokyo
www.hiramatsu.co.jp/restaurants/hiramatsu-hiroo

JAPANESE

Hirosaku
ひろ作

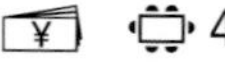

4

A friendly couple welcomes you to this simple dining room with its nostalgic Showa feel. The abalone is cooked salty-sweet; the *watari-gani* is dipped in a sauce made to a secret recipe. The light taste of the simmered Japanese branquillo is enhanced by the fine broth. As the last dish, enjoy glossy handmade soba noodles; they slide down smoothly and are in perfect harmony with the slightly sweet sauce. Good value lunch prices.

■ Opening hours, last orders
Lunch = 11:45-13:00 (L.O.)
Dinner = 18:00-20:00 (L.O.)

■ Annual and weekly closing
Closed mid-August, late December-early January, Saturday, Sunday and Public Holidays

■ Price
Lunch = set ¥ 8,400-12,600
Dinner = set ¥ 26,250-31,500

TEL. 03–3591–0901
3-6-13 Shinbashi, Minato-ku, Tokyo

Hishinuma
菱沼

Owner-chef Takayuki Hishinuma's goal is to 'serve society through food'. While Japanese cuisine is the base, he combines it with meat and creative Western-inspired dishes. A vegetarian menu is offered along with a *Hiyoko-san* menu for children to provide them with nutritional education. His love of wine allows him to suggest pairings. The tranquil, modern restaurant includes a wide counter, table seating and two private rooms.

■ Opening hours, last orders
Lunch = 11:30-13:30 (L.O.)
Dinner = 17:30-22:00 (L.O.)

■ Annual and weekly closing
Closed mid-August, late December-early January, Sunday and Public Holidays

■ Price
Lunch = set ¥ 3,570-7,350
Dinner = set ¥ 12,600-18,900
Service charge = 10%

TEL. 03-3568-6588
Axis Building B1F,
5-17-1 Roppongi, Minato-ku,
Tokyo

JAPANESE SUKIYAKI

Hiyama
日山

In 1935, a meat store opened a *sukiyaki kappo* restaurant on the 2nd floor of its building, built in the style of a tea-ceremony house. There are various sized rooms, and evidence of repeated extensions can be seen. The Hiyama *wagyu* is from the butcher's shop downstairs and its quality is constant; seasonal vegetables like *mitsuba* and mushrooms are used. There are dedicated cooking staff, allowing you to simply enjoy the food.

■ Opening hours, last orders
Lunch = 11:30-14:00
Dinner = 17:00-21:00

■ Annual and weekly closing
Closed mid-August, late December-early January, Sunday and Public Holidays

■ Price
Lunch = set ¥ 6,825-9,975
Dinner = set ¥ 8,400-18,900
Service charge = 10%

TEL. 03–3666–2901
2-5-1 Nihonbashiningyocho,
Chuo-ku, Tokyo
www.hiyama-nihonbashi.co.jp

FRENCH

Hommage NEW

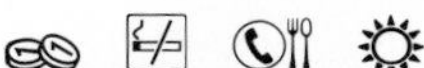

As the name suggests, the humble owner-chef has a respectful attitude in everything. Using ingredients from all over the world, he identifies their unique characteristics and then prepares them using French techniques. He uses Japanese ingredients for the *dengaku miso* French toast accompanying the foie gras, and the bean sprout *kuzuyose* side dish. Sometimes dishes are playful, like the Asakusa speciality, 'Kaminariokoshi'.

■ Opening hours, last orders
Lunch = 11:30-13:30 (L.O.)
Dinner = 18:00-21:00 (L.O.)

■ Annual and weekly closing
Closed late December-early January and Monday except Public Holidays

■ Price
Lunch = set Tue.-Fri.¥ 2,900-6,300
Sat.,Sun.¥ 3,800-6,300
Dinner = set ¥ 6,300-10,500
Service charge = 10% (dinner)

TEL. 03-3874-1552
4-10-5 Asakusa, Taito-ku, Tokyo

www.hommage-arai.com

JAPANESE

Horikane
堀兼

Owner-chef Hidehiro Horiuchi's kitchen is a place of focused concentration. Combining Chinese and Japanese styles, a spiced stew of Jinhua ham and vegetables is served on steamed papaya while *shirako* risotto is topped with white truffles from Alba; in winter, *shabu-shabu* of yellowtail and wild *nameko* mushrooms is delicious. The hotpot dish is served all year round. In Nittozakashita, near the entrance to the Shirogane Tunnel.

■ Opening hours, last orders
Dinner = 18:30-23:00 L.O.21:00

■ Annual and weekly closing
Closed Golden week, mid-August, late December-early January, Sunday and Public Holidays

■ Price
Dinner = set ¥ 21,000-24,000

TEL. 03-3280-4629
5-10-13 Shirokanedai,
Minato-ku, Tokyo

JAPANESE

Hosokawa
ほそ川

The owner-chef of this restaurant - operated out of a corner of a commercial building - went from dietician to chef. The cosy interior makes you forget the bustle of the city, and the menu is full of vegetable dishes. The *ohitashi* is boiled just before serving and seasoned only with salt to bring out the flavours. The meal ends with white rice cooked in an earthenware pot. The entrance is to the right from the elevator.

■ Opening hours, last orders
Dinner = 18:00-23:00

■ Annual and weekly closing
Closed late December-early January, Sunday and Public Holidays

■ Price
Dinner = set ¥ 3,800-10,500

TEL. 03–3581–8886
HK Shinbashi Building 5F,
2-12-2 Shinbashi, Minato-ku,
Tokyo

JAPANESE

Hyo-tei NEW
瓢亭

The current owner-chef's grandfather opened a restaurant during the Taisho period and, while the name has an exclusive ring to it, it took on a more casual atmosphere when it relocated. There is *bento* but we recommend the *kaiseki* cuisine, passed down through the generations. The famous Hyo-tei *tamago*, an unlikely success story, is on every menu and sashimi uses traditional techniques like slight boiling and *hegizukuri*.

■ Opening hours, last orders
Lunch = 11:30-14:30 L.O.13:30
Dinner = 17:30-22:00 L.O.20:00

■ Annual and weekly closing
Closed mid-August and late December-early January

■ Price
Lunch = set ¥ 8,000-15,000
Dinner = set ¥ 8,000-15,000

TEL. 03-5779-7477
1-10-8 Ikejiri, Setagaya-ku, Tokyo

JAPANESE

Ibuki NEW
一二岐

The owner-chef opened in 2010 and serves Japanese cuisine unfettered by convention, with a sense of largesse and freedom. Fish comes from a port in Kochi, the speciality being straw-smoked *katsuo*. There are also creative dishes like grilled cutlass fish with *uni* garnished with *daikon* topped with *karasumi*. The rice offers a range of delightful contrasts, from slightly undercooked right through to somewhat burnt round the edges.

■ Opening hours, last orders
Lunch = 11:30-15:00 L.O.14:00
Dinner = 17:30-23:00 L.O.22:00

■ Annual and weekly closing
Closed mid-August, late December-early January, Sunday and Public Holiday Mondays

■ Price
Lunch = set ¥ 1,300-5,000
Dinner = set ¥ 9,450-15,750

TEL. 03-6278-8110
Daini Matsuoka Building B1F,
2-14-6 Ginza, Chuo-ku, Tokyo

ITALIAN

Icaro

This small restaurant feels bigger than it is, thanks to the large window, and it has a casual, trattoria-style atmosphere. The chef uses his 7 years of experience in Italy, and his brother, a wine connoisseur, handles the service. The speciality is the braised Hokkaido deer *pappardelle* with sauce; the Japanese beef cheek goulash is northern Italian, a cuisine in which the chef excels. The wine is also reasonably priced.

■ Opening hours, last orders
Dinner = 18:00-1:00
Saturday 18:00-24:00

■ Annual and weekly closing
Closed late December-early January and Sunday

■ Price
Dinner = set ¥ 5,250
à la carte ¥ 5,500-8,000
Seat charge = ¥500/person

TEL. 03–5724–8085
Coms Nakameguro 4F,
2-44-24 Kamimeguro,
Meguro-ku, Tokyo

www.icaro-miyamoto.com

JAPANESE

Ichie
一会

Junichi Watanabe became a chef at the age of 35, having previously pursued a different career path. Only set menus are offered. Giant abalone, a staple dish, steamed for over four hours in sake and very tender, fills your mouth with its flavour; served in a clay pot, Koshihikari rice from Aizu Kitakata region rounds off the meal. Chef prepares all the dishes himself but the wait is worth it as he puts his heart into them.

■ Opening hours, last orders
Dinner = 18:00-23:00 L.O.21:00

■ Annual and weekly closing
Closed mid-August, late December-early January and Tuesday

■ Price
Dinner = set ¥ 10,500
Service charge = 10%

TEL. 03-3280-1439
Excel Shirota Building B1F,
5-16-16 Hiroo, Shibuya-ku, Tokyo

JAPANESE ODEN

Ichigo
一期

Enjoy *oden* at this atmospheric restaurant that resembles a bar, with jazz in the background. The base stock is made from eight ingredients and no effort is spared in bringing out essential flavours, such as *yuba* – fried for a pleasant aroma – and the soft-boiled eggs marinated in stock. After *sashimi*, charbroiled *ichiyaboshi* and other dishes, have your favourite *oden* items. We recommend *chameshi* with *oden-dashi* to end with.

■ Opening hours, last orders
Dinner = 17:30-24:00 L.O.23:30

■ Annual and weekly closing
Closed Monday

■ Price
Dinner = set ¥ 6,800
à la carte ¥ 5,500-10,000
Service charge = 10%
Seat charge=¥ 840/person

TEL. 03–5772–2936
My-Corner Building B1F,
2-5-14 Azabujuban, Minato-ku,
Tokyo

www.azabu-ichigo.com

JAPANESE

Ichimonji
一文字

14

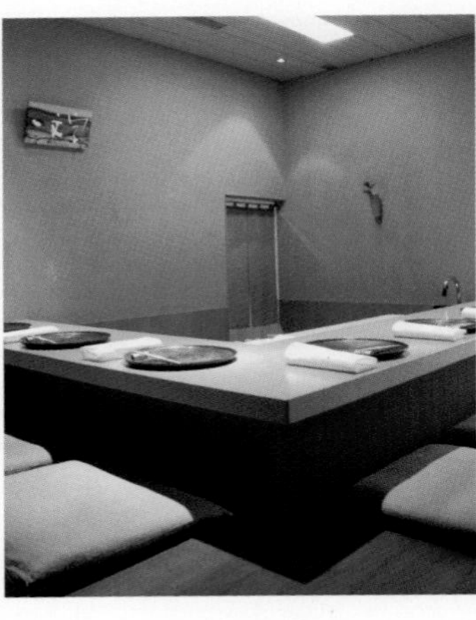

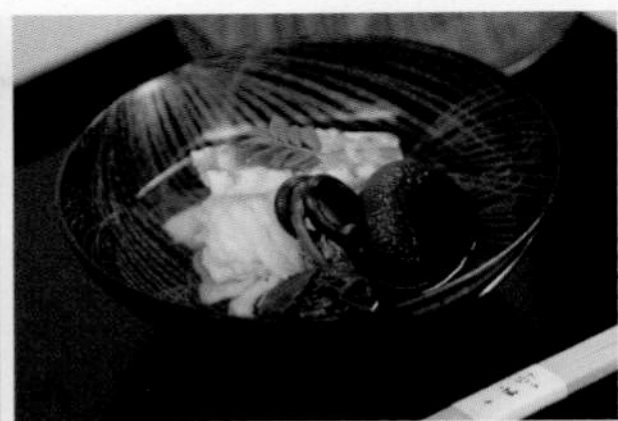

Kazuhiko Hirose catered for tea ceremonies for 13 years (and continues to do so) before opening here in 2005. Each dish is in harmony with the colour and feel of the tableware on which it is served; soft, plump *hotate-shinjo* served with Kintoki carrot and *yuzu* is a colourful dish with the white, red and yellow standing out in the clear soup. There is sunken seating at the counter on the 1st floor and a tatami room on the 2nd.

■ Opening hours, last orders
Lunch = 12:00-14:00 (L.O.)
Dinner = 18:00-21:00 (L.O.)

■ Annual and weekly closing
Closed Golden week, mid-August and late December-early January

■ Price
Lunch = set ¥ 8,400-16,800
Dinner = set ¥ 12,600-21,000
Private room fee = ¥5,250
Service charge = 10%

TEL. 03–5206–8223
3-6 Kagurazaka, Shinjuku-ku, Tokyo

JAPANESE

Ichirin 

一凛

The owner-chef serves traditional cuisine based on his extensive experience but does not get trapped in form. First and last harvest ingredients are used in the *hassun* to draw thoughts to the slowly changing seasons. At the end comes *takikomi-gohan*, prepared for each group. There is also a selection of sake and wine. Lunch requires reservations at least 2 days in advance and a party of at least 4 on regular closing days.

■ Opening hours, last orders
Lunch = 12:00-13:00 (L.O.)
Dinner = 18:00-21:00 (L.O.)

■ Annual and weekly closing
Closed mid-August, late December-early January, Sunday and Public Holidays

■ Price
Lunch = set ¥ 3,300-11,000
Dinner = set ¥ 11,000-20,000
Service charge = 10% (5% for lunch)

TEL. 03–6410–7355
Azuma Building 2F,
2-19-5 Jingumae, Shibuya-ku,
Tokyo

JAPANESE

Ikku NEW
一空

Enjoy seasonal set menus developed around natural *anago*. The large *anago* are about 500g each and are aged for 2 days. Sashimi is cut into beautiful, chrysanthemum-shaped slices and has a delicate taste; chargrilled items are creatively garnished with *yuzu* or *sudachi* froth. There are also other carefully prepared specialities including soups and vinegar-based dishes. A popular end to the meal is *chazuke* with fragrant sesame.

■ Opening hours, last orders
Lunch = 12:00-14:30 L.O.13:30
Dinner = 17:30-22:00 L.O.19:30

■ Annual and weekly closing
Closed mid-August, late December-early January and Wednesday

■ Price

Lunch = set	¥ 2,200-4,200
Dinner = set	¥ 5,250-10,500

TEL. 03-6795-0117
5-7-12 Yanaka, Taito-ku, Tokyo

JAPANESE TEMPURA

Ise
いせ

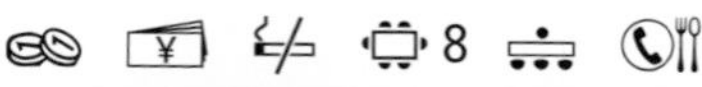

The owner-chef goes to Tsukiji to select the seafood himself; vegetables are from all over the country and the live young *saimaki ebi* come directly from Amakusa. In spring, his father sends edible wild plants from the mountains of Tohoku. The ingredients are fried in a homemade blend of cotton seed oil; the salt is also homemade. Prices are reasonable for what is included and once the rice runs out, the restaurant closes.

■ Opening hours, last orders
Lunch = 11:30-14:00 L.O.13:30
Dinner = 17:30-22:00 L.O.20:30

■ Annual and weekly closing
Closed mid-August, late December-early January and Sunday

■ Price
Lunch = set ¥ 950-3,000
Dinner = set ¥ 4,200-8,800
à la carte ¥ 5,000-8,000

TEL. 03-3768-0750
3-29-8 Minamioi, Shinagawa-ku, Tokyo

Ishibashi
いし橋

Established in 1879, this restaurant serves finely-marbled sirloin cuts from black-haired cattle beef from throughout Japan. The secret to the *sukiyaki* sauce, known only to the proprietress, has been passed down the generations. Staff take care of the pot and the serving, allowing you to enjoy the food and entertain your guests. Prices depend on the quality of meat; we recommend the *ojiya* in a *sukiyaki* pot to conclude the meal.

■ Opening hours, last orders
Dinner = 17:00-21:30 L.O.20:30

■ Annual and weekly closing
Closed Golden week, mid-August, late December-early January, Saturday, Sunday and Public Holidays

■ Price
Dinner = set ¥ 8,400-10,500
Service charge = ¥1,365/person

TEL. 03–3251–3580
3-6-8 Sotokanda, Chiyoda-ku, Tokyo

JAPANESE UNAGI

Ishibashi
石ばし

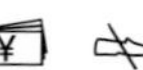

The *unagi* comes from a designated farm in Shizuoka, with the feed, cultivation period, etc. all specified by Ishibashi's owner. Preparation begins only once the customer has arrived so expect something of a wait. The broiled eel, free of excess oil, is served on rice in a Wajima lacquered box with a light, slightly tangy sauce to flavour the rice. The pickles, prepared using rice bran in a time-honoured way are also good.

■ Opening hours, last orders
Lunch = 11:30-13:30 (L.O.)
Saturday 11:30-14:00 (L.O.)
Dinner = 18:00-19:30 (L.O.)
Saturday 17:30-20:00 (L.O.)

■ Annual and weekly closing
Closed mid-August, late December-early January, Sunday, Monday and Public Holidays

■ Prices
Lunch = set ¥ 7,500-10,000
à la carte ¥ 2,500-10,000
Dinner = set ¥ 10,000-12,000
à la carte ¥ 2,500-10,000
Service charge = 10% (Tatami room)

TEL.03–3813–8038
2-4-29 Suido, Bunkyo-ku, Tokyo

www.unagi-ishibashi.com

JAPANESE

Ishikawa
石かわ

✿✿✿

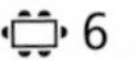

Hideki Ishikawa's cuisine is described as 'Ishikawa-style', bound only by his imagination. Innovative touches are incorporated to highlight the unique characteristics of each ingredient. Stewed beef tendon and wax gourd in stock is refined and creamy; the spiny lobster and abalone add an element of luxury. Sake is mainly from chef's birthplace of Niigata and the Hokuriku region. Look for a black fence behind Bishamonten Zenkokuji Temple.

■ Opening hours, last orders
Dinner = 17:30-24:00 L.O.22:00

■ Annual and weekly closing
Closed mid-August, late December-early January, Sunday and Public Holidays

■ Price
Dinner = set ¥ 15,750-19,950
Service charge = 10%

TEL. 03–5225–0173
5-37 Kagurazaka, Shinjuku-ku, Tokyo

JAPANESE SHOJIN

Itosho
いと正

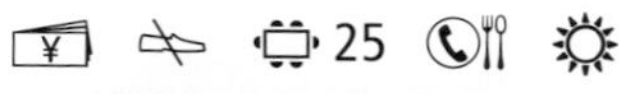

Opened by Hiroji Ito in 1960 in order to introduce Takayama meat-free cuisine, rooted in Zen Buddhism. He uses vegetables from all over the country, including Takayama, and stock made from kelp, *shiitake*, dried gourd shavings and other ingredients. The colourful appetiser, matcha jelly mixed with yams, laver boiled down in soy sauce and raw wheat gluten are eaten with a rich sauce with tofu, sesame and walnuts.

■ Opening hours, last orders
Lunch = 12:00-15:00 L.O.13:00
Dinner = 17:30-21:30 L.O.19:30

■ Price
Lunch = set ¥ 6,300
Dinner = set ¥ 8,400-10,500
Service charge = 10%

TEL. 03-3454-6538
3-4-7 Azabujuban, Minato-ku, Tokyo

JAPANESE FUGU

Izumi
い津み

✿ XXX

12

The *omakase* comes in two types: *fugu kaiseki* and *fugu ryori*. If you are looking for *chirinabe* and *zosui*, we recommend the latter; the former is made up of several dishes that include *fugu*, like *nikogori* and *nanbanni*. *Sashimi* is cut thick and placed on a white porcelain dish. The speciality is the *zosui*; the rice is cooked in stock to fully absorb the flavour of the *fugu*. There are separate entrances for the 1st and 2nd floors.

■ Opening hours, last orders
Dinner = 17:00-22:00

■ Annual and weekly closing
Closed August, late December-early January, Saturday and Public Holidays from April-September and Sunday

■ Price
Dinner = set ¥ 21,000-29,400
à la carte ¥ 20,000-30,000
Service charge = 15%

TEL. 03–3582–0101
6-11-11 Akasaka, Minato-ku, Tokyo

www.izumi-akasaka.jp

JAPANESE FUGU

Jirocho NEW

治郎長

18

Miharakoji's speciality from October to March is *fugu* and, from April to September, charbroiled *tai*. The proprietress, a licensed *fugu* chef and sommelier, maintains the spirit of its founding. Natural *fugu* is from Shimonoseki; *tsukuri* is prepared in thick strips and the pot served on a clay charcoal brazier; the *shuko* is also of repute. Across the street is the 'Ofuku' annexe; if you want a counter seat, ask for 'Jirocho'.

■ Opening hours, last orders
Dinner = 17:30-23:00 L.O.21:30

■ Annual and weekly closing
Closed mid-August, late December-early January, Saturday, Sunday and Public Holidays

■ Price
Dinner = set ¥ 26,250-31,500
Service charge = 10%

TEL. 03-3571-3819
5-9-18 Ginza, Chuo-ku, Tokyo

FRENCH CONTEMPORARY

Joël Robuchon

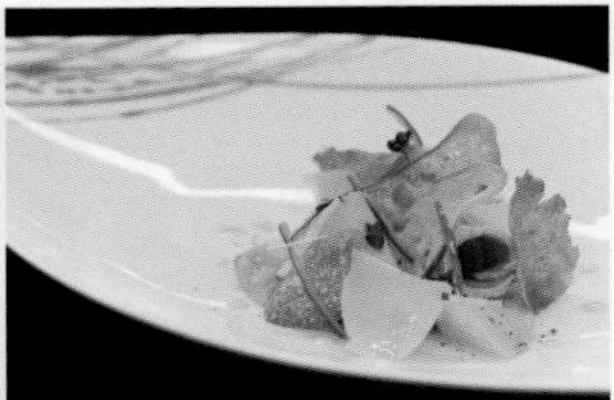

Located on the 2nd floor of an 18C French-style château at Yebisu Garden Place and under the auspices of the eponymous chef, Joël Robuchon. The room is furnished in black with Swarovski crystal adorning the golden walls and a dazzling Baccarat chandelier. The house specialities, ossetra caviar and crustacean gelée served with cauliflower cream, and ravioli stuffed with langoustine and truffles, are highly recommended.

■ Opening hours, last orders
Lunch = 11:30-14:00 (L.O.)
Sat., Sun. and Public Holidays 12:00-14:00 (L.O.)
Dinner = 18:00-21:30 (L.O.)

■ Price
Lunch = set ¥ 6,000-12,300
à la carte ¥ 15,000-30,000
Dinner = set ¥ 22,500-36,000
à la carte ¥ 15,000-30,000
Service charge = 12% (private room 15%)

TEL. 03–5424–1347
Yebisu Garden Place,
1-13-1 Mita, Meguro-ku, Tokyo

www.robuchon.jp/ebisu

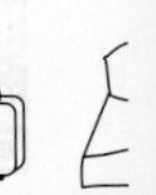

JAPANESE

Jushu NEW
壽修

The name comes from Chinese philosopher Mencius – live each day to the fullest. The owner-chef's focus is on capturing the seasons, following nature's ways and respecting ingredients. He rises to the occasion with a pantry of produce that always feel just right: sprouting mountain vegetables and bamboo shoots in spring, vegetables full of summer goodness, nuts and cereals harvested in fall, and root crops from the winter soil.

■ Opening hours, last orders
Dinner = 18:00-24:00

■ Annual and weekly closing
Closed mid-August, late December-early January, Sunday and Public Holidays

■ Price
Dinner = set ¥ 12,000

TEL. 03-6427-5167
2-16-1 Nishiazabu, Minato-ku, Tokyo

JAPANESE

Kadowaki
かどわき

Toshiya Kadowaki's creativity is the attraction here. Along with local ingredients, he looks to Western produce like truffles and foie gras to help him make 'dishes to impress'. In April, *hanasansho* hotpot with fish or beef is available; in autumn, *matsutake* and beef *shabu-shabu* is recommended. *Soba* with foie gras sauce is also good and truffle rice is a speciality. There are private rooms but we recommend the counter.

■ Opening hours, last orders
Dinner = 18:00-1:00 L.O.23:00
Saturday L.O.22:00

■ Annual and weekly closing
Closed Golden week, mid-August, late December-early January, Sunday and Public Holidays

■ Price
Dinner = set ¥ 21,000-26,250
Service charge = 10%

TEL. 03–5772–2553
2-7-2 Azabujuban, Minato-ku, Tokyo

www.azabu-kadowaki.com

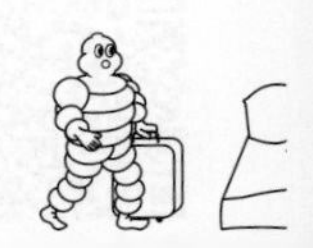

JAPANESE

Kagura
花楽

This restaurant was born in 2010 out of a collaboration between Kanazawa brewery Fukumitsuya and the Kyoto-born proprietress. The chef trained at a *ryotei* in Tokushima and the menu offers plenty of vegetable dishes; one of the standards is the *kagurazuke* – vegetables pickled in sake lees. Traditional techniques are used in familiar dishes like *okara* and *shiraae*. Try also the salt-grilled sweetfish and the monthly hotpot.

■ Opening hours, last orders
Lunch = Mon.-Fri. except Public Holidays 11:30-14:00 L.O.13:30
Dinner = 17:30-23:00 L.O.22:00

■ Annual and weekly closing
Closed mid-August, late December-early January and Sunday

■ Price
Lunch = set ¥ 1,500-3,500
Dinner = set ¥ 8,400-15,750
à la carte ¥ 5,000-15,000
Private room fee = ¥ 10,500
Service charge = 10% (dinner)

TEL. 03-3585-3030
5-5-9 Akasaka, Minato-ku, Tokyo
www.kagura-akasaka.com

JAPANESE

Kamiya Nogizaka
神谷 乃木坂

12

Masataka Kamiya expands the possibilities of Japanese cuisine by also using French, Italian and Chinese ingredients. Meishanton pork loin is used for the *shabu-shabu*, while the belly is cooked with black vinegar and topped with a scallion sauce. French duck is slowly cooked in its own fat and flavoured with a red wine sauce that includes soy sauce. The handmade *soba* served before dessert is another memorable feature.

■ Opening hours, last orders
Lunch = 11:30-15:00 L.O.14:30
Dinner = 17:30-22:00 L.O.21:30

■ Annual and weekly closing
Closed Golden week, mid-August, late December-early January, Sunday and Public Holidays

■ Price
Lunch = set ¥ 3,150-10,500
Dinner = set ¥ 10,500-21,000
Private room fee = ¥ 1,050/person
Service charge = 10%

TEL. 03-3497-0489
8-11-19 Akasaka, Minato-ku, Tokyo

www.kamiya-m.com/nogizaka

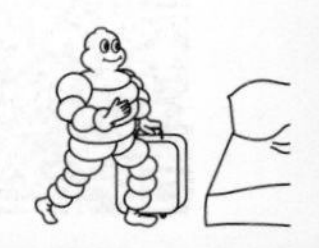

JAPANESE

Kanda
かんだ

6

Hiroyuki Kanda makes the most of the natural flavour of quality ingredients to create dishes bursting with originality. The springtime broad bean cakes have a rich sweetness and pleasant texture. Tomatoes are used in the sweet *waridashi* for the beef *sukiyaki*, eaten with whipped eggs. Close attention is even paid to garnishes and the chef understands his customers' preferences and adjusts tastes and quantity to satisfy them.

■ Opening hours, last orders
Dinner = 17:30-22:00 (L.O.)

■ Annual and weekly closing
Closed mid-August, late December-early January, Sunday and Public Holidays

■ Price
Dinner = set ¥ 15,750-24,150
Service charge = 10%

TEL. 03–5786–0150
3-6-34 Motoazabu, Minato-ku, Tokyo

JAPANESE

Kasane NEW
かさね

The multifarious set menu items, which vary from day to day, could include 'Tsuyu Anago no Arai' featuring the light aroma of eggplants and myoga ginger; *ayu*, salted and dried overnight, with all bones removed; *oshizushi* of lightly grilled saury with a piquant and fragrant *yuzu*-pepper dressing; and squid *sashimi* with Hokkaido yama-wasabi instead of regular *wasabi*. The *hiyashijiru-gohan* at the end is available year-round.

■ Opening hours, last orders
Dinner = 18:00-22:00 (L.O.)

■ Annual and weekly closing
Closed mid-August, late December-early January, Saturday except December, Sunday and Public Holidays

■ Price
Dinner = set ¥ 10,000

TEL. 03-3589-0505
Sanemu Akasaka 3F, 3-18-10 Akasaka, Minato-ku, Tokyo

http://kasanetokyoakasaka.com

JAPANESE TONKATSU

Katsuzen
かつぜん

This restaurant is run by a family of four. In charge of the fluffy batter is the daughter, who sifts the bread crumbs by hand with a special sifter. The *tonkatsu*, enveloped in a delicate batter, is not oily and is accompanied by white rice that whets the appetite. The *miso* soup, made with sardine stock, is prepared while the *tonkatsu* is fried. The entrance to the *tatami* room is small, like a tea ceremony hut, so watch your head.

■ Opening hours, last orders
Lunch = 11:30-14:30 L.O.14:00
Sat.,Sun. and Public Holidays
11:30-15:00 L.O.14:30
Dinner = 17:00-22:30 L.O.21:30
Sat., Sun. and Public Holidays
17:00-21:30 L.O.20:00

■ Annual and weekly closing
Closed late December-early January and Monday

■ Price
Lunch = à la carte ¥ 2,500-8,000
Dinner = set ¥ 7,500-12,000
à la carte ¥ 3,500-10,000
Service charge = 10% (dinner)

TEL. 03–3289–8988
Kojun Building 4F,
6-8-7 Ginza, Chuo-ku, Tokyo

JAPANESE

Kikuchi
き久ち

The owner-chef of this cosy *kappo* restaurant trained in a range of restaurants to learn various cuisines. To sample different ingredients, order *tsukuri* - the two varieties are served side-by-side. For roast dishes, try the charcoal-grilled seasonal fish. Rice cooked in kelp stock is served in small iron pots. Since he runs the restaurant on his own and purchases only enough ingredients for the day, book as early as possible.

■ Opening hours, last orders
Dinner = 18:00-21:30 (L.O.)

■ Annual and weekly closing
Closed early January and Sunday

■ Price
Dinner = set ¥ 10,500-15,750

TEL. 03-6313-5599
Minatoya Sohonten Building 2F,
2-17-17 Nishiazabu, Minato-ku,
Tokyo

JAPANESE

Kikunoi
菊乃井

25

Third-generation owner-chef Yoshihiro Murata reflects the seasons through exquisite dishes, prepared according to the restaurant's long-held traditions. April's grilled dish is smoked and grilled cherry salmon from Himi; it's first dipped in *miso* paste, sake, *mirin* and soy sauce. On the 1st floor are two counters; upstairs, a tearoom and *tatami* rooms are based on the *sukiya* style of architecture employed for tea houses.

■ Opening hours, last orders
Lunch = Tue.-Sat. 12:00-13:00 (L.O.)
Dinner = 17:00-21:00 (L.O.)

■ Annual and weekly closing
Closed mid-August, late December-early January and Sunday

■ Price
Lunch = set ¥ 10,500
Dinner = set ¥ 15,750-21,000
Service charge = 10% (tatami room 15%)

TEL. 03–3568–6055
6-13-8 Akasaka, Minato-ku, Tokyo

www.kikunoi.jp/akasaka.htm

JAPANESE

Kisaku
喜作

Opened in 2010, the restaurant is named after the owner-chef's grandfather, who invented a technique for artificially cultivating *shiitake*. Prices are relatively low as he wants young people to enjoy Japanese cuisine. The elaborate *hassun*, thinly sliced white-fleshed sashimi with liver, and summer vegetable *nibitashi* are recommended. *Omakase* set menus are served but, after 8:30pm, à la carte dishes can also be ordered.

■ Opening hours, last orders
Lunch = 11:30-13:30 (L.O.)
Dinner = 17:00-22:00 (L.O.)

■ Annual and weekly closing
Closed mid-August, late December-early January, Sunday and Public Holidays

■ Price
Lunch = set ¥ 4,000
Dinner = set ¥ 11,550-15,750
à la carte ¥ 8,000-12,000

TEL. 03–5419–7332
Coms Azabu Jyuban 5F,
3-3-9 Azabujuban, Minato-ku,
Tokyo

FRENCH

Kitajima-tei NEW
北島亭

In contrast to its modest appearance, this restaurant is known for the grand flavours and techniques of traditional French cuisine. The chef trained for 6 years at several places, including Troisgros. He goes to Tsukiji each morning to select the ingredients and prepares dynamic dishes – his favourite is grilled lamb rack in rock salt or pie crust. The chef explains his dishes by displaying the ingredients that he will use.

■ Opening hours, last orders
Lunch = 11:30-13:30 (L.O.)
Dinner = 18:00-19:30 (L.O.)

■ Annual and weekly closing
Closed mid-August, late December-early January, Wednesday, 1st and 3rd Tuesday

■ Price
Lunch = set ¥ 3,700-10,500
Dinner = set ¥ 8,400-15,750
Service charge = 10%

TEL. 03-3355-6667
7 San-eicho, Shinjuku-ku, Tokyo

FRENCH

KM NEW

A touch of creativity makes these traditional dishes memorable. The chef, who trained in France, prepares the food by himself. He learnt creativity in the Brittany region, and dedication to his craft in Paris. His taste can be seen in the serving dishes and throughout the elegant interior, while his wife's courteous service leaves a lasting impression. With just 8 counter seats and 4 table seats, reservations are required.

■ Opening hours, last orders
Lunch = 12:00-14:30 L.O.13:30
Dinner = 18:00-22:30 L.O.20:30

■ Annual and weekly closing
Closed late December-early January and Monday

■ Price
Lunch = set ¥ 8,800-12,800
Dinner = set ¥ 8,800-12,800
Service charge = 10%

TEL. 03-6252-4211
Iseyoshi Building 6F, 8-8-19
Ginza, Chuo-ku, Tokyo

www.km-french.jp

JAPANESE CONTEMPORARY

Kodama
こだま

Owner-chef Tsutomu Kodama is self-taught and guided by his instincts. Emphasis is on the ingredients' true taste and food is transformed into inventive dishes. One of the most popular is *awabi-soba* and *tai-meshi*. The fish bone soup is made from seasonal fish after it has been stewed, and contains plenty of gelatine, bone marrow and other nutrients. In autumn, the *matsutake* ice cream is particularly innovative.

■ Opening hours, last orders
Dinner = 18:00-22:00 L.O.20:00

■ Annual and weekly closing
Closed Golden week, mid-August, 30,31 December, Sunday and Public Holidays

■ Price
Dinner = set ¥ 15,750-21,000
Private room fee = 10%
Service charge = 10%

TEL. 03-3408-8865
Nishiazabu 1106 2F,
1-10-6 Nishiazabu, Minato-ku, Tokyo

Kogetsu
湖月

Whilst not spacious, it goes back a long way and has nine counter seats plus a further room. House specialities include *kasujiru* -the sake lees soup- with eight kinds of vegetables, steamed Shogoin turnip with conger eel, and thinly sliced crossbred duck loin cooked in a bonito and kelp stock. To finish, we recommend the fish roe with rice or sea bream with rice. The friendly chef previously taught Japanese cuisine overseas.

■ Opening hours, last orders
Dinner = 18:00-21:30

■ Annual and weekly closing
Closed mid-August, late December-early January, Sunday and Public Holidays

■ Price
Dinner = set ¥ 13,650-15,750

TEL. 03-3407-3033
5-50-10 Jingumae, Shibuya-ku, Tokyo

www.aoyama-kogetsu.com

JAPANESE CONTEMPORARY

Kohaku NEW
虎白

In charge of this restaurant is Koji Koizumi who is thoroughly au fait with the features and flavours of ingredients and never ventures too far outside the box. Skilful meal planning, that takes even tableware into account, makes for a pleasing flow to the meal. This skill extends to the ingredients; the idea for the white *miso* soup with firm, fragrant sautéed *sakura ebi* and spicy *dou ban jiang* came from shrimp bisque.

■ Opening hours, last orders
Dinner = 17:30-24:00 L.O.22:30
Saturday 17:00-24:00 L.O.22:30

■ Annual and weekly closing
Closed mid-August, late December-early January, Sunday and Public Holidays

■ Price
Dinner = set ¥ 13,650-17,850
Service charge = 5%

TEL. 03-5225-0807
3-4 Kagurazaka, Shinjuku-ku, Tokyo

Koju
小十

The name comes from close friend and ceramicist Koju Nishioka. Toru Okuda says he aims to use choice ingredients to excite his customers. In addition to seafood ordered from Omaezaki, red sea bream, *hamo*, tilefish, prawns and others are sent daily from Naruto in Tokushima. The *unagi* is thick and both the *shirayaki* and *kabayaki* are tasty. For dessert, strawberry sherbet with champagne rosé shows the chef's creativity.

■ Opening hours, last orders
Dinner = 17:30-1:00 L.O.23:30
Saturday 17:30-24:00 L.O.21:30

■ Annual and weekly closing
Closed mid-August, late December-early January, Sunday and Public Holidays

■ Price
Dinner = set ¥ 13,650-26,250
Service charge = 10%

TEL. 03-6215-9544
8-5-25 Ginza, Chuo-ku, Tokyo
www.kojyu.jp

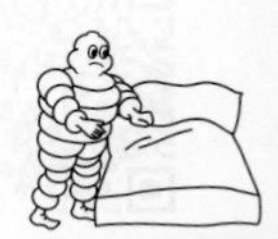

Komuro
小室

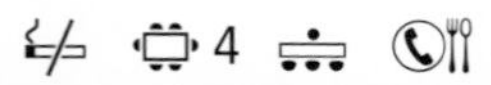

Having trained at a *chakaiseki* restaurant, Mitsuhiro Komuro's philosophy is to use only choice domestic ingredients and emphasise seasonal flavours. The summer *hamo zukushi* menu is a treat and includes *tsukuri*, *oshizushi* and other *hamo* dishes. Chat with him while enjoying food served in bowls by Seika Suda and Tosai Sawamura. Go up Kagurazaka-dori Avenue, take the side road just before Bishamonten Zenkokuji Temple until the white sign.

■ Opening hours, last orders
Lunch = Tue.-Sat. 12:00-13:00 (L.O.)
Dinner = 18:30-20:00 (L.O.)

■ Annual and weekly closing
Closed mid-August, 21 December-16 January, Sunday and Public Holidays

■ Price
Lunch = set ¥ 8,400-12,600
Dinner = set ¥ 16,800-63,000
Service charge = 10%

TEL. 03-3235-3332
13 Wakamiyacho, Shinjuku-ku, Tokyo

JAPANESE TEMPURA

Kondo
近藤

Fumio Kondo opened this *tempura* restaurant in 1991, from a desire to treat customers to generous helpings of delicious vegetables. Because he wants to provide the tastes of the season, he travels to the production areas himself to buy ingredients directly. One 'must' is sweet potato: after frying, the cylindrical slices are left to cook in the remaining heat. Also worth trying is zucchini stuffed with *yuba*, his original recipe.

■ Opening hours, last orders
Lunch = 12:00-15:00 L.O.13:30
Dinner = 17:00-22:30 L.O.20:30

■ Annual and weekly closing
Closed Golden week, mid-August, late December-early January, Sunday and Public Holiday Mondays

■ Price
Lunch = set ¥ 6,300-8,400
Dinner = set ¥ 10,500-17,850

TEL. 03–5568–0923
Sakaguchi Building 9F,
5-5-13 Ginza, Chuo-ku, Tokyo

Kurogi
くろぎ

Jun Kurogi relocated to a traditional Japanese house in 2007. Besides standard items like aromatic *goma-dofu* and tender tongue stew, the menu is determined by the day's ingredients. Prices are relatively low as he wants to introduce people to Japanese cuisine. The number of lunches served is limited; the *tai chazuke* comes with small appetisers and dessert. The name was changed from 'Yushima 121' to 'Kurogi' in autumn 2010.

■ Opening hours, last orders
Lunch = Tue.-Fri. 11:30-12:30 and 12:30-13:30
Dinner = 17:00-22:00 (L.O.)

■ Annual and weekly closing
Closed mid-August, late December-early January, Sunday and Public Holidays

■ Price
Lunch = set ¥ 1,000
Dinner = set ¥ 12,600-21,000
Service charge = 10% (dinner)

TEL. 03-5846-3510
3-35-1 Yushima, Bunkyo-ku, Tokyo

www.kurogi.co.jp

Kuwano
くわ野

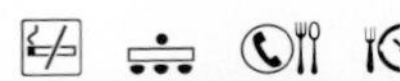

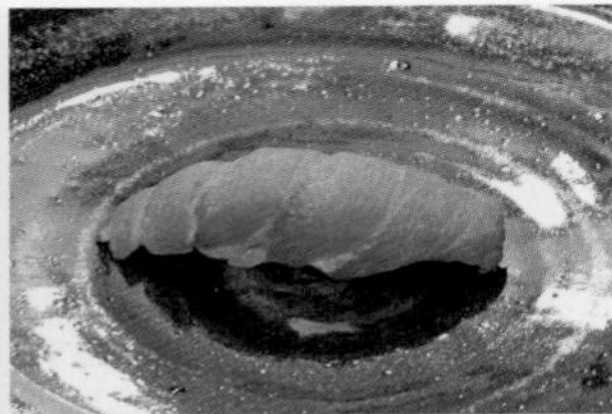

Tatsuya Kuwano opened in 2005, having spent many years as chef of a sushi restaurant in Akasaka. Appetisers before the sushi could include oysters steamed in sake, tasty *kobashira* kebab seasoned with red pepper flakes or the grilled spicy marinated pollock roe. Examples of the sushi are gizzard shad and the prawn, which is boiled on the spot. Although a little pricey, the effort Kuwano puts into his work is worth it.

■ Opening hours, last orders
Dinner = 17:00-24:00 L.O.23:00

■ Annual and weekly closing
Closed Golden week, mid-August, late December-early January, Sunday and Public Holidays

■ Price
Dinner = set ¥ 20,000-25,000

TEL. 03–3573–6577
Hiratsuka Building 3F,
8-7-6 Ginza, Chuo-ku, Tokyo

JAPANESE SOBA

Kyoraku-tei
蕎楽亭

The faint sound of a *shamisen* drifting in from a music studio suits the atmosphere here. It is well-regarded for its stone-ground, hand-kneaded *soba* noodles made with *soba* flour from Aizu, the owner's home town. For a summer treat try the tomato *soba*. There are drinking snacks like *zarudofu*, uncooked *yuba* and *anago tempura*, so be sure to order some sake. *Udon* is also a favourite. It fills up fast at lunch, so arrive early.

■ Opening hours, last orders
Lunch = Tue.-Sat. 11:30-15:00 L.O.14:30
Dinner = 17:00-21:00 L.O.20:30

■ Annual and weekly closing
Closed early January, mid-August, Sunday and Public Holidays

■ Price
Lunch = à la carte ¥ 1,500-5,000
Dinner = à la carte ¥ 1,500-5,000

TEL. 03–3269–3233
3-6 Kagurazaka, Shinjuku-ku, Tokyo

www.kyourakutei.com

JAPANESE CONTEMPORARY

La Bombance

Although underpinned by Japanese culinary traditions, the cooking uses a variety of non-Japanese ingredients – one is unlikely to find these dishes elsewhere. With freshness as his credo, the owner-chef buys only the day's ingredients. He serves a monthly changing menu and foie gras appears as a constant. A degustation menu, with sake pairings, is also available. The amiable owner-chef gives his customers his full attention.

■ Opening hours, last orders
Dinner = 18:00-22:00 (L.O.)

■ Annual and weekly closing
Closed mid-August, late December-early January, Sunday and Public Holidays

■ Price
Dinner = set ¥ 10,800
Service charge = 10%

TEL. 03–5778–6511
New City Residence Twin Tower I B1F, 2-26-21 Nishiazabu, Minato-ku, Tokyo

www.bombance.com

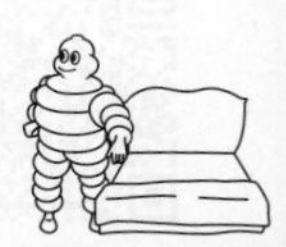

FRENCH

L'Anneau d'Or

A husband and wife team run this small restaurant, ideal for family gatherings. He buys ingredients from all over the country to create rich but never heavy cuisine. Specialities include soft-steamed egg in a small cocotte with a sauce of truffles and foie gras, Lacan pigeon with a light salmis sauce, and roasted Challans duck served with a Rouennaise sauce. The two-plate business lunch is served only on weekdays.

■ Opening hours, last orders
Lunch = 12:00-13:30 (L.O.)
Dinner = 18:00-20:00 (L.O.)

■ Annual and weekly closing
Closed mid-August, late December-early January and Wednesday

■ Price
Lunch = set Tue.,Thu.¥ 5,000-21,000
Fri.-Mon.¥ 10,000-21,000
Dinner = set ¥ 10,000-21,000
Service charge = 10% (lunch 5%)

TEL. 03–5919–0141
Yotsuya Sun Heights B1F,
4-6-1 Yotsuya, Shinjuku-ku, Tokyo
www.lanneaudor-tokyo.com

ITALIAN

L'Asse NEW

This young chef, who trained for 3 years at Dal Pescatore in Lombardy, opened his own restaurant in 2011. He produces original arrangements of specialities from Northern Italy and turns them into refined dishes. His own speciality is ravioli with 4 Italian cheeses. Dinner consists of a set menu of 5-6 dishes; the lunch set is similar but at a discounted price. There is also a selection of primarily French and Italian wines.

■ Opening hours, last orders
Lunch = 12:00-15:00 L.O.13:30
Dinner = 18:00-23:00 L.O.21:30

■ Annual and weekly closing
Closed late December-early January, and Sunday

■ Price
Lunch = set ¥ 2,500-4,200
Dinner = set ¥ 7,500-10,500
Service charge = 10%

TEL. 03-6417-9250
Verona Meguro B1F, 1-4-15 Meguro, Meguro-ku, Tokyo

http://lasse.jp

FRENCH CONTEMPORARY

La Table de Joël Robuchon

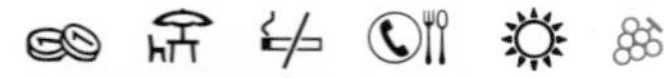

French *convivialité* is the underlying theme of the restaurant and a favourite word of Joël Robuchon. The cuisine is contemporary, with original recipes combining Spain (gazpacho soup), Italy (millefeuille of eggplant, tomato and mozzarella cheese) and France (quail with a caramelised layer stuffed with foie gras). A special feature is an hors d'oeuvre of consommé jelly-covered sea urchin, served with fennel cream.

■ Opening hours, last orders
Lunch = 11:30-14:00 (L.O.)
Dinner = 18:00-21:30 (L.O.)

■ Price
Lunch = set Mon.-Fri. ¥ 2,950-8,500
Sat., Sun. ¥ 3,850-8,500
à la carte ¥ 7,000-14,000
Dinner = set ¥ 6,300-16,000
à la carte ¥ 7,000-14,000
Service charge = 10%

TEL. 03–5424–1338
Yebisu Garden Place,
1-13-1 Mita, Meguro-ku, Tokyo

www.robuchon.jp/ebisu

FRENCH CONTEMPORARY

L'Atelier de Joël Robuchon

The stylish red and black interior is dominated by a long counter with seating for 44, in the style of a sushi restaurant or Spanish bar. The open kitchen is lively; the chefs and waiting team a friendly lot. Carefully selected ingredients include seafood from Japan, foie gras, asparagus and poultry from France and, from Spain, Jamón Ibérico de Bellota. The Dégustation menu allows guests to try a variety of à la carte dishes.

■ Opening hours, last orders
Lunch = 11:30-14:30 (L.O.)
Sat., Sun. and Public Holidays
11:30-15:00 (L.O.)
Dinner = 18:00-23:00 L.O.21:30

■ Price
Lunch = set ¥ 2,950-5,400
à la carte ¥ 5,000-16,000
Dinner = set ¥ 4,800-14,800
à la carte ¥ 5,000-16,000
Service charge = 10%

TEL. 03–5772–7500
Roppongi Hills Hillside 2F,
6-10-1 Roppongi, Minato-ku,
Tokyo
www.robuchon.jp/roppongi

FRENCH

La Tour

12

Owner-chef Tadaaki Shimizu refined his skills at La Tour d'Argent in Paris and Tokyo. The Royale de Foie Gras is a house speciality: foie gras is cooked for four hours at 110℃, flavoured with Sauternes and refined by the sweetness of honey. Also recommended are duck dishes, which go well with the green pepper, fig or citrus sauces. There is also a wide choice of French cheeses. The restaurant uses classic French techniques.

■ Opening hours, last orders
Lunch = 11:30-15:00 L.O.13:30
Dinner = 18:00-23:00 L.O.20:30

■ Annual and weekly closing
Closed mid-August, 31 December, 1 January and Monday

■ Price
Lunch = set ¥ 4,500-8,000
Dinner = set ¥ 12,500-18,500
à la carte ¥ 14,000-19,000
Service charge = 10%

TEL. 03-3569-2211
Kojun Building 5F,
6-8-7 Ginza, Chuo-ku, Tokyo

www.ginzalatour.com

FRENCH

La Tour d'Argent

The venerable Parisian institution serving diners since 1582, opened this Tokyo outpost in 1984. The restaurant spells graceful luxury at every turn. Among the specialities is roast duckling, imported from France. Two sauces are recommended: 'Tour d'Argent' is a rich sauce made from consommé and duck blood and liver - adjusted with cognac and Madeira, and 'Marco Polo,' a duck stock seasoned with four types of pepper.

■ Opening hours, last orders
Dinner = 17:30-21:00 (L.O.)

■ Annual and weekly closing
Closed Monday

■ Price
Dinner = set ¥ 18,000-25,000
à la carte ¥ 15,000-25,000
Private room fee = less than 12 persons ¥ 21,000
Service charge = 10%

TEL. 03-3239-3111
New Otani Hotel The Main 2F,
4-1 Kioicho, Chiyoda-ku, Tokyo

www.newotani.co.jp/tokyo

Lauburu

Push the pig's foot shaped door knob to enter, and the sounds of Radio France, combined with the interior, will make you feel as though you've stepped into Basque Country. The chef works with pork to this day, placing importance on the teachings of Madame Juliette. The menu includes pork dishes made from various parts, and the portions are large. Ham is all carefully home-cured; pork loin is cooked slowly over a charcoal flame.

■ Opening hours, last orders
Dinner = 18:00-21:30 (L.O.)

■ Annual and weekly closing
Closed mid-August, late December-early January and Sunday

■ Price
Dinner = à la carte ¥ 3,500-7,000
Service charge = 10%

TEL. 03–3498–1314
6-8-18 Minamiaoyama,
Minato-ku, Tokyo

FRENCH

Le Bouchon NEW

Specialities are asparagus with hollandaise sauce in spring; abalone risotto in summer; sautéed foie gras and chestnut soup in autumn; and wild game dishes in winter. The chef is adept at highlighting ingredients by using truffles and sometimes takes classic recipes from Raymond Olivier and gives them a modern touch. He went to France at the age of 27 and studied for 2 years at places like Vivarois and Lucas Carton.

■ Opening hours, last orders
Lunch = 11:30-14:00 (L.O.)
Dinner = 18:00-22:00 (L.O.)

■ Annual and weekly closing
Closed late December-early January and Sunday

■ Price
Lunch = set ¥ 2,800-7,800
Dinner = set ¥ 5,500-10,000
à la carte ¥ 6,500-12,000
Service charge = 10% (dinner)

TEL. 03-5652-0655
2-22-3 Nihonbashihamacho,
Chuo-ku, Tokyo

www.lebouchon-cigal.com

FRENCH

Le Bourguignon

Based on traditional French regional cuisine, the dishes of owner-chef Yoshinaru Kikuchi are refined according to his own style. His speciality is the *boudin noir* terrine with apple salad and purée: the dish is delicately flavoured. As offal is the chef's strong suit, the menu consists of many varied meat dishes, including a number of winter game dishes. Good wines, primarily from Burgundy, are offered at reasonable prices.

■ Opening hours, last orders
Lunch = 11:30-15:30 L.O.13:00
Dinner = 18:00-23:30 L.O.21:00

■ Annual and weekly closing
Closed 2 weeks in July, late December-early January, Wednesday and 2nd Tuesday

■ Price
Lunch = set ¥ 2,625-4,725
à la carte ¥ 7,000-11,000
Dinner = set ¥ 5,775-10,500
à la carte ¥ 7,000-11,000
Service charge = 10%

TEL. 03–5772–6244
3-3-1 Nishiazabu, Minato-ku, Tokyo

FRENCH

Le Coq NEW

XX

This 4-table restaurant is run by a quiet, sober chef and his attentive wife. The atmosphere is more like a studio than a restaurant, with the round table in front of the serving window reserved for regulars. Staple dishes are home-smoked salmon and Japanese beef steak. The chef studied under Joël Robuchon and takes a disciplined approach to cooking, minimizing preparation; his dishes are well worth waiting for.

■ Opening hours, last orders
Lunch = 12:00-13:00 (L.O.)
Dinner = 18:00-22:00 (L.O.)

■ Price
Lunch = set ¥ 3,150-4,725
Dinner = set ¥ 5,250-8,400
à la carte ¥ 5,000-8,000
Service charge = 5% (lunch 10%)

TEL. 03-3770-1915
2-7-2 Ebisunishi, Shibuya-ku,
Tokyo

FRENCH CONTEMPORARY

L'Effervescence NEW

10

The chef has been with the restaurant since it opened, having spent time at Michel Bras Toya Japon in Hokkaido and The Fat Duck in England. Ingredients come from outside Japan too, including parsnips from England; his speciality is whole cooked turnip. Set menus called 'en chemin' (through the pathway) and 'à côté la prairie' (near the ranch) feature creative dishes that tell a story. Booth seating is for parties of 2 or 3.

■ Opening hours, last orders
Lunch = 12:00-14:00 (L.O.)
Dinner = 18:00-21:00 (L.O.)

■ Annual and weekly closing
Closed mid-August, late December-early January and Monday except Public Holidays

■ Price
Lunch = set ¥ 4,800-7,500
Dinner = set ¥ 15,750
Private room fee = less than 4 persons ¥20,000
Service charge = 10%

TEL. 03-5766-9500
2-26-4 Nishiazabu, Minato-ku, Tokyo

www.leffervescence.jp

FRENCH CONTEMPORARY

Le Jeu de l'Assiette

XX

The second-generation chef's experiences in France inform his creative dishes, which do not use too much oil. The assortment of ingredients is original and the delicate seasoning is exquisite. Specialities are Tasmanian ocean trout, roasted duck breast and chocolate sphere rose. As the name of the restaurant – "play on the plate" – implies, the appealing, whimsical presentation of the food makes for a delightful experience.

■ Opening hours, last orders
Lunch = 11:30-13:30 (L.O.)
Dinner = 18:00-21:00 (L.O.)

■ Annual and weekly closing
Closed mid-August, late December-early January and Monday

■ Price
Lunch = set ¥ 3,500-10,000
Dinner = set ¥ 7,500-13,500
Service charge = 10%

TEL. 03-6415-5100
Sun Village Daikanyama 2F,
2-17-5 Ebisunishi, Shibuya-ku,
Tokyo

www.lejeudelassiette.com

Le Mange-Tout

Chef Noboru Tani is an avid follower of Auguste Escoffier and offers traditional French cuisine but with a modern twist. In winter expect game dishes using Japanese deer and boar from West Izu in Shizuoka; game consommé is based on a classic venison dish with sauce poivrade. *Omble chevalier*, a European mountain trout, is served lightly smoked. The *pêche Melba* combines juicy peach, vanilla ice cream and raspberry sauce.

■ Opening hours, last orders
Lunch = 1st, 3rd and 5th Saturday
12:00-15:00 L.O.13:00
Dinner = 18:30-21:00 (L.O.)

■ Annual and weekly closing
Closed late December-early January and Sunday

■ Price
Lunch = set ¥ 5,800
Dinner = set ¥ 12,600
Service charge = 10%

TEL. 03-3268-5911
22 Nandomachi, Shinjuku-ku, Tokyo

www.le-mange-tout.com

L'Embellir

After relocating to its current spot an adjoining patisserie offering elaborate desserts was opened. The chef now uses more domestic ingredients, but the delicate seasoning and beautiful presentation remain the same. Specialities should be ordered when making reservations and include vegetable terrine, *akaza ebi* wrapped in crispy potatoes, and almond blancmange. Just a monthly changing *omakase* set menu is offered.

■ Opening hours, last orders
Lunch = 11:30-14:00 (L.O.)
Dinner = 18:00-21:00 (L.O.)

■ Annual and weekly closing
Closed mid-August and late December-early January

■ Price
Lunch = set ¥ 5,250-10,500
Dinner = set ¥ 13,650
Private room fee = ¥ 10,500
Service charge = 10%

TEL. 03–6427–3209
R2-A B1F, 5-2-11 Minamiaoyama, Minato-ku, Tokyo

www.lembellir.com

Les Créations de Narisawa

Yoshihiro Narisawa offers creative and modern dishes which are underpinned by the basics of French cuisine, hence the restaurant's name. Take note, too, of the novel combinations of ingredients. Organic vegetables come directly from farmers, while fish is sourced nationwide and delivered on the same day as caught. Located in the courtyard of a modern building, this chic restaurant is ideally suited for special occasions.

■ Opening hours, last orders
Lunch = 12:00-13:00 (L.O.)
Dinner = 18:30-21:00 (L.O.)

■ Annual and weekly closing
Closed Sunday

■ Price
Lunch = set ¥ 7,350-21,000
Dinner = set ¥ 21,000
Service charge = 10%

TEL. 03–5785–0799
2-6-15 Minamiaoyama, Minato-ku, Tokyo

www.narisawa-yoshihiro.com

FRENCH

Les Enfants Gâtés

8

Beside the mid-century-style bar is a collection of terrines, which are the speciality here. Choose an appetiser from several terrines, the standard dishes being country-style and duck foie gras. Flavours vary from traditional to inventive; texture and colour are taken into account. The chef hired in 2011 uses the same techniques as his predecessor. The art deco design of the dining room adds to the sophisticated feel.

■ Opening hours, last orders
Lunch = 12:00-14:00 (L.O.)
Dinner = 18:00-21:30 (L.O.)

■ Annual and weekly closing
Closed late December-early January and Monday except Public Holidays

■ Price
Lunch = set ¥ 3,150-5,775
Dinner = set ¥ 7,140-11,550
à la carte ¥ 6,000-11,000
Service charge = 10%

TEL. 03-3476-2929
2-3 Sarugakucho, Shibuya-ku, Tokyo

www.terrine-gates.com

FRENCH

Les Rosiers Eguzkilore NEW

Dishes at this restaurant were developed by a French chef who draws her inspiration from Basque cuisine; two Japanese chefs preside over the cooking and use Japanese and Basque ingredients to create modern arrangements. The speciality is fish grilled in chorizo sauce with squid and a coco blanc bean crème; the combinations of ingredients are unique and balanced. Ask for a booth if there are 2 or 3 in your party, or the terrace.

■ Opening hours, last orders
Lunch = 11:00-16:00 L.O.14:30
Dinner = 17:00-23:00 L.O.21:00

■ Annual and weekly closing
Closed 1 January

■ Price
Lunch = set ¥ 3,990-9,450
Dinner = set ¥ 3,990-12,600
Service charge = 10%

TEL. 03-3561-7020
Ginza Mitsukoshi Department Store 12F,
4-6-16 Ginza, Chuo-ku, Tokyo

www.lesrosiers-eguzkilore.com

Les Saisons

The 'classic-modern' style fuses traditional design elements with a contemporary elegance. While the menu is grounded in tradition, dishes incorporate a modern spirit. For example, roast flounder with truffles and a white asparagus purée; and Bresse chicken breast stuffed with morels and served with Comté cheese gnocchi. The spacious dining has warmly lit oak walls and, in addition to 4 private rooms, also has a cigar salon.

■ Opening hours, last orders
Lunch = 11:30-14:30 (L.O.)
Dinner = 17:30-22:00 (L.O.)

■ Price
Lunch = set ¥ 6,800-10,500
à la carte ¥ 13,000-28,000
Dinner = set ¥ 16,800-27,500
à la carte ¥ 13,000-28,000
Private room fee = ¥ 10,500-21,000
Service charge = 10%

TEL. 03–3539–8087
Imperial Hotel-Main Building M2F,
1-1-1 Uchisaiwaicho, Chiyoda-ku,
Tokyo

www.imperialhotel.co.jp

FRENCH

Lugdunum Bouchon Lyonnais

Owner-chef Christophe Paucod was born in Lyon and in tribute to his hometown has faithfully replicated a typical *bouchon* restaurant. As well as Lyonnaise salad and *boudin noir*, there are other dishes that add touches of creativity and lightness to tradition. Burgundy and Rhône wines account for the majority of the wine list. French music plays in the background and Mr Paucod provides friendly service in fluent Japanese.

■ Opening hours, last orders
Lunch = 11:30-14:30 (L.O.)
Dinner = 18:00-22:00 (L.O.)

■ Annual and weekly closing
Closed 2 weeks in August, late December-early January, Monday except Public Holidays and 3rd Tuesday

■ Price
Lunch = set Tue.-Fri. ¥ 1,850-3,850
Sat., Sun.¥ 2,850-3,850
Dinner = set ¥ 3,850-4,850
à la carte ¥ 4,000-6,000

TEL. 03–6426–1201
4-3-7 Kagurazaka, Shinjuku-ku, Tokyo

www.lyondelyon.com

Maison Paul Bocuse

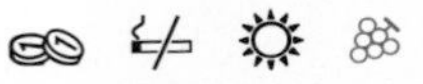

A partnership between celebrated chef Paul Bocuse and Hiroyuki Hiramatsu; this is the main restaurant out of several in the chain and is popular for weekend wedding receptions. Although somewhat expensive, we recommend the à la carte where you can try specialities from the chef's Lyon restaurant, like the oven-baked black truffle consommé with pie dough - served in 1975 to then French President Valéry Giscard d'Estaing.

■ Opening hours, last orders
Lunch = 12:00-13:30 (L.O.)
Dinner = 18:00-20:30 (L.O.)

■ Annual and weekly closing
Closed early January and Monday except Public Holidays

■ Price
Lunch = set ¥ 3,500-4,800
à la carte ¥ 12,600-23,300
Dinner = set ¥ 6,800-21,000
à la carte ¥ 12,600-23,300
Service charge = 10%

TEL. 03–5458–6324
Daikanyama Forum B1F,
17-16 Sarugakucho, Shibuya-ku,
Tokyo

www.hiramatsu.co.jp/restaurants/maison-paulbocuse

JAPANESE

Makimura
まき村

Since relocating in 2010, Akio Makimura has been spending even more time and effort on perfecting his cooking. He uses a light stock and two kinds of dried bonito - with or without *chiai*. The former makes a richer stock for the fried eggplant; the latter is used for the clear soup of pike conger and egg tofu. Rice from the stove comes into its own with the *tai-chazuke* speciality, which has also been refined over the years.

■ Opening hours, last orders
Lunch = Sat. 12:00-14:00 L.O.13:00
Dinner = 18:00-22:00 L.O.21:00

■ Annual and weekly closing
Closed Golden week, mid-August, late December-early January, Sunday and Public Holiday Mondays

■ Price
Lunch = set ¥ 8,400
Dinner = set ¥ 10,500-13,650
Service charge = 10%

TEL. 03–3768–6388
3-11-5 Minamioi, Shinagawa-ku, Tokyo

CHINESE

Masa's Kitchen 47

6

Dishes are largely traditional and from all over China - but primarily Sichuan - and are prepared in a modern style so as not to be too heavy. The predominant feature is the delicate seasoning, which highlights the freshness of the ingredients, as seen with the cold eggplant and raw sea urchin, the white asparagus tofu, whole jellyfish and endive *aemono*. At lunch, set menus with pork dumplings and noodles are also offered.

■ Opening hours, last orders
Lunch = 11:30-14:00 (L.O.)
Dinner = 18:00-23:30 L.O.22:30

■ Annual and weekly closing
Closed Golden week, mid-August, late December-early January and Monday

■ Price
Lunch = set ¥ 3,500-5,500
à la carte ¥ 1,400-20,000
Dinner = set ¥ 7,850-15,750
à la carte ¥ 4,500-20,000
Service charge = 10% (dinner)

TEL. 03–3473–0729
Comforia Ebisu Building B1F,
1-21-13 Ebisu, Shibuya-ku, Tokyo

Masumi
ます味

Using the techniques he learned at a *kaiseki* restaurant, Tsukasa Masui serves a wide variety of *anago* dishes. The thinly sliced *tsukuri* resembles *fugu* and is served with *ponzu*, and in summer *anago shabu-shabu*, reminiscent of *hamo*, comes with plum pulp sauce. Staples include the fluffy *shirayaki* and the seared *anago* hotpot with thinly sliced burdock served in an iron pot. The *anago* should keep you coming back for more.

■ Opening hours, last orders
Lunch = 12:00-14:00 L.O.13:00
Dinner = 17:00-22:30 L.O.21:00

■ Annual and weekly closing
Closed mid-August, late December-early January, Sunday and Public Holidays

■ Price
Lunch = set ¥ 3,885-5,565
Dinner = set ¥ 6,825-14,700
Service charge = 15%

TEL. 03-3356-5938
Hokuto Yotsuya Building B1F,
11-2 Arakicho, Shinjuku-ku,
Tokyo

KOREAN

Matsunomi NEW
松の実

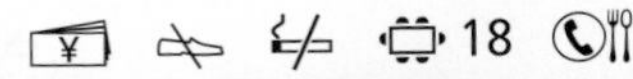

You will find this warmly run, homely restaurant in a cobblestoned alley across from Bishamonten Zenkokuji Temple in Kagurazaka. The self-taught cook is the owner's mother; her beautiful, colourful arrangements of Korean dishes are lightly seasoned with salt and soy sauce. The *gujeolpan* is prepared according to the 'five taste, five colour' philosophy and typifies court cuisine; at the end, comes *samgyetang*, stewed for 2 days.

■ Opening hours, last orders
Dinner = 17:30-22:30 L.O.20:00
Sat. and Public Holidays
17:30-22:00 L.O.19:30

■ Annual and weekly closing
Closed late December-early January and Sunday

■ Price
Dinner = set ¥ 6,800

TEL. 03-3267-1519
4-2 Kagurazaka, Shinjuku-ku, Tokyo

JAPANESE TEMPURA

Mikawa Zezankyo
みかわ 是山居

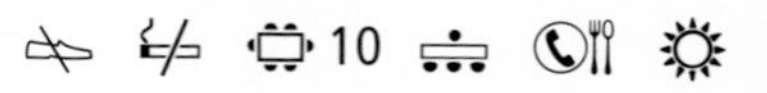

Tetsuya Saotome opened this restaurant in 2009, as the realisation of his dream. Nostalgic yet also contemporary, its interior is truly a work of art and was produced by 20 different artists. The flow of the meal goes from light to strongly flavoured items, moving from *makiebi* to smelt-whiting, squid, *megochi* and *anago;* their degree of cooking also varies. The soup is a rare experiment for a *tempura* restaurant.

■ Opening hours, last orders
Lunch = 11:30-13:00 (L.O.)
Dinner = 17:00-21:00 (L.O.)

■ Annual and weekly closing
Closed mid-August, late December-early January and Wednesday

■ Prices
Lunch = set ¥ 10,500
Dinner = set ¥ 15,750-16,800

TEL. 03–3643–8383
1-3-1 Fukuzumi, Koto-ku, Tokyo

JAPANESE

Minoichi
未能一

Owner-chef Yasuji Tatsumi and his wife run this small but charming *kappo* restaurant, paying attention to the smallest of details. Each dish leaves you with a real appreciation of the skill of a traditional Japanese chef. The *konnyaku* and scallion mixed with salted and fermented bonito gut is perfectly seasoned and provides a nice chewy texture, while the sea urchin pickled in *miso* is richly flavoured and satisfying.

■ Opening hours, last orders
Dinner = 17:30-22:30 L.O.21:00

■ Annual and weekly closing
Closed Golden week, mid-August, late December-early January and Sunday

■ Price
Dinner = set ¥ 12,600-21,000
Service charge = 10%

TEL. 03–3289–3011
Suzuryu Building 5F,
8-7-19 Ginza, Chuo-ku, Tokyo

JAPANESE TEMPURA

Mitsuta
三ツ田

14

Diners sit on *tatami* at this *tempura* restaurant, opened in 1958. Through a specially made glass cover you can watch the chef at work. Meals begin with several *makiebi*, thinly battered and fried, with a raw centre to bring out their sweetness. The taste of the pickled vegetables, *miso* soup and *tentsuyu* dipping sauce comes from a secret recipe from the proprietress' aunt. Don't forget to remove your shoes at the entrance.

■ Opening hours, last orders
Lunch = 12:00-14:30 (L.O.)
Dinner = 17:30-20:30 (L.O.)

■ Annual and weekly closing
Closed mid-August, late December-early January, Sunday and Public Holidays

■ Price
Lunch = set ¥ 14,700
Dinner = set ¥ 16,800
Service charge = 10%

TEL. 03–3541–5577
1-12-15 Tsukiji, Chuo-ku, Tokyo

CHINESE

Momonoki
桃の木

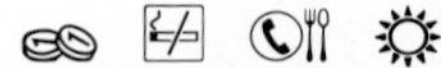

Although the menu mostly consists of Cantonese and Shanghainese dishes, those from Beijing and Sichuan are not overlooked. Takeshi Kobayashi prefers 'less familiar home-style dishes' and avoids pricey dried ingredients like shark's fin and abalone. Lightly fried *A-sai* and *fu ru* is their specialty. *Mapo tofu*, a typical Sichuan offering, is made using hot pepper rather than *dou ban jiang*. One unique Beijing dish is duck tongue.

■ Opening hours, last orders
Lunch = Tue., Thu.-Sun.
11:30-14:30 L.O.14:00
Dinner = 17:30-22:30 L.O.21:30

■ Annual and weekly closing
Closed mid-August, late December-early January, Wednesday and 2nd Tuesday

■ Price
Lunch = set ¥ 2,500-15,000
à la carte ¥ 3,000-6,500
Dinner = set ¥ 8,500-20,000
à la carte ¥ 3,000-6,500

TEL. 03–5443–1309
2-17-29 Mita, Minato-ku, Tokyo
www.mitamachi-momonoki.com

Monnalisa Ebisu

The menu changes quarterly, with new dishes being added each year. In spring, examples could include *blanc-manger d'asperges blanches et crevettes*; in summer you might find *rocace de tomate farcie au crabe et laitue*. Only a minimal amount of butter is ever used and all dishes beautifully match the plates designed by the chef himself. A smaller portion à la carte menu is available only at lunch on weekdays.

■ Opening hours, last orders
Lunch = 11:30-15:30 L.O.14:00
Dinner = 17:30-23:30 L.O.21:30

■ Annual and weekly closing
Closed late December-early January

■ Price
Lunch = set ¥ 5,064-10,550
Dinner = set ¥ 7,174-15,825
à la carte ¥ 8,000-15,000
Service charge = 10%

TEL. 03–5458–1887
1-14-4 Ebisunishi, Shibuya-ku, Tokyo

www.monnalisa.co.jp

FRENCH

Monnalisa Marunouchi

Toru Kawano favours set menus and offers a large variety of seasonal dishes, making sure that the cooking methods and seasoning combinations do not overlap. He also looks to indigenous ingredients – wild plants in spring, and ginkgo and *matsutake* in autumn – to create a distinctly Japanese sense of season. The speciality is roast lamb with a herb and salt pie dough. Wide windows offering a city panorama are another treat.

■ Opening hours, last orders
Lunch = 11:30-15:30 L.O.14:00
Dinner = 17:30-23:30 L.O.21:30

■ Annual and weekly closing
Closed 1 January

■ Price
Lunch = set ¥ 3,956-10,550
Dinner = set ¥ 7,174-16,880
à la carte ¥ 8,000-15,000
Service charge = 10%

TEL. 03–3240–5775
Marunouchi Building 36F,
2-4-1 Marunouchi, Chiyoda-ku,
Tokyo

www.monnalisa.co.jp

KOREAN

Moranbong NEW
モランボン

16

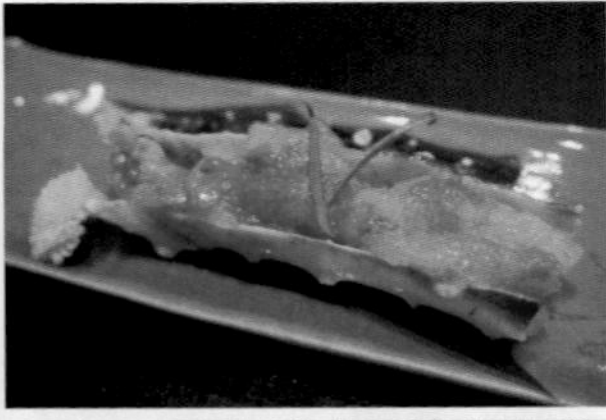

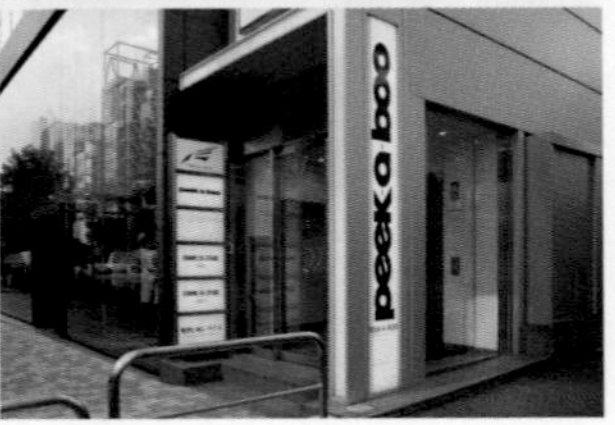

Moranbong carries on the life's work of the founder, whose wish it was to spread Korean cuisine in Japan. Catering to Japanese preferences, the seasoning is elegant and items are served on individual plates. The set menu ends with *wagyu* cooked on view over a *bincho* grill; a mild saltiness brings out the flavour of the beef tongue, cooked using a rock salt plate. The restaurant reopens December 2011 following refurbishment.

■ Opening hours, last orders
Dinner = 17:00-22:30 L.O.20:00

■ Annual and weekly closing
Closed Sunday and Monday

■ Prices
Dinner = set ¥ 12,000-18,000
Service charge =5%

TEL.03-6419-1775
m² Harajuku Building B1F,
6-27-8 Jingumae, Shibuya-ku

www.moran-bong.com/jingumae

Motoyoshi
元吉

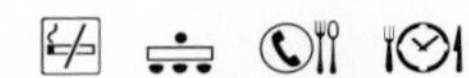

Offering three *omakase* set menus, owner-chef Kazuhito Motoyoshi says he is keen to see people eat lots of vegetables, which is why the menu ends up with so many vegetable dishes. Be sure to try the standard 'kakumorokoshi' summer dish and the firm asparagus. The savoury *mizunasu* is kept juicy, and the *kamonasu* is cooked slowly to draw out the flavour. Open late; after 9pm you can order your favourite dishes or just *tencha*.

■ Opening hours, last orders
Dinner = 17:30-23:00 (L.O.)

■ Annual and weekly closing
Closed mid-August, late December-early January and Sunday

■ Prices
Dinner = set ¥ 7,350-10,500
Service charge =10 %

TEL.03–3401–0722
Central Aoyama No.6 B1F
3-2-4 Minamiaoyama, Minato-ku, Tokyo
www.motoyoshi-1120.com

JAPANESE

Muroi
室井

Masao Muroi opened his restaurant in 1980 and the 'Muroi-style' results from his culinary flexibility. Original dishes include curry made with a bonito and kelp broth and others using wild plants. The wild mushrooms collected by the chef and his staff in autumn are another appealing feature; about 40kg of over 70 varieties are picked in a single day. The wild mushroom set menu offers a pasta dish, a risotto and a clear soup.

■ Opening hours, last orders
Dinner = 17:30-22:00 (L.O.)

■ Annual and weekly closing
Closed Golden week, mid-August, late December-early January, Sunday and Public Holidays

■ Price
Dinner = set ¥ 15,750-31,500
Service charge = 10%

TEL. 03-3571-1421
Suzuryu Building 2F,
8-7-19 Ginza, Chuo-ku, Tokyo

JAPANESE SOBA

Muto
むとう

Soft lighting and background jazz set the mood. The *soba* flour arrives daily from a long-time supplier in Nagano. It is basically *juwari*, but a small amount of flour is added depending on the weather. The noodles are thick and glossy, while rich sauce made with 2-year old dried bonito accents the aroma and sweetness of the *soba*. At dinner, there is only a set menu featuring *sashimi* and broiled fish, ending with *soba*.

■ Opening hours, last orders
Lunch = 11:30-14:30 L.O.14:00
Sat. 12:00-16:00 L.O.15:30
Dinner = Mon.-Fri. 17:30-21:00
L.O.20:30

■ Annual and weekly closing
Closed early January, mid-August, Sunday , 2nd and 4th Saturday and Public Holidays

■ Price
Lunch = set ¥ 4,000
à la carte ¥ 2,000-5,000
Dinner = set ¥ 5,250-7,350
Service charge = 5% (dinner)

TEL. 03–3231–7188
1-13-1 Nihonbashimuromachi,
Chuo-ku, Tokyo

Nabeya
なべ家

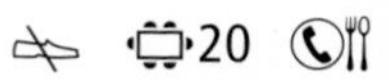

Hiroshi Fukuda, the second-generation owner-chef of this restaurant founded in 1935, is an expert in Edo cuisine. Kelp is not used in the stock; instead, it is made with sake and *katsuo-bushi*. The *katsuo sashimi* with mustard and the sweet fried eggs are good examples of *Edomae* cuisine. Look for *negima* hotpot in April, brook trout in May, *ayu* from June to August, *matsutake* in September, and *fugu* and *Horai nabe* in winter.

■ Opening hours, last orders
Dinner = 17:00-21:00

■ Annual and weekly closing
Closed mid-August, late December-early January, Sunday and Public Holidays

■ Prices
Dinner = set ¥ 15,750-23,100
Service charge = 10%

TEL. 03–3941–2868
1-51-14 Minamiotsuka,
Toshima-ku, Tokyo

http://www.gourmet.ne.jp/nabeya/

JAPANESE

Nadaman Honten Sazanka-so
なだ万本店 山茶花荘

All four rooms, named from *The Tale of Genji*, have a view of the manicured garden from the veranda. Waiting staff in kimono offer polished service, making this a suitable venue for a reception. The traditional cuisine focuses on seasonal tastes; one example in winter is yellowtail covered with turnip; simmered beef cheek and Sakurajima radish dish is also tasty. Prices may not be that low but lunch menus are less expensive.

■ Opening hours, last orders
Lunch = 11:30-15:00
Dinner = 17:00-22:00

■ Annual and weekly closing
Closed late December-early January

■ Price
Lunch = set ¥ 21,000-42,000
Dinner = set ¥ 42,000
Private room fee = ¥ 8,000/person (Mon.-Fri. for dinner)
Service charge = 20%

TEL. 03-3264-7921
New Otani Hotel Japanese Garden, 4-1 Kioicho, Chiyoda-ku, Tokyo
www.nadaman.co.jp/sazankaso

JAPANESE

Nagazumi
ながずみ

The name comes from the owner-chef's hometown in Fukuoka City. He stands behind the 10-seater, U-shaped counter, wearing a white *samue* with his hair pulled back. There are three *omakase* set menus, featuring creative combinations of aromas and textures. The *oden*, which is the speciality, features a stock made not only from kelp and *katsuo-bushi* but also flying fish and small horse mackerel. It is always lively at night.

■ Opening hours, last orders
Dinner = 18:00-22:30 (L.O.)

■ Price
Dinner = set ¥ 7,000-10,000

TEL. 03–5410–1919
1-5-3 Motoakasaka, Minato-ku, Tokyo

Nakajima
中嶋

Owner-chef Sadaharu Nakajima can trace his culinary roots back to his grandfather and creates original cuisine guided by Kansai traditions, while remaining loyal to his family's craft. He pays close attention to both his cooking and his customers. Figs express the changing of the seasons; served with white *miso* at the beginning and wild boar at the end of the season. At lunch, customers can choose set menus featuring sardines.

■ Opening hours, last orders
Lunch = 11:30-14:00 L.O.13:45
Dinner = 17:30-22:00 L.O.20:30

■ Annual and weekly closing
Closed mid-August, late December-early January, Sunday and Public Holidays

■ Price
Lunch = set ¥ 800-5,250
Dinner = set ¥ 8,400-13,650
Service charge = 10%

TEL. 03–3356–4534
Hihara Building B1F,
3-32-5 Shinjuku, Shinjuku-ku,
Tokyo

www.shinjyuku-nakajima.com

JAPANESE

Nico
二戀

First timers may be a little confused by the members-only like appearance. The platinum finished walls and interior were designed by Yasumichi Morita. The chef honed his skills at a Naniwa *kappo* restaurant and places emphasis on natural flavours. Only set menus are available, but creative dishes using Western ingredients are combined with more traditional ones. The kimono-clad staff all leave a favourable impression.

■ Opening hours, last orders
Dinner = 18:00-22:00 (L.O.)

■ Annual and weekly closing
Closed mid-August, late December-early January and Sunday

■ Price
Dinner = set ¥ 11,550-15,750
Service charge = 10%

TEL. 03–3498–3330
4-2-9 Nishiazabu, Minato-ku, Tokyo

www.nico-nishiazabu.jp

JAPANESE SOBA

Nigyo NEW
仁行

Formerly 'Kosetsu', Jin Ishii changed the name to Nigyo when he moved from Ginza. This is very much a place to enjoy delicate *soba* with *shuko*. The focus is on set menus, so single items can only be ordered at certain times. Firm yet lush, the super-fine *juwari* soba blends several buckwheat flours for a consistent flavour that goes well with the mild sauce. At lunch, the Soba Zen is popular; Soba Kaiseki requires reservations.

■ Opening hours, last orders
Lunch = 11:30-14:00 L.O.13:30
Dinner = 18:00-22:00 L.O.21:00
(Set 20:00)

■ Annual and weekly closing
Closed mid-August, late December-early January and Sunday

■ Price
Lunch = set ¥ 5,250
à la carte ¥ 3,000-4,000
Dinner = set ¥ 6,300-8,400
à la carte ¥ 3,000-4,000
Service charge = dinner 5%
(tatami room 10%)

TEL. 03-5695-8117
Green Building 4F, 6-16
Nihonbashikobunacho, Chuo-ku,
Tokyo
www.nigyou.sakura.ne.jp.com

Nodaiwa
野田岩

25

5th-generation owner-chef Kanejiro Kanemoto keeps alive a family tradition as this is one of the few places serving natural *unagi*. Numbers are decreasing, but between mid-April to early December, he receives *unagi* caught at Kasumigaura, the Tone River and the Ariake. The *shirayaki*, the steamed *unagi* with its excess fat removed, is normally eaten with *wasabi* and rock salt, but try it here with caviar, an original combination.

■ Opening hours, last orders
Lunch = 11:00-13:30 (L.O.)
Dinner = 17:00-20:00 (L.O.)

■ Annual and weekly closing
Closed mid-August, late December-early January and Sunday

■ Price
Lunch = set ¥ 4,500-15,700
à la carte ¥ 2,100-10,000
Dinner = set ¥ 4,500-15,700
à la carte ¥ 2,100-10,000
Service charge = 10%

TEL. 03–3583–7852
1-5-4 Higashiazabu, Minato-ku, Tokyo

Obana
尾花

Lines form before it opens and the hall with rows of small dining tables is reminiscent of the Showa era. The *unagi* is prepared once an order is placed and takes at least 40 minutes, so try drinking snacks like *koi-no-arai*, *umaki* and *uzaku* while waiting. The almost melting *shirayaki* is eaten with soy sauce and *wasabi*; the *unaju* is packed tight in the multi-tiered box with just the right amount of sauce soaking into the rice.

■ Opening hours, last orders
Lunch = 11:30-13:30
Sat., Sun. and Public Holidays
11:30-19:30
Dinner = 16:00-19:30

■ Annual and weekly closing
Closed mid-August, late December-early January and Monday

■ Prices
Lunch = à la carte ¥ 3,500-12,000
Dinner = à la carte ¥ 3,500-12,000

TEL.03–3801–4670
5-33-1 Minamisenju,
Arakawa-ku, Tokyo

SPANISH CONTEMPORARY

Ogasawara Hakushaku-tei
小笠原伯爵邸

The current owner renovated this Spanish-style building, which was once the residence of Count Nagayoshi Ogasawara. Its air of elegance allows your mind to wander back in time to the life of the nobles. The Spanish chef offers colourful dishes based on Spanish cuisine with a modern twist, using Japanese ingredients. Only one set menu consisting of many small dishes is served. Suitable for both business or private occasions.

■ Opening hours, last orders
Lunch = 11:30-15:00 L.O.13:00
Dinner = 18:00-23:00 L.O.20:00

■ Annual and weekly closing
Closed late December-early January

■ Price
Lunch = set ¥ 7,350
Dinner = set ¥ 10,500-15,750
Private room fee = ¥ 10,500
Service charge = 10%

TEL. 03–3359–5830
10-10 Kawadacho, Shinjuku-ku, Tokyo

www.ogasawaratei.com

FRENCH

Ohara's

Kei Ohara honed his skills in a number of famous restaurants in France, where he lived for a decade. He offers traditional French cuisine, placing particular attention on the pairing of sauces: Choron sauce is used for fish dishes and béarnaise is paired with grilled Hiba beef. The *boudin noir* served with herb salad is particularly recommended. Warm service provided by the chef's German wife makes for a friendly atmosphere.

■ Opening hours, last orders
Lunch = 11:30-15:00 L.O.14:00
Dinner = 18:00-23:00 L.O.21:00

■ Annual and weekly closing
Closed late December-mid-January, Monday and 3rd Tuesday

■ Price
Lunch = set ¥ 3,150-7,350
à la carte ¥ 7,000-13,000
Dinner = set ¥ 7,350-10,500
à la carte ¥ 7,000-13,000
Service charge = 10%

TEL. 03–5436–3255
Yacmo Building B1F,
5-4-18 Osaki, Shinagawa-ku,
Tokyo

JAPANESE SOBA

Okina

翁

The proprietress is an 8th-generation descendant of the founder of a long-established Sarashina *soba* restaurant. The buckwheat noodles are made and boiled on the spot for maximum freshness. While set menus ending with *soba* are generally served, other dishes can also be enjoyed: seaweed; fish and shellfish. Unique *soba* dishes are also available: tea flavoured *soba* with *yuzu* and winter *soba* kneaded with black or white truffles.

■ Opening hours, last orders
Dinner = 18:00-22:30 (L.O.)

■ Annual and weekly closing
Closed early January, Sunday and Public Holidays

■ Price
Dinner = set ¥ 15,750-26,250
Service charge = 10%

TEL. 03–3477–2648
Five Annex B1F,
1-3-10 Ebisunishi, Shibuya-ku,
Tokyo

ITALIAN

Ostü NEW

The chef, who trained in northern Italy for 6 years, specialises in the cuisine of Piedmont and shows off his skills in an open kitchen. Handmade pasta uses only the yolk of the egg for firmness; the *agnolotti* speciality is stuffed with meat in summer and fondue cheese in winter. The name means 'cafeteria' so the atmosphere is down-to-earth. Wine from Barolo holds a place in the chef's heart and goes well with meat dishes.

■ Opening hours, last orders
Lunch = 11:30-15:30
Dinner = 18:00-23:00

■ Annual and weekly closing
Closed late December-early January and Wednesday

■ Price
Lunch = set ¥ 2,800-4,500
à la carte ¥ 5,000-7,000
Dinner = set ¥ 6,000-6,500
à la carte ¥ 5,000-7,000
Seat charge = ¥ 500/person (dinner)

TEL. 03-5454-8700
5-67-6 Yoyogi, Shibuya-ku, Tokyo
www.ostu.jp

JAPANESE SUSHI

Otaninosushi NEW
大谷之鮨

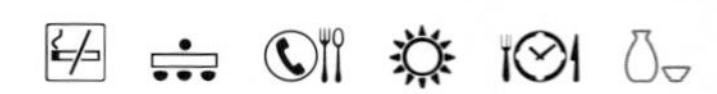

Regulars make this a lively spot but first-timers are also cheerfully welcomed. Start with a snack, move on to hand-pressed sushi or have some *shuko* in between; the dexterous owner-chef will respond flexibly to your preferences. Squid innards with *miso*, frozen at -60, is a delicate snack – preparations take time as, for example, the arch shell is opened just before serving and the squid is peeled after sitting in iced water.

■ Opening hours, last orders
Dinner = 18:00-23:00 (L.O.)

■ Annual and weekly closing
Closed mid-August, late December-early January

■ Price
Dinner = set ¥ 16,800-21,000
Service charge = 5%

TEL. 03-5468-8880
4-11-7 Nishiazabu, Minato-ku, Tokyo

www.otanino.com

JAPANESE

Ozaki
おざき

12

As the son of a sushi chef, Ichiro Ozaki sticks to what he knows best: he offers an *omakase* menu which naturally includes sushi. After appetisers, two pieces of tasty tuna sushi are served as a 'greeting'. Grilled crab in its shell follows as a year-long dish; cold sea-urchin *chawanmushi* is a seasonal favourite. Demonstrating his talent along with his young cooks, he also carefully explains dishes when asked.

■ Opening hours, last orders
Dinner = 18:00-24:00 L.O.22:00

■ Annual and weekly closing
Closed late December-early January and Sunday

■ Price
Dinner = set ¥ 21,000
Service charge = 10%

TEL. 03–3454–1682
3-4-5 Azabujuban, Minato-ku, Tokyo

FRENCH

Pachon

André Pachon, who has lived in Japan for about 40 years, has contributed to the cultures of both France and Japan, thanks to his classic French cuisine. You may be surprised by the firewood stove burning all year long until learning that it is used to cook the lamb, duck, suckling pig and other fine ingredients. The speciality is *cassoulet* and, as the chef is from Carcassonne, he puts an extra touch into this hometown dish.

■ Opening hours, last orders
Lunch = 11:30-15:30 L.O.14:00
Dinner = 18:00-22:00 (L.O.)
Sun. and Public Holidays 18:00-21:00 (L.O.)

■ Annual and weekly closing
Closed late December-early January

■ Price
Lunch = set ¥ 3,200-8,400
à la carte ¥ 4,500-6,500
Dinner = set ¥ 6,300-16,800
à la carte ¥ 9,000-24,000
Service charge = 10%

TEL. 03–3476–5025
Hillside Terrace B1F,
29-18 Sarugakucho, Shibuya-ku, Tokyo

www.pachon.co.jp

ITALIAN

Piatto Suzuki

Located by Azabujuban Station, which is a constant hive of activity. Owner-chef Yahei Suzuki serves traditional, regional Italian cuisine and the strictness with which he runs his kitchen is palpable. *Agu* pork, a delicacy, is ordered from Okinawa; chicken comes from Miyazaki and beef fillet from Hitachi in Ibaraki; most of the vegetables come directly from Kyoto. There's also a wide choice of Italian and French desserts.

■ Opening hours, last orders
Dinner = 18:00-2:00 L.O.24:00

■ Annual and weekly closing
Closed Golden week, late December-early January, Sunday and Public Holiday Mondays

■ Price
Dinner = set ¥ 10,500
à la carte ¥ 6,500-12,000

TEL. 03–5414–2116
Hasebeya Building 4F,
1-7-7 Azabujuban, Minato-ku,
Tokyo

FRENCH CONTEMPORARY

Pierre Gagnaire

Opened in 2010 by famous chef Pierre Gagnaire, this restaurant serves creative dishes prepared with Japanese and French ingredients in set menus. Each dish is served on multiple plates for an enjoyable mix of tastes and arrangements. For lunch there is also a low-priced 'Express Gourmet' set consisting of the weekly appetiser and a main dish. The cityscape can be enjoyed from the bench seats, which are ideal for couples.

■ Opening hours, last orders
Lunch = 11:30-14:00 (L.O.)
Dinner = 18:00-21:00 (L.O.)

■ Annual and weekly closing
Closed Monday except Public Holidays

■ Price
Lunch = set Tue.-Fri.¥ 3,800-15,000
Sat., Sun.¥ 6,000-10,000
Dinner = set ¥ 12,000-26,500
Service charge = 10%

TEL. 03–3505–1111
ANA Intercontinental Hotel 36F,
1-12-33 Akasaka, Minato-ku,
Tokyo

www.anaintercontinental-tokyo.jp

FRENCH CONTEMPORARY

Quintessence

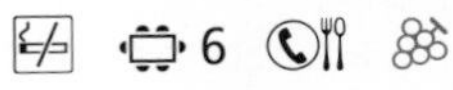

After training in Japan, Chef Shuzo Kishida perfected his skills in France, notably at Parisian restaurant, Astrance. So inspired was he that he bases the menu *carte blanche* -under which different dishes are created for each table - on available ingredients as well as his own inclination. Particular care is paid to the roasting and broiling of meat and fish. Reservation calls are only accepted 09:30-11:00 and 15:30-17:00.

■ Opening hours, last orders
Lunch = 12:00-15:00 L.O.13:00
Dinner = 18:30-23:00 L.O.20:30

■ Annual and weekly closing
Closed late December-early January and Sunday

■ Price
Lunch = set ¥ 7,875
Dinner = set ¥ 16,800
Service charge = 10%

TEL. 03-5791-3715
5-4-7 Shirokanedai, Minato-ku, Tokyo

www.quintessence.jp

JAPANESE TEMPURA

Raku-tei

楽亭

A subdued atmosphere and a plain wooden counter with seating for 12 greet you at this *tempura* restaurant. There is a choice of two set menus and the mild oil is specially blended to enhance the flavour of sesame and gives the *tempura* a light, pleasant taste. Owner-chef Shuji Ishikura fries *makiebi* only after receiving an order. The oil temperature for each ingredient is adjusted; while it is being changed try some *sashimi*.

■ Opening hours, last orders
Lunch = 12:00 (L.O.)
Dinner = 17:00-20:30 (L.O.)

■ Annual and weekly closing
Closed Golden week, mid-August, late December-early January and Monday

■ Price
Lunch = set ¥ 10,500-12,600
Dinner = set ¥ 10,500-12,600

TEL. 03–3585–3743
6-8-1 Akasaka, Minato-ku, Tokyo

JAPANESE YAKITORI

Ranjatai
蘭奢待

The passionate owner-chef uses Hinai chicken and says that, while it is difficult to prepare for *yakitori*, its strong flavours come out through careful roasting. As well as *yakitori*, the soft-boiled quail eggs, firm lotus root stuffed with meat, and mushrooms are also popular, as are the salad and kumquat. First-timers should try the set menu, which includes liver pâté, 6 spit-roasts and rice, and add other items if desired.

■ Opening hours, last orders
Dinner = Mon.-Fri. 17:00-24:00 L.O.23:00
Sat. 17:00-22:00 L.O.21:00

■ Annual and weekly closing
Closed mid-August, late December-early January, Sunday and Public Holidays

■ Price
Dinner = set ¥ 2,200-3,200
à la carte ¥ 4,000-6,000
Seat charge=¥ 500/person

TEL. 03–3263–0596
2-12-3 Kandajinbocho,
Chiyoda-ku, Tokyo

www.ranjatai.com

CHINESE

Reikasai
厲家菜

The female chef has access to imperial recipes, thanks to her grandfather who was a high-ranking courtier in the Qing Dynasty and supervised the preparation of meals for Empress Dowager Cixi. The chef's choice menu, which includes dishes such as smoked pork flavoured with jasmine and peanuts and coloured with beetroot, is bound to satisfy. Each colourful, memorable dish offers a sense of the rich history of the Li family.

■ Opening hours, last orders
Lunch = 11:30-15:30 L.O.13:30
Dinner = 18:00-23:30 L.O.20:30

■ Price
Lunch = set ¥ 6,300-47,250
Dinner = set ¥ 10,500-47,250
Service charge = 10%

TEL. 03-5413-9561
Roppongi Hills Residence B, 3F,
6-12-2 Roppongi, Minato-ku,
Tokyo

JAPANESE

Ren
蓮

The sacred lotus (*ren*) symbolises purity and is used in the restaurant's name to express the approach of cooking with a pure heart. Dishes that deliver honest flavours are prepared behind the counter, like the bamboo shoots, charbroiled skin and all, and *hamo*, placed in the stock with onions. The young chef's interaction with the customers is just right. Only an *omakase* is offered, but after 9pm there are small set menus.

■ Opening hours, last orders
Dinner = 17:30-24:00 L.O.22:30

■ Annual and weekly closing
Closed mid-August, late December-early January, Sunday and Public Holidays

■ Price
Dinner = set ¥ 12,600
Service charge = 5%

TEL. 03–6265–0177
Omiya Building 4F,
4-3-2 Kagurazaka,
Shinjuku-ku, Tokyo

FRENCH

Restaurant-I

20

The glass-enclosed dining room, surrounded by trees, has a spacious feel. The chef also owns a restaurant in Nice, but here dishes are prepared primarily with ingredients from the outskirts of Tokyo. The speciality is Edo vegetable and foie gras terrine, which goes well with *miso* sauce. Whole pigs are purchased, and each part is prepared using the most suitable technique. Dessert is the Harajuku crepe, which changes monthly.

■ Opening hours, last orders
Lunch = 11:30-15:00 L.O.13:30
Dinner = 18:00-23:00 L.O.21:00

■ Annual and weekly closing
Closed mid-August and late December-early January

■ Price
Lunch = set ¥ 3,500-9,000
Dinner = set ¥ 6,800-16,000
Service charge = 10%

TEL. 03–5772–2091
1-4-20 Jingumae, Shibuya-ku, Tokyo

www.restaurant-i.jp

FRENCH CONTEMPORARY

Révérence NEW

The most recent chef arrived at this restaurant, owned by a sommelier, in 2011 and together they collaborate to produce a unique gastronomic world. There are two set menus for different palates: 'Éternel' features traditional dishes, while 'Tourbillon' showcases his creativity. The staple dish is the popular boudin noir; the rest of the menu changes monthly. Whimsical dish names like 'Black Tie' Pigeon all tell a story.

■ Opening hours, last orders
Lunch = 12:00-13:30 (L.O.)
Dinner = 18:00-21:30 (L.O.)

■ Annual and weekly closing
Closed mid-August, late December-early January and Tuesday

■ Price
Lunch = set ¥ 3,900-5,800
Dinner = set ¥ 8,400-12,600
Service charge = 10%

TEL. 03-5475-3290
4-12-4 Minamiazabu, Minato-ku, Tokyo

www.rest-reverence.jp

ITALIAN CONTEMPORARY

Ristorante Aso

20

Ristorante Aso opened in 1997, with chef Tatsuji Aso's original and creative cooking going far beyond the boundaries of Italian and French cuisine. Dishes overflow with innovation, both in their arrangement and their colour combinations. Quality aged beef is grilled on charcoal and served with peppered mascarpone; sautéed foie gras is topped with zabaione and black truffle sauce. Customers leave immeasurably satisfied.

■ Opening hours, last orders
Lunch = 12:00-15:30 L.O.13:30
Dinner = 18:00-23:00 L.O.20:30

■ Annual and weekly closing
Closed early January, Saturday, Sunday and Public Holidays

■ Price
Lunch = set ¥ 5,250-7,350
à la carte ¥ 11,500-15,000
Dinner = set ¥ 9,450-15,750
à la carte ¥ 11,500-15,000
Service charge = 13%

TEL. 03-3770-3690
29-3 Sarugakucho, Shibuya-ku, Tokyo

www.hiramatsu.co.jp/restaurants/aso

ITALIAN CONTEMPORARY

Ristorante Honda

Tetsuya Honda's menu is characterised by sophisticated dishes, full of originality in the way the food is arranged and the colour combinations. His distinct approach is also reflected in his cooking methods which, although based on Italian cuisine, incorporate some French elements. The tableware is also unique. *Tagliolini* with sea urchin is a year-long speciality. Dishes on the set menus can be ordered individually.

■ Opening hours, last orders
Lunch = 12:00-15:00 L.O.14:00
Dinner = 18:00-22:00 (L.O.)

■ Annual and weekly closing
Closed late December-early January and Monday except Public Holidays

■ Price
Lunch = set ¥ 2,940-6,825
Dinner = set ¥ 8,400-12,600
Service charge = 10%

TEL. 03-5414-3723
2-12-35 Kitaaoyama, Minato-ku, Tokyo

www.ristorantehonda.jp

Ristorante La Primula

   3 

The chef spent three years studying Italian cuisine in northern Italy; his last position, in Friuli, was at a restaurant called Primula (primrose), from which this establishment takes its name. *Cjalçons*, pasta stuffed with potato purée, cinnamon, mint and raisins and topped with smoked Gouda cheese, is one of the Friulian specialities. Only set menus are served and they showcase the flavours of regional Italian cuisine.

■ Opening hours, last orders
Lunch = Wed.-Sat. 12:00-14:30 L.O.13:00
Dinner = 18:00-23:00 L.O.21:00

■ Annual and weekly closing
Closed late December-early January, Sunday and 3rd Monday

■ Price
Lunch = set ¥ 1,260-5,500
Dinner = set ¥ 6,300-15,750
Service charge = 10%

TEL. 03–5439–9470
Patio Azabu Juban 3F,
2-8-10 Azabujuban, Minato-ku, Tokyo

JAPANESE KUSHIAGE

Rokukaku-tei
六覺燈

This *kushikatsu* restaurant, originally from Nipponbashi in Osaka, opened in Ginza in 2004. It has a single set menu which varies in price depending on the number of skewers ordered - the standard being twenty. The minced white-fleshed fish is wrapped in *oba*, fried and topped with *tonburi*, and there is also lotus root stuffed with curry-flavoured minced beef. The sliced and stacked *konnyaku* has an interesting texture.

■ Opening hours, last orders
14:00-22:30 (L.O.)

■ Annual and weekly closing
Closed mid-August, late December-early January and Tuesday

■ Price
Dinner = set ¥ 10,500
Service charge = 10%

TEL. 03-5537-6008
Kojun Building 4F,
6-8-7 Ginza, Chuo-ku, Tokyo

CHINESE

Ryuan

劉安

Specialities are the *kanpo* herbal soups reproduced according to books passed down over thousands of years. The set menus include 1 of 9 varieties of soup, each with its own health benefit and eaten before other liquids to ensure it is absorbed. Try also the fried vegetable dish, made up of over 20 different vegetables. Passionate about health through food, the owner-chef opened a clinical *kanpo* research institute in Beijing.

■ Opening hours, last orders
Lunch = 12:00-15:00 L.O.14:00
Dinner = 17:30-23:00 L.O.21:00

■ Annual and weekly closing
Closed mid-August, late December-early January and Monday

■ Price
Lunch = set ¥ 6,500-28,800
à la carte ¥ 3,000-30,000
Dinner = set ¥ 10,000-28,800
à la carte¥ 3,000-30,000
Service charge = 10% (dinner)

TEL. 03–3448–1978
5-13-35 Shirokanedai, Minato-ku, Tokyo

www.shirokane-ryuan.com

JAPANESE CONTEMPORARY

Ryugin 

龍吟

The owner-chef Seiji Yamamoto says that new things can be created by bringing together various classics. Focusing on Japanese cuisine, he exercises his natural curiosity in the pursuit of new possibilities and original dishes. He shaves the dried bonito after receiving the order so that the stock is at its tastiest when served. A daily-changing *omakase* set menu is available and its contents vary according to the season.

■ Opening hours, last orders
Dinner = 18:00-1:00 L.O.22:30

■ Annual and weekly closing
Closed mid-August, late December-early January, Sunday and Public Holidays

■ Price
Dinner = set ¥ 23,100
à la carte ¥ 10,000-20,000
Service charge = 10% (private room 15%)

TEL. 03–3423–8006
7-17-24 Roppongi, Minato-ku, Tokyo

www.nihonryori-ryugin.com

FRENCH

Ryuzu NEW

The owner-chef opened his restaurant in 2011 and focuses on the harmony between fragrance and texture. In the foie gras and Kamo eggplant dish, eggplant is simmered in broth to give it a texture similar to foie gras; sautéed abalone comes with a sauce made from abalone stock and liver to bring out the ocean fragrance. The crispness of the *shiitake* tart is of high repute. Book a counter seat early if you want to chat with him.

■ Opening hours, last orders
Lunch = 12:00-14:00 (L.O.)
Dinner = 18:00-21:30 (L.O.)

■ Annual and weekly closing
Closed early January, mid-August and Monday

■ Price
Lunch = set ¥ 3,600-8,400
Dinner = set ¥ 8,400-17,800
à la carte ¥ 6,000-12,000
Service charge = 10%

TEL. 03-5770-4236
Urban Style Roppongi B1F, 4-2-35 Roppongi, Minato-ku, Tokyo

www.restaurant-ryuzu.com

Sakuragawa
櫻川

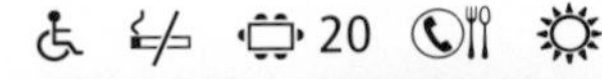

Owner-chef Yoshiaki Kurahashi named the restaurant after his hometown to remember his heritage. Keeping traditional sensibilities alive, seasonal flowers and leaves are used for *hassun*; *warabimochi* dessert, sprinkled with salt-pickled cherry blossom petals, is served with *matcha*. The set menu changes monthly and so does the tableware, with motifs depicting seasonal blossoms such as cherry, camellia, plum, iris and hydrangea.

■ Opening hours, last orders
Lunch = 12:00-15:30 L.O.14:00
Dinner = 18:00-22:00 L.O.20:00

■ Annual and weekly closing
Closed mid-August

■ Price
Lunch = set ¥ 6,050
Dinner = set ¥ 13,200
Private room fee=¥3,150-5,250 (lunch)
¥5,250-10,500 (dinner)

TEL. 03–3279–0039
Mitsui Tower 2F,
2-1-1 Nihonbashimuromachi,
Chuo-ku, Tokyo

Sanda
さんだ

This *kappo* restaurant serves Japanese beef, with an emphasis on offal. The thinly sliced Achilles tendon is reminiscent of *fugu* skin, and there is variety in the cooking techniques and seasoning. The rumen is seasoned with curry powder and salt; soft-boiled cheek has a Western taste and there's a hint of *wamono* in the beef tongue *tsumire* soup with cartilage. Well priced and suitable for casual business dinners.

■ Opening hours, last orders
Dinner = 17:30-23:30 L.O.21:30
Saturday 17:30-23:00 L.O.21:00

■ Annual and weekly closing
Closed mid-August, late December-early January, Sunday and Public Holidays

■ Price
Dinner = set ¥ 6,300

TEL. 03–3423–2020
4-5-9 Roppongi, Minato-ku, Tokyo

Sangoan
三合菴

Hiroyuki Kato opened his restaurant in 2000. Recently renovated, it is now half its original size but the warm lighting creates a soothing atmosphere. The *toichi soba* is made with 10 parts buckwheat and 1 part wheat flour; it includes moderate amounts of the black inner skin of the buckwheat, making it fragrant and visually pleasing. The slightly strong sauce served with the *seiro* brings out the sweetness of the *soba*.

■ Opening hours, last orders
Lunch = 11:30-14:00 L.O.13:30
Dinner = 17:30-21:30 L.O.21:00

■ Annual and weekly closing
Closed early January, early September, Wednesday and 3rd Thursday

■ Price
Lunch = à la carte ¥ 2,000-5,000
Dinner = set ¥ 6,500
à la carte ¥ 2,000-5,000
Seat charge=¥ 850/person (dinner à la carte only)

TEL. 03–3444–3570
5-10-10 Shirokane, Minato-ku, Tokyo

JAPANESE

Sankame
三亀

  LUNCH  6

Sankame has been serving Kansai-style cuisine since 1946. As well as set menus, à la carte dishes are available at dinner; only *teisyoku* are served at lunch. Try the simmered *zenmai*, its bitterness removed by being plunged in water, or steamed tilefish wrapped in glutinous rice and cherry tree leaves. The restaurant is always lively with a diverse clientele. Owner-chef Isao Nanjo's personality and humour add to the appeal.

■ Opening hours, last orders
Lunch = 12:00-14:00 L.O.13:00
Dinner = 17:00-22:00 L.O.21:30

■ Annual and weekly closing
Closed mid-August, late December-early January, Saturday in July-August, Sunday and Public Holidays

■ Price
Lunch = set ¥ 1,950-2,950
Dinner = set ¥ 13,650
à la carte ¥ 8,000-12,000

TEL. 03-3571-0573
6-4-13 Ginza, Chuo-ku, Tokyo

SPANISH CONTEMPORARY

Sant Pau

8

This is the Tokyo branch of Sant Pau, near Barcelona. Diners can experience traditional Spanish cuisine that makes much of Catalonia's natural bounty, albeit with extra twists courtesy of Carme Ruscalleda, the owner-chef of the parent restaurant. Ingredients such as Iberico pork, salted cod, olive oil, Majorca salt and dried pimientos are imported from Catalonia, while others are sourced locally. Presentation is also original.

■ Opening hours, last orders
Lunch = 11:30-15:30 L.O.13:30
Dinner = 18:00-23:30 L.O.21:00

■ Annual and weekly closing
Closed 1 January and Monday

■ Price
Lunch = set ¥ 5,500-22,000
à la carte ¥ 16,000-17,000

Dinner = set ¥ 18,000-22,000
à la carte ¥ 16,000-17,000
Private room fee = ¥10,000 (lunch), ¥18,000 (dinner)
Service charge = 10%

TEL. 03-3517-5700
Coredo Nihonbashi Annex,
1-6-1 Nihonbashi, Chuo-ku,
Tokyo

www.santpau.jp

JAPANESE

Sanyukyo
三友居

    4 

Opened by Kyoto's *chakaiseki* catering establishment Sanyukyo, out of a desire to have people enjoy their cooking in a casual atmosphere and to make lives even richer. Most ingredients arrive daily from Kyoto. The main item of the set menus changes with the seasons and is prepared in several different ways to keep your taste buds guessing. The thick sesame seed dressing accompanying the Kyoto vegetables has a rich taste.

■ Opening hours, last orders
Lunch = 11:30-15:00 L.O.14:00
Dinner = 17:30-21:30 L.O.20:00

■ Annual and weekly closing
Closed late December-late January and Monday

■ Price
Lunch = set ¥ 4,700
Dinner = set ¥ 8,900

TEL. 03-5449-7155
1-27-19 Takanawa, Minato-ku, Tokyo

JAPANESE SUSHI

Sawada
さわ田

Koji Sawada is a sushi chef with an unusual background because, before setting up his restaurant, he worked in the transport industry. One of the features here is the chef's commitment to maturing each ingredient, allowing their full flavour to come out. Rice is cooked slightly hard and is well seasoned with white vinegar so that its flavour is as distinctive as that of the ingredients that top it. Sawada is reservation-only.

■ Opening hours, last orders
Lunch = 12:00-14:00
Dinner = 18:00-21:00 and
22:00-1:00 L.O.22:00
Sat. and Sun. 17:00-20:00 L.O.17:00

■ Annual and weekly closing
Closed mid-August, late December-early January and Monday

■ Price
Lunch = set ¥ 21,000-35,000
Dinner = set ¥ 32,000-35,000

TEL. 03–3571–4711
MC Building 3F,
5-9-19 Ginza, Chuo-ku, Tokyo

JAPANESE TEMPURA

Seiju
清壽

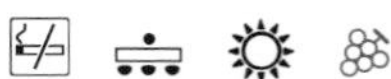

In such a dignified atmosphere you may feel obliged to sit up straight, but Yoshiaki Shimizu's friendly manner creates a sense of ease. There is only one *omakase* set menu, but drinking snacks can be added as desired. The specialities are prawn and kidney beans from the owner's parents' farm. During the new sake season, rare sake lees *tempura* is available. Along with sake are reasonably priced wines selected by the sommelier.

■ Opening hours, last orders
Dinner = 17:00-21:00 (L.O.)

■ Annual and weekly closing
Closed Golden week, mid-August, late December-early January and Monday

■ Price
Dinner = set ¥ 12,600
Service charge = 5%

TEL. 03-3546-2622
Urban Mates Building B1F,
3-16-9 Tsukiji, Chuo-ku, Tokyo

JAPANESE

Seika Kobayashi
青華 こばやし

The owner-chef of this homely restaurant says he opened it after collecting a full set of serving dishes. The set menus are largely comprised of seafood, except when bamboo shoots, wax gourds, turnips and *ebi-imo* are in season; sugar and *mirin* are used sparingly and the volume is plentiful. At the end comes rice from his parents' farm prepared in an earthenware pot. Only one party is served at lunch and two at dinner.

■ Opening hours, last orders
12:00-21:30 (L.O.)

■ Annual and weekly closing
Closed late December-early January

■ Price
Lunch = set ¥ 10,000-13,800
Dinner = set ¥ 13,800-18,000

TEL. 03–6459–2210
7-10-30 Roppongi, Minato-ku, Tokyo

www.seikakobayashi.com

JAPANESE

Seisoka
青草窠

  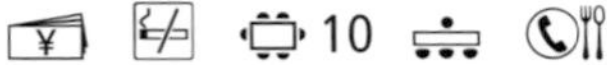  10  

Hidden on the 1st floor of a building near Tengenji Temple. The *mukozuke* features serving dishes made in the middle of the Edo era by Sonyu, the 5th-generation Raku family potter who continued the techniques of Chojiro. The *hassun* comes on lotus leaves laid out, according to the restaurant, on a Tenpyo roof tile from the Nara era (710-794) which exemplifies traditional beauty. The easy-going hospitality makes you feel at home.

■ Opening hours, last orders
Lunch = 12:00-15:00
Dinner = 17:30-23:00

■ Annual and weekly closing
Closed mid-August, late December-early January and Sunday

■ Price
Lunch = set ¥ 6,300-20,000
Dinner = set ¥ 20,000
Service charge = 10%

TEL. 03-3473-3103
4-2-34 Minamiazabu, Minato-ku, Tokyo

JAPANESE

Sekiho-tei
赤寶亭

10

Traditional techniques and high quality ingredients are used here. Stock is made only with the core parts of back meat and belly of a special kind of bonito produced in Makurazaki; water comes from Shiga to highlight the taste of the Rishiri kelp. Cards that read '*risshun daikichi* (with luck on the first day of spring)' are placed on plates in February; and *chimaki-zushi* are served on the May 5 Boys' Festival.

■ Opening hours, last orders
Lunch = Wed.-Sat.12:00-14:30 L.O.13:30
Dinner = 18:00-22:30 L.O.21:30

■ Annual and weekly closing
Closed Golden week, mid-August, late December-early January and Sunday

■ Price
Lunch = set ¥ 5,250-18,900
Dinner = set ¥ 11,500-18,900
Private room fee = ¥ 3,000-5,000
Service charge = 10%

TEL. 03-5474-6889
3-1-14 Jingumae, Shibuya-ku, Tokyo

Sekine NEW
勢きね

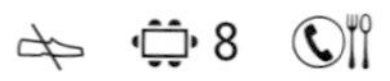

The owner-chef became interested in *unagi* at university and went on to study *unagi* and *kaiseki* cuisine in Hamamatsu. He prefers 1 to 1½ year-old *unagi* with lean, strong-tasting meat; whether or not it is steamed is determined by its texture, but he places more emphasis on taste than on tenderness. The basic sauce is rich, but there is also a light *Kanto*-style sauce available. Only three groups are served per day at dinner.

■ Opening hours, last orders
Lunch = 11:30-14:00 (L.O.)
Dinner = 17:30-20:00 (L.O.)

■ Annual and weekly closing
Closed late December-early January and Sunday

■ Price
Lunch = set ¥ 5,500-7,500
Dinner = set ¥ 10,000-15,000
Service charge = 10% (Lunch 8%)

TEL. 03-5410-1500
9-1-7 Akasaka, Minato-ku, Tokyo

KOREAN

Sennohana NEW
千の花

Enjoy a fusion of Korean Royal Court cuisine and *yakiniku*. First comes a small serving of congee to protect the stomach. As the true flavour of *kimchi* can only be produced under the climatic conditions in Korea, the fermentation is done there. Appetisers include *samgyetang* and pig's foot in gelatine. The 'food is medicine' concept is seen in dishes like beef tongue with ginseng salt and *galbi* in a *yakuzen* sauce.

■ Opening hours, last orders
Dinner = 17:00-23:00 L.O.22:00

■ Annual and weekly closing
Closed mid-August, late December-early January

■ Prices
Dinner = set ¥ 10,000-15,000
à la carte ¥ 8,000-15,000
Private room fee = ¥5,000
Service charge = 10%

TEL.03-3599-6662
1-3-5 Daiba, Minato-ku, Tokyo

www.sennohana.com

CHINESE

Sense

18

The Japanese chef prepares modern Cantonese cuisine based on traditional recipes, with the focus on set menus. Authentic Chinese ingredients and seasonings are used, such as Napoleon fish – a Hong Kong favourite – local grouper, and Chinese vegetables grown in Japan, cooked according to each diner's preference. A casual lunch is always appealing, but ambient lighting and panoramic city views make dinner even more attractive.

■ Opening hours, last orders
Lunch=11:30-14:30 (L.O.)
Sat., Sun. and Public Holidays
11:30-16:00 (L.O.)
Dinner=17:30-22:00 (L.O.)

■ Price
Lunch = set Mon.-Fri. ¥ 3,800-8,800
Sat.,Sun. ¥ 5,500-12,000
à la carte ¥ 7,000-29,000

Dinner = set ¥ 14,000-26,000
à la carte ¥ 7,000-35,000
Private room fee = ¥10,000
Service charge = 13%

TEL. 03–3270–8188
Mandarin Oriental Hotel 37F,
2-1-1 Nihonbashimuromachi,
Chuo-ku, Tokyo

www.mandarinoriental.co.jp/tokyo

7chome Kyoboshi
七丁目 京星

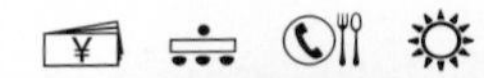

Shigeya Sakakibara's Kyoto-style *tempura* is made of only the best seasonal ingredients, small enough to be popped into the mouth whole: sweet *saimaki ebi*, purple asparagus, abalone, quail eggs and figs. *Ten-cha* is recommended to finish. His constant trial of ingredients accounts for his wide repertoire, allowing diners to savour some rare treats, albeit at a price. Weekend reservations must be made two days in advance.

■ Opening hours, last orders
Lunch = 12:00-15:00 (L.O.)
Dinner = 17:00-21:00 (L.O.)

■ Annual and weekly closing
Closed mid-August and late December-early January

■ Price
Lunch = set ¥ 33,600-38,850
Dinner = set ¥ 33,600-38,850

TEL. 03-3572-3568
Ozio Ginza Building 6F,
5-5-9 Ginza, Chuo-ku, Tokyo

JAPANESE

Shigeyoshi
重よし

10

This *itamae kappo* restaurant was opened 40 years ago. We recommend the counter seats where you can sit and chat with the owner-chef, Kenzo Sato. He serves choice ingredients, carefully prepared, and every dish is flavoursome and refined. Madaka abalone is procured from Boshu, while *tai, hamo, uni,* and other seafood all come from Naruto. In early summer try the Amami Oshima passion fruit gelatine.

■ Opening hours, last orders
Lunch = 12:00-13:30 (L.O.)
Dinner = 17:30-22:00 L.O.21:00

■ Annual and weekly closing
Closed Golden week, mid-August, late December-early January, Sunday and Public Holiday Mondays

■ Price
Lunch = set ¥ 5,250-15,750
Dinner = set ¥ 18,900-31,500
Private room fee = 10%

TEL. 03–3400–4044
Co-op Olympia 1F,
6-35-3 Jingumae, Shibuya-ku,
Tokyo

JAPANESE IZAKAYA

Shinsuke
シンスケ

Once an established liquor store, it became a Japanese-style pub in 1924 and is now run by the fourth-generation of the family. The onion *nuta* with mustard-vinegar-*miso* dressing offers a nostalgic taste; the *Kitsune Raclette* with cheese inside deep-fried tofu is popular. Try draft sake ordered by the barrel between autumn and spring. Seats on the 1st floor, which has a Showa feel to it, cannot be reserved so arrive early.

■ Opening hours, last orders
Dinner = 17:00-22:00

■ Annual and weekly closing
Closed mid-August, late December-early January, Sunday and Public Holidays

■ Prices
Dinner = à la carte ¥ 4,500-8,000
Seat charge=¥ 315/person

TEL.03–3832–0469
3-31-5 Yushima, Bunkyo-ku, Tokyo

JAPANESE

Shofukuro
招福楼

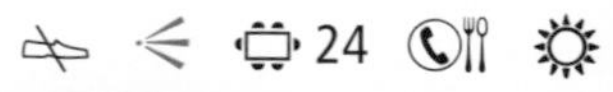

Boasting a prime location on the top floor of Marunouchi Building, this restaurant has counter seats, *tatami* rooms and table seating, all with views of the Imperial Palace and northern Tokyo. There are more modern rooms but the elegant *tatami* rooms offer traditional Japanese beauty. The way the *suiji* (the soup) is prepared depends on the season to bring out the sweetness of the *kombu* and the natural flavour of the *katsuo*.

■ Opening hours, last orders
Lunch = 11:30-15:00
Dinner = 17:00-23:00
Sun. and Public Holidays 17:00-22:00

■ Annual and weekly closing
Closed 1 January

■ Price
Lunch = set ¥ 6,300-31,500
Dinner = set ¥ 12,600-31,500
Private room fee = ¥ 1,050/person
Service charge = 10%

TEL. 03-3240-0003
Marunouchi Building 36F,
2-4-1 Marunouchi, Chiyoda-ku,
Tokyo

www.shofukuro.jp

JAPANESE

Shunnoaji Ichi
旬の味 いち

Enjoy seasonal seafood fresh from the port and vegetables from the owner-chef's parents' home. In spring, regulars come for the nearly 10 different wild plants cooked in various ways: in summer tomato *surinagashi*, in autumn pacific saury with rice, and in winter *sawani nabe* with boar meat and plenty of edible roots. We recommend the *omakase* and adding meat dishes and rice according to how hungry you are. Prices are reasonable.

■ Opening hours, last orders
Dinner = 18:30-24:00

■ Annual and weekly closing
Closed late December-early January, Sunday and Public Holidays

■ Price
Dinner = set ¥ 3,500-10,500
Service charge = 10%

TEL. 03–3402–9424
7-10-30 Roppongi, Minato-ku, Tokyo

Signature

XXXX

10

The chef uses French and Japanese produce to create delicate, refined, contemporary French cuisine. Using sweet and sour flavours from fruits and accents of herbs and spices, he makes each dish stand out. Specialities include toasted scallops, foie gras and persimmon two ways and laurel-roasted wild partridge with sauerkraut. The reasonably priced lunch menus are very appealing. Ask for a window table to enjoy the cityscape.

■ Opening hours, last orders
Lunch = 11:30-14:30 (L.O.)
Dinner = 17:30-22:00 (L.O.)

■ Price
Lunch = set weekday ¥ 5,000-12,000
Sat.,Sun. ¥ 5,500-12,000
à la carte ¥ 12,000-19,000
Dinner = set ¥ 14,000-20,000
à la carte ¥ 12,000-19,000
Private room fee = ¥10,000
Service charge = 13%

TEL. 03–3270–8188
Mandarin Oriental Hotel 37F,
2-1-1 Nihonbashimuromachi,
Chuo-ku, Tokyo

www.mandarinoriental.co.jp/tokyo

Soba Miwa NEW

蕎麦 みわ

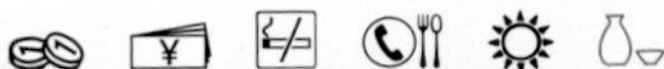

The owner-chef buys *marunuki* and grinds it himself for *soba*. The basic selections are 'seiro', 'tebiki' and 'inakaseiro', the latter two limited to 15 servings each; all go well with the full-bodied sauce made from *kombu* and *katsuobushi* stock. Wild vegetables from Nagano and Tohoku are available in spring. We recommend the 'tenseiro' and the 'hiyakake soba' in summer. Various artists worked on the interior and serving dishes.

■ Opening hours, last orders
Lunch = 11:30-14:30 L.O.14:15
Dinner = 17:30-21:00 L.O.20:45
Sun. and Public Holidays 17:30-20:30 L.O.20:15

■ Annual and weekly closing
Closed mid-August, early January, 1st and 3rd Tuesday, Monday except Public Holidays

■ Price
Lunch = à la carte ¥ 2,000-4,000
Dinner = set ¥ 3,150-4,725
à la carte ¥ 2,000-4,000

TEL. 03-3394-3837
3-15-3 Igusa, Suginami-ku, Tokyo

www.sobamiwa.jp

JAPANESE SUSHI

Sukiyabashi Jiro Honten
すきやばし 次郎 本店

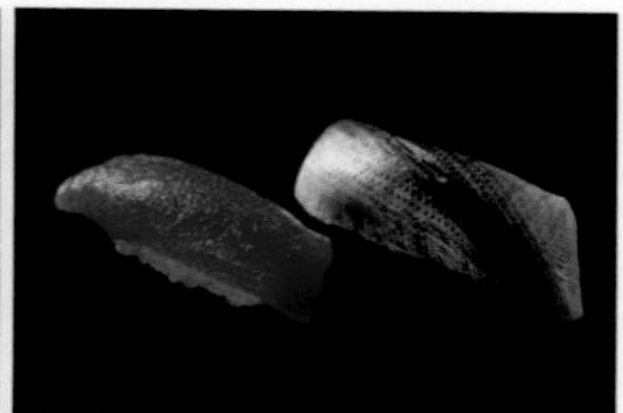

The 'left-handed master craftsman', Jiro Ono, creates the finest sushi with swift, fluid movements. At his authentic sushi restaurant, he serves only *omakase nigiri* sushi and nothing more; and don't be surprised to be finished within 30 minutes. The 20 or so pieces may not come cheap but just consider the exquisite tastes. Everything is carefully timed so be punctual - and if you don't speak Japanese, go with someone who does.

■ Opening hours, last orders
Lunch = 11:30-14:00
Dinner = Mon.-Fri. 17:30-20:30

■ Annual and weekly closing
Closed mid-August, late December-early January, Sunday and Public Holidays

■ Price

Lunch = set	¥ 31,500
Dinner = set	¥ 31,500

TEL. 03–3535–3600
Tsukamoto Sozan Building B1F,
4-2-15 Ginza, Chuo-ku, Tokyo

www.sushi-jiro.jp

JAPANESE SUSHI

Sukiyabashi Jiro Roppongi
すきやばし 次郎 六本木

A branch of 'Sukiyabashi Jiro', this is run by Takashi Ono, second son of the world-famous sushi master, Jiro Ono. His creed is 'No compromise' and the occasional reprimand to the young cooks is an expression of this attitude. Try the 15-item *omakase* for lunch and the 20-item *omakase* for dinner. The rice is carefully cooked so that each grain stands out. Prices may be high but the restaurant attracts plenty of sushi lovers.

■ Opening hours, last orders
Lunch = 11:30-14:00
Dinner = 17:00-21:00

■ Annual and weekly closing
Closed late December-early January and Wednesday

■ Price
Lunch = set ¥ 17,850
Dinner = set ¥ 25,200

TEL. 03–5413–6626
Roppongi Hills Residence B, 3F,
6-12-2 Roppongi, Minato-ku,
Tokyo

Sushi Aoki Ginza
鮨 青木 銀座

Toshikatsu Aoki, the owner-chef, uses *Edomae* techniques handed down from his father but also seeks out new ideas. Specialities inherited from his father are still favourites: simmered octopus; smelt-whiting between sheets of kelp; and pickled young tiger prawns. Perch or red rockfish are good either as snacks, or lightly seared, served as sushi. Popular and well-priced *okimari* and *chirashi-zushi* are offered at lunch.

■ Opening hours, last orders
Lunch = 12:00-14:00
Dinner = 17:00-22:00

■ Annual and weekly closing
Closed late December-early January

■ Price
Lunch = set ¥ 2,300-20,000
Dinner = set ¥ 21,000

TEL. 03-3289-1044
Ginza Takahashi Building 2F,
6-7-4 Ginza, Chuo-ku, Tokyo

www.sushiaoki.com

JAPANESE SUSHI

Sushi Fukumoto
鮨 福元

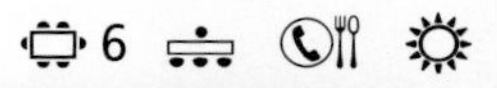

A menu listing the items of the day and where they were produced sits on the counter. An appetiser of Chinese yam and sea urchin dressed with soy sauce is one speciality; conger eel and ark shells *shiroyaki* is also flavoursome. Rice is boiled quite hard and blended with a mild *akazu*. It's fun to have sake with the sushi while listening to his owner-chef's stories about fish. A dental clinic's green board acts as a marker.

■ Opening hours, last orders
Dinner = 18:00-23:00 (L.O.)
Sun. and Public Holidays 17:00-21:00 (L.O.)

■ Annual and weekly closing
Closed mid-August, late December-early January and Wednesday

■ Price
Dinner = set ¥ 14,667
Service charge = 5%

TEL. 03–5481–9537
Hanabu Building B1F,
5-17-6 Daizawa, Setagaya-ku,
Tokyo

www17.ocn.ne.jp/~fuku3411

JAPANESE SUSHI

Sushiichi

鮨一

The entrance is on the first floor, not noticeable from the street; alert the staff over the intercom and they will come to greet you. Thought has gone into the modern interior, the tableware and chopsticks. Red vinegar and rice vinegar are used with the rice to cut down on the sweetness; chub mackerel and *nodoguro* are grilled, and white-fleshed fish are garnished with salt and *sudachi*. There are several *omakase* set menus.

■ Opening hours, last orders
Lunch = 12:00-14:30 L.O.14:00
Dinner = 17:30-23:00 L.O.21:30
Sat. and Public Holidays
17:30-22:00 L.O.20:30

■ Annual and weekly closing
Closed Golden week, mid-August, late December-early January, Sunday and Public Holiday Mondays

■ Price
Lunch = set ¥ 3,150-30,000
Dinner = set ¥ 10,500-30,000

TEL. 03–3567–0014
3-4-4 Ginza, Chuo-ku, Tokyo

www.3567-0014.com

JAPANESE SUSHI

Sushi Imamura
鮨 いまむら

The counter runs alongside the kitchen, so you can watch the food being prepared. The rice blend is cooked firm in a cast iron rice cooker and seasoned with *akazu*, rice vinegar and salt. The salt-vinegar mix for the gizzard shad is perfect, the bitterness complementing the sweetness of the rice. *Anago* is boiled soft and then charbroiled and pressed gently onto the rice. The owner-chef's wife provides meticulous service.

■ Opening hours, last orders
Lunch = Sat. and Sun. 12:00-14:00
Dinner = 18:00-23:30
Sat., Sun. and Public Holidays
18:00-22:00

■ Annual and weekly closing
Closed mid-August, late December-early January and Monday

■ Price
Lunch = set ¥ 5,250
Dinner = set ¥ 12,600

TEL. 03–5789–3637
5-8-13 Shirokane, Minato-ku, Tokyo

JAPANESE SUSHI

Sushi Isshin Asakusa

鮨 一新 浅草

Abalone from Chiba is a house appetiser. *Maguro-no-zuke* sees tuna marinated in a blend of dried tuna stock and soy sauce to ensure a richer taste. Winter dishes include *karasumi* and seared *shirako*. Rice is steamed on charcoal and seasoned with *akazu*. Popular sushi toppings include gizzard, conger eel, boiled clams and spear squid with egg in spring and salmon roe. Asakusa-4 Post Office or the Police Station act as landmarks.

■ Opening hours, last orders
Dinner = 18:00-22:00 (L.O.)

■ Annual and weekly closing
Closed mid-August, late December-early January, Sunday and Public Holidays

■ Price
Dinner = set ¥ 15,750

TEL. 03–5603–1108
4-11-3 Asakusa, Taito-ku, Tokyo

www.sushi-issin.com

Sushi Isshin Ginza

鮨 一新 銀座

This Ginza branch of an Asakusa sushi restaurant is run single-handedly by the owner-chef's right-hand man. It shares the same philosophy as the parent restaurant, but offers a bigger selection of drinking snacks, and the sushi is a little smaller. The standard dish is the *nidako*, cooked in *bancha* together with red beans; boiled *anago* is cooked on a charcoal stove for a smoky flavour. Items include *nihamaguri* and *zuke-maguro*.

■ Opening hours, last orders
Dinner = 18:00-23:00 (L.O.)

■ Annual and weekly closing
Closed mid-August, late December-early January, Sunday and Public Holidays

■ Price
Dinner = set ¥ 18,900-21,000

TEL. 03–3575–0150
MC Building B1F,
5-9-19 Ginza, Chuo-ku, Tokyo

www.sushi-issin.com/pc/free01.html

Sushi Iwa
鮨 いわ

Located near Taimei Elementary School, in a narrow alleyway. To ensure the best flavour of the tuna, Iwa leaves the cut slices to sit for a while before transforming them into sushi and uses several sections of the tuna, including *harakami*, a delicacy. Three pieces of sushi - topped respectively with *akami*, *chu-toro* and *o-toro* - are served in well-timed succession. This is an intimate restaurant that is good for small groups.

■ Opening hours, last orders
Lunch = 12:00-14:00
Dinner = 17:00-23:00
Sun. and Public Holidays
12:00-20:00

■ Annual and weekly closing
Closed late December-early January

■ Price
Lunch = set ¥ 4,725-8,400
Dinner = set ¥ 15,750-26,250

TEL. 03-3571-7900
6-3-17 Ginza, Chuo-ku, Tokyo

JAPANESE SUSHI

Sushi Kanesaka
鮨 かねさか

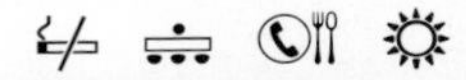

While the owner-chef Shinji Kanesaka attaches much importance to *Edomae* sushi techniques, new ideas are also adopted in pursuit of the ultimate taste: this is the style of 'Sushi Kanesaka'. The basic rules are still observed: priority is given to the freshness of ingredients and close attention paid to the way they are matured. The oft-felt barrier of respect between customers and sushi chefs gives way to a cosy atmosphere.

■ Opening hours, last orders
Lunch = 11:30-14:00 L.O.13:00
Dinner = 17:00-22:00 L.O.21:00

■ Annual and weekly closing
Closed mid-August and late December-early January

■ Price
Lunch = set ¥ 5,250-15,750
Dinner = set ¥ 15,750-21,000

TEL. 03–5568–4411
Misuzu Building B1F,
8-10-3 Ginza, Chuo-ku, Tokyo

JAPANESE SUSHI

Sushi Mizutani
鮨 水谷

The appeal lies in the quality of ingredients and Hachiro Mizutani's sushi-making techniques. It is slightly more slender than usual and beautifully crafted. Innovative ideas are used to enhance the taste of the toppings, which include fragrant steamed abalone, high-quality tuna, and smoked bonito. Two time slots are available for dinner - it's easier to get a lunch booking. Sushi Mizutani moved to its address here in 2010.

■ Opening hours, last orders
Lunch = 11:30-13:30
Dinner = 17:00-21:30

■ Annual and weekly closing
Closed Golden week, mid-August, late December-early January, Sunday and Public Holidays

■ Price
Lunch = set ¥ 18,000-30,000
Dinner = set ¥ 18,000-30,000

TEL. 03-3573-5258
Juno Ginza Seiwa Building 9F,
8-7-7 Ginza, Chuo-ku, Tokyo

JAPANESE SUSHI

Sushi Nakamura
鮨 なかむら

As well as fish from Tsukiji market, white fish and shellfish come from Noto. Masanori Nakamura is particular about tuna: in summer it's from Sado and in winter from Oma. Sun-dried rice from Fukushima is steamed at a high heat, seasoned with aged black vinegar from Kagoshima and a mild salt from Okinawa for a good match with the tuna. A summer soup of boiled abalone slices is recommended. It is open late and always busy.

■ Opening hours, last orders
Dinner = 18:00-24:00 L.O.23:00

■ Annual and weekly closing
Closed Golden week, mid-August, late December-early January, Sunday and Public Holidays

■ Price
Dinner = set ¥ 16,800

TEL. 03–3746–0856
7-17-16 Roppongi, Minato-ku, Tokyo

JAPANESE SUSHI

Sushi Saito
鮨 さいとう

As you enter the parking lot of the Nihon Jitensha Kaikan building, this restaurant, with its counter for six, is on your right – there is no sign. Takashi Saito takes great care to achieve the right balance between rice, topping, *wasabi* and *nikiri*. The texture of each grain of rice is constant; seasoning is slightly saltier than usual, the red vinegar milder. This is ideal for tuna, of which the chef is particularly proud.

■ Opening hours, last orders
Lunch = 12:00-14:00 (L.O.)
Dinner = 17:00-22:00 (L.O.)

■ Annual and weekly closing
Closed mid-August, late December-early January, Sunday and Public Holiday Mondays

■ Price
Lunch = set ¥ 5,250-15,750
Dinner = set ¥ 15,750-26,250

TEL. 03–3589–4412
Nihon Jitensha Kaikan 1F,
1-9-15 Akasaka, Minato-ku,
Tokyo

JAPANESE SUSHI

Sushi Shin
鮨真

Shintaro Suzuki looks to traditional *Edomae* techniques and the ingredients are salted, vinegared or seared - sometimes with straw. Rice is a blend of two from Niigata and Ibaraki; *nigari* is added and it is cooked quite hard so that the texture of each grain is distinguishable. The sushi is comparatively large but can be adjusted. Sea bream is used as a topping with radish and kelp; gizzard shad is combined with shredded kelp.

■ Opening hours, last orders
Lunch = Wed. and Fri. 12:00-13:30
Sun. 12:00-14:30
Dinner = 17:30-22:30

■ Annual and weekly closing
Closed Monday

■ Price
Lunch = set ¥ 5,750-10,500
Dinner = set ¥ 16,800-21,000

TEL. 03–5485–0031
4-18-20 Nishiazabu, Minato-ku, Tokyo

JAPANESE SUSHI

Sushi Yoshitake NEW

鮨 よしたけ

The restaurant relocated from Roppongi in 2010 and serves only an *omakase*. Snacks come before the sushi; sweet and plump *uni* pudding is a summer staple and is replaced in winter by monkfish liver steamed in *akazake*. White fleshed sashimi is wrapped in *kombu* and eaten with a mixture of fish bone stock and soy sauce; the red vinegar-based rice is mildly sour. Boiled in its juices, the *kurumaebi* is accentuated with shrimp *miso*.

■ Opening hours, last orders
Dinner = 18:00-24:00 L.O.23:00

■ Annual and weekly closing
Closed mid-August, late December-early January, Sunday and Public Holidays

■ Price
Dinner = set ¥ 21,000
Private Room Fee = ¥ 2,100/person

TEL. 03-6253-7331
Suzuryu Building 3F,
8-7-19 Ginza, Chuo-ku, Tokyo

http://sushi-yoshitake.com

JAPANESE

Suzuki
すずき

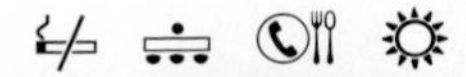

Chinese and French techniques combine with Suzuki's flair to bring out natural flavours, while the menu is determined by what's good at the market each day. Bamboo shoots brought in directly from Tanba offer a taste of spring; tilefish is soaked in salted water, dried then roasted. As he offers a home-cooking class in his kitchen every day at noon, only one lunch reservation is accepted and *tatami* seating is the only option.

■ Opening hours, last orders
Lunch = 12:00-14:00 L.O.12:30
Dinner = 18:00-22:00 L.O.21:00

■ Annual and weekly closing
Closed Golden week, mid-August, late December-early January and Monday

■ Price
Lunch = set ¥ 6,300
Dinner = set ¥ 10,500-15,750

TEL. 03-3710-3696
2-16-3 Takaban, Meguro-ku, Tokyo

www.kappou.jp

JAPANESE

Suzunari NEW
鈴なり

After working for 13 years at Nadaman main branch, owner-chef Sazanka-so opened his own restaurant aged 31. The name is a combination of his children's and represents his pledge to love the restaurant as if it were his child. Using a combination of first and last harvest and seasonal ingredients, he takes care not to overdo the preparations. The soft *chawanmushi* 'tamajimushi' is available year-round; but his specialty is tuna.

■ Opening hours, last orders
Dinner = 18:00-24:00 L.O.22:00

■ Annual and weekly closing
Closed Golden week, mid-August, late December-early January, Sunday and Public Holidays

■ Price
Dinner = set ¥ 4,500-10,000
Service charge = 10%

TEL. 03-3350-1178
7-9 Arakicho, Shinjuku-ku, Tokyo
www.suzu-nari.com

JAPANESE SOBA

Tajima
たじま

The *shin-soba,* from summer to autumn, comes from Hokkaido, Ibaraki, Fukui and Nagano. De-hulled buckwheat is blended according to the quality that year and the day's weather; it is then ground both coarse and fine, and the flours are mixed to make the *soba*. The sauce gives off a savoury *katsuo* aroma. There are also drinking snacks that include *itawasa* and *dashimaki*. The fixed priced menu is ideal for those who like vegetables.

■ Opening hours, last orders
Lunch = Tue.-Sat. and Public Holiday Mondays 11:30-14:30 (L.O.)
Dinner = 17:30-21:30 (L.O.)
Public Holidays 17:30-20:30 (L.O.)

■ Annual and weekly closing
Closed early January, Sunday and last Monday

■ Price

Lunch = set		¥ 3,000-5,100
	à la carte	¥ 2,000-5,000
Dinner = set		¥ 3,000-5,100
	à la carte	¥ 2,000-5,000

TEL. 03–3445–6617
3-8-6 Nishiazabu, Minato-ku, Tokyo

www.sobatajima.jp

Takahashi
たかはし

Yuji Takahashi opened here in 2005, having previously had a French restaurant. He works alone so order the chicken liver terrine and wine while waiting. Influences from western cuisines are adapted: chicken oysters come with violet mustard, and the *eringi* mushrooms are seasoned with *pancetta* and olive oil. To conclude, try the spicy *keema* curry. There are two starting times for dinner; at lunch only *oyakodon* is available.

■ Opening hours, last orders
Dinner = 17:00-20:00 and
20:15-22:30

■ Annual and weekly closing
Closed mid-August, late December-early January, Sunday, 1st and 3rd Mondays

■ Price
Dinner = à la carte ¥ 2,800-8,000
Seat charge = ¥300/person

TEL. 03–5436–9677
Pragma. G-Tower 2F,
1-7-1 Nishigotanda, Shinagawa-ku, Tokyo

Taku
拓

Co-owned by a sushi chef and sommelière, Taku offers interesting pairings of sushi and wine. Takuya Sato trained in Japanese cuisine which gives extra depth to his sushi craftsmanship; the high-quality fish, for example, is seasoned with kelp or salt before being served, to bring out its natural flavour. The *omakase* begins with a wide variety of elaborate appetisers including *sashimi*, before moving on to *nigiri*. Open late.

■ Opening hours, last orders
Dinner = 18:00-1:00 (L.O.)

■ Annual and weekly closing
Closed mid-August, late December-early January, Sunday and Public Holidays

■ Price
Dinner = set ¥ 16,800-21,000

TEL. 03–5774–4372
2-11-5 Nishiazabu, Minato-ku, Tokyo

JAPANESE SUSHI

Takumi Tatsuhiro NEW
匠 達広

Inside a building with many restaurants is one resembling a hideaway. It's quite unique in that it serves small, hand-pressed sushi and snacks in an alternating fashion and using two types of sushi rice depending on the item. The basic techniques are pure *edomae*, like the hand-pressed *kasugodai* sushi oborozuke. As there are only nine seats at the *hinoki* counter, it's worth booking early. At lunch there is only *barachirashi*.

■ Opening hours, last orders
Lunch = 11:30-13:30 (L.O.)
Dinner = 18:00-22:30 (L.O.)
Sat., Sun 17:00-22:30 (L.O.)

■ Annual and weekly closing
Closed mid-August, late December-early January and Monday

■ Price
Lunch = à la carte ¥ 1,700
Dinner = set ¥ 15,000

TEL. 03-6457-7570
PAX Shinjuku Youth Building 6F,
4-1-9 Shinjuku, Shinjuku-ku,
Tokyo

FRENCH CONTEMPORARY

Tateru Yoshino Ginza

The Ginza branch of Yoshino's restaurant group is its third. As with the other locations, the focus is on what the chef calls '*terroir* cooking', although here the modern presentation of the food and its lighter seasoning set it apart. Specialities include 'Stella Maris-style pâté en croûte' and 'red tuna and eggplant millefeuille with Ossetra caviar'. The set lunch menu is quite a bargain and includes the specialities.

■ Opening hours, last orders
Lunch = 11:30-14:00 (L.O.)
Dinner = 18:00-21:00 (L.O.)

■ Annual and weekly closing
Closed late December-early January and Tuesday

■ Price
Lunch = set ¥ 4,800-21,000
Dinner = set ¥ 10,000-21,000
Private room fee = ¥ 3,150 (lunch)
¥ 5,250 (dinner)
Service charge = 10%

TEL. 03–3563–1511
Pias Ginza 12F,
4-8-10 Ginza, Chuo-ku, Tokyo

www.tateruyoshino.

FRENCH

Tateru Yoshino Shiba

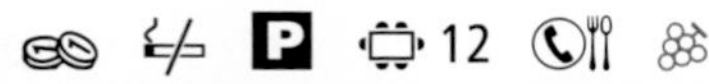

Tateru Yoshino is also the owner-chef of Stella Maris in Paris. *Duo de foie gras* is a duck foie gras terrine infused with dried fruits, while *saumon fumé mi-cuit à la Stella Maris* is Yoshino's fish speciality. *Tourte de gibier*, wild game meat pie, is a traditional winter dish that uses several types of game and foie gras. Compared to his other locations, dishes here are more classic. An extensive wine list is also available.

■ Opening hours, last orders
Lunch = 11:30-14:00 (L.O.)
Dinner = Mon.-Sat. 18:00-21:00 (L.O.)

■ Annual and weekly closing
Closed Monday

■ Price
Lunch = set ¥ 3,675-15,750
à la carte ¥ 10,000-17,000
Dinner = set ¥ 4,725-15,750
à la carte ¥ 10,000-17,000
Service charge = 10%

TEL. 03–5405–7800
Shiba Park Hotel Annex 1F,
1-5-10 Shibakoen, Minato-ku,
Tokyo

www.tateruyoshino.com

FRENCH CONTEMPORARY

Tateru Yoshino Shiodome

✿ XXX

28

The compact dining room is on the 25th floor of the Shiodome Media Tower. Menus are mainly fixed price but there is also a chef's choice menu available. Accent is placed on the combination of classic ingredients and dishes are kept quite light to please today's palate. We recommend the roast lamb with rock salt. Bar à vins Tateru Yoshino, the adjacent wine bar, offers a collection of wines from France and other countries.

■ Opening hours, last orders
Lunch = 11:30-14:00 (L.O.)
Dinner = 18:00-21:00 (L.O.)

■ Price
Lunch = set ¥ 3,675-8,400
Dinner = set ¥ 7,875-15,750
Private room fee = ¥ 5,250-29,400
Service charge = 10%

TEL. 03–6252–1155
Park Hotel Shiodome Media Tower 25F,
1-7-1 Higashishinbashi,
Minato-ku, Tokyo

www.tateruyoshino.com

JAPANESE

Tatsumura
たつむら

8

There is just one set menu, consisting of about 10 dishes. Masahiko Miyagawa employs various techniques so as not to bore diners' palates: he uses a different soup stock base (bonito flakes, scallops or clams) depending on the dish to add variety and the *takikomi-gohan* changes each season. The interior is simple but is often used for business occasions. One of their *tatami* rooms has a lovely view of the spring cherry blossom.

■ Opening hours, last orders
Dinner = 17:30-23:00 L.O.21:00

■ Annual and weekly closing
Closed mid-August, late December-early January, Sunday and Public Holidays

■ Price
Dinner = set ¥ 12,600
Private room fee = 10%

TEL. 03–3585–7285
Trade Akasaka Building 2F,
5-4-14 Akasaka, Minato-ku,
Tokyo

JAPANESE TEMPURA

Tenmo
てん茂

This family-operated *tempura* restaurant opened in 1885. Today, third-generation owner-chef Nobuo Okuda looks after the customers and his son does the cooking. Traditional flavours are preserved through the use of sesame oil, as has always been the practice. Seasonal tastes include ice fish and butterbur sprouts in spring, young *ayu* and the *Edomae anago*. The specialities are abalone in summer and fried chestnuts in the autumn.

■ Opening hours, last orders
Lunch = 12:00-14:00 L.O.13:30
Dinner = 17:00-20:00 L.O.19:00

■ Annual and weekly closing
Closed mid-August, late December-early January, Saturdays in August, Sunday and Public Holidays

■ Price
Lunch = set ¥ 6,300-12,600
Dinner = set ¥ 9,450-12,600

TEL. 03-3241-7035
4-1-3 Nihonbashihoncho, Chuo-ku, Tokyo

www.tenmo.jp

JAPANESE

Tetsuan
哲庵

The quiet owner-chef's personality is reflected in the restaurant's tranquil atmosphere. There are three set menus, each offering a different number of dishes, including *nabe ryori* and *takikomi-gohan*. In summer, *nabe* is served cold with ice made from stock; in winter, *mizore-nabe* is flavoured with *yuzu* and tilefish. The stock varies depending on the dish, while salt is used for seasoning in summer and soy sauce in winter.

■ Opening hours, last orders
Dinner = 18:00-21:30 (L.O.)

■ Annual and weekly closing
Closed early January and Monday

■ Price
Dinner = set ¥ 10,500-16,800

TEL. 03–3423–1850
1-5-26 Azabujuban, Minato-ku, Tokyo

JAPANESE

Tomura
と村

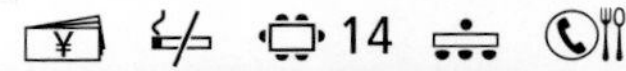

Chiba-native Kimio Tomura not only selects ingredients each day from Tsukiji, he also buys items not available in Tokyo directly from the producing area. The steamed lobster is a speciality served all year round; after cooking, he carefully peels off the shell in front of you. The meal concludes either with *jakomeshi* or a noodle dish. The warm and friendly owner-chef will happily answer questions about ingredients or dishes.

■ Opening hours, last orders
Dinner = 18:00-21:30 (L.O.)

■ Annual and weekly closing
Closed Golden week, mid-August, late December-early January, Sunday and Public Holiday Mondays

■ Price
Dinner = set ¥ 24,150-52,500
Service charge = 10%

TEL. 03–3591–3303
1-11-14 Toranomon, Minato-ku, Tokyo

Toriki
とり喜

Yasuhito Sakai serves up varieties of free-range poultry, including Daisen chicken and Tokyo *shamo* gamecock; carefully skewered, lightly salted and then grilled. In addition to individual kebabs, there are also set menus comprised of 8 yakitori and 4 vegetable skewers. To end the meal, we recommend the *chazuke* featuring refined chicken stock; the *kiji-chazuke* is a particularly rare delight. Phone between 10:00-16:00.

■ Opening hours, last orders
Dinner = Mon.-Fri. 17:30-22:00 (L.O.)
Sat. 17:00-22:00 (L.O.)

■ Annual and weekly closing
Closed Golden week, mid-August, late December-early January, Sunday and Public Holidays

■ Price
Dinner = set ¥ 2,835-4,200
à la carte ¥ 3,000-7,000
Seat charge=¥ 630/person

TEL. 03-3622-6202
1-8-13 Kinshi, Sumida-ku, Tokyo

JAPANESE YAKITORI

Torishiki
鳥しき

The main feature of the menu here is *omakase*, ensuring a nicely balanced assortment of various cuts and parts; simply indicate when you've had enough. The vegetables are succulent, and the date chicken has a light texture with sweet skin. The outside is cooked with a fuller flame to seal in the juices, and the inside is cooked slowly with the residual heat, so you may have to wait although the regulars never seem to mind.

■ Opening hours, last orders
Dinner = 18:00-23:00

■ Annual and weekly closing
Closed mid-August, late December-early January, Monday and Public Holidays

■ Price
Dinner = set ¥ 4,000-5,500
Seat charge=¥ 500/person

TEL. 03–3440–7656
2-14-12 Kamiosaki,
Shinagawa-ku, Tokyo

JAPANESE

Totoya Uoshin
とゝや魚新

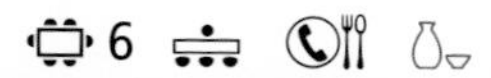

As the name suggests - Totoya means 'fish dealer'- dishes revolve around seasonal fish. A word or two with the chef will have him serve you your favourite. The Pacific sea bream comes in various ways, including *sashimi*, *kombujime*, *ushiojiru*, *arataki*, and also the steamed *kotsumushi*. There is a large selection of sake, chosen by the head chef who visits small breweries all over the country - ask the chefs for recommendations.

■ Opening hours, last orders
Lunch = 11:30-14:00 (L.O.)
Dinner = 17:30-21:30 (L.O.)

■ Annual and weekly closing
Closed mid-August, late December-early January, Sunday and Public Holidays

■ Price
Lunch = set ¥ 5,250-7,350
Dinner = set ¥ 10,500-15,750
Private room fee = ¥ 3,150 (lunch)
¥ 5,250 (dinner)
Service charge = 10% (dinner)

TEL. 03–3585–4701
5-1-34 Akasaka, Minato-ku, Tokyo

JAPANESE

Tsujitome
辻留

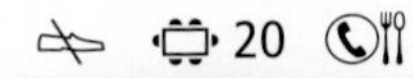

The chef serves *kaiseki* dishes with respect for the *chanoyu* spirit. *Tofu-dengaku* dressed with *miso* is a March dish; in September, *maruage-dofu* is used in a soup to recreate the season inside the bowl. As in *chakaiseki*, *usucha* finishes the meal. Attention to detail is apparent in everything, from the alcove with its hanging scrolls and *ikebana* to the attractive tableware and the service of the waiters in neat, simple *kimono*.

■ Opening hours, last orders
Lunch = 12:00-14:00
Dinner = 17:00-21:00

■ Annual and weekly closing
Closed Golden week, mid-August, late December-early January and Sunday

■ Price
Lunch = set ¥ 15,750-36,750
Dinner = set ¥ 26,250-45,150
Service charge = 10%

TEL. 03–3403–3984
1-5-8 Motoakasaka, Minato-ku, Tokyo

www.tsujitome.co.jp

Tsukasa
司

Opened in 1960, this warm and friendly *kappo* restaurant serves high-grade, natural white tiger puffer fish. There is a set menu, which can be a little expensive, but you can talk with the chef and order what you like. The *sashimi* is thickly sliced and the milt soup is a popular item and features strong-tasting dried bonito stock, white *miso* and smooth, seasoned milt. The hotpot is made with green onions, tofu and *shungiku*.

■ Opening hours, last orders
Dinner = 17:00-22:30

■ Annual and weekly closing
Closed 16 April-10 September

■ Price
Dinner = set ¥ 31,500-39,900
à la carte ¥ 25,000-40,000
Private room fee = 10%

TEL. 03–3405–9397
1-9-1 Minamiaoyama, Minato-ku, Tokyo

JAPANESE FUGU

Tsukiji Yamamoto
つきじ やまもと

✿✿ XXX

12

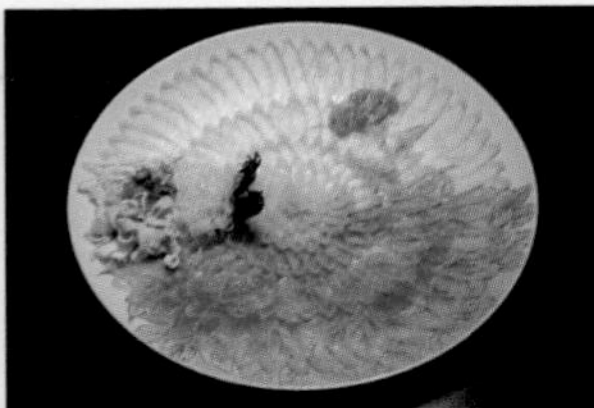

Run by the same family for three generations, Yamamoto is in a traditional house; its antique scrolls and decorative pieces chosen by the owner-chef. *Tora-fugu* features, with traditional dishes such as *kiku-zukuri* and *nikogori*, alongside original ones like milt crêpes and clear soup made with *fugu* skin. English menus, with drawings of *fugu* done by the chef, are available so it's a good place to entertain foreign nationals.

■ Opening hours, last orders
Dinner = 17:00-22:30

■ Annual and weekly closing
Closed April-September, Sunday and Public Holidays

■ Price
Dinner = set ¥ 36,750
Service charge = 10%

TEL. 03–3541–7730
2-15-4 Tsukiji, Chuo-ku, Tokyo
www8.plala.or.jp/tsukijiyamamoto

JAPANESE TEMPURA

Uchitsu
うち津

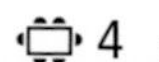

Uchitsu is a new style of *tempura* restaurant, opened by Takahisa Uchitsu in 2008. Just a set menu is usually served, which includes staples like *anago* and smelt-whiting as well as seasonal items such as summer oyster, pike conger and crab meat. Assorted items, including raw vegetables, are served in between the various tempura pieces. You will see a private room on your left and a cypress counter at the end of a stone path.

■ Opening hours, last orders
Dinner = 18:00-23:00 L.O.21:00

■ Annual and weekly closing
Closed mid-August, late December-early January, Sunday except Public Holidays and Public Holiday Mondays

■ Price
Dinner = set ¥ 15,750-18,900

TEL. 03-6408-9591
5-25-4 Hiroo, Shibuya-ku, Tokyo
www.tempura-uchitsu.com

JAPANESE

Uchiyama
うち山

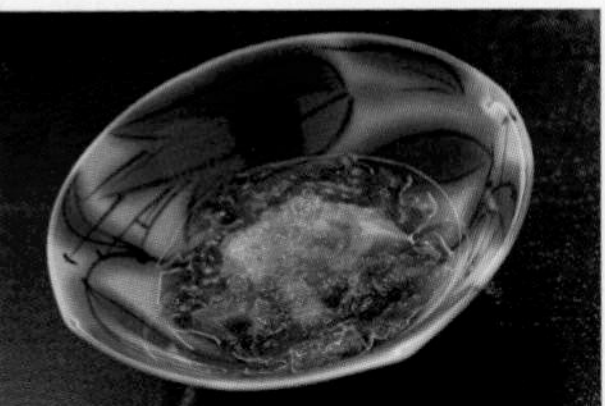

The spirit of *chakaiseki* holds special importance for the owner-chef and the purchasing of *tai* and abalone is done with his own keen eye. His modesty and the staff's friendly service is expressed in the 'the spirit of tea'. Specialities are sesame tofu, with its fragrant skin and soft inner texture, and *ochazuke*-style rice and broth with raw sea bream. The dessert *kuzukiri* is made from Yoshino *kudzu* and Okinawan *kuromitsu*.

■ Opening hours, last orders
Lunch = 11:30-14:00 (L.O.)
Dinner = 17:00-23:00
Sun. and Public Holidays
17:00-22:00

■ Annual and weekly closing
Closed late December-early January

■ Price
Lunch = set ¥ 5,000-15,000
à la carte ¥ 1,500-3,500
Dinner = set ¥ 13,650-26,250
Service charge = 10% (dinner)

TEL. 03–3541–6720
Light Building B1F,
2-12-3 Ginza, Chuo-ku, Tokyo

www.nk-net.jp/uchiyama

JAPANESE

Uemura Honten
植むら 本店

12

The head chef uses Kyoto vegetables like Kamo eggplants, carrots and Shogoin turnips, as well as seafood from various parts of the country. The *hassun* features elaborate seasonal arrangements; sweet tomato soup made with chicken stock and *junsai* is a refreshing dish in summer. Each floor offers a different seating option: table seating, private rooms or a large main room; the counter on the 1st floor only opens in the evening.

■ Opening hours, last orders
Lunch = 11:30-15:00 L.O.14:00
Dinner = 17:00-22:00 L.O.20:00

■ Annual and weekly closing
Closed Golden week, mid-August, late December-early January, Sunday and Public Holidays

■ Price
Lunch = set ¥ 7,000-25,000
Dinner = set ¥ 7,000-25,000

TEL. 03-3541-1351
1-13-10 Tsukiji, Chuo-ku, Tokyo
www.tukijiuemura.com/shop/101

JAPANESE TEPPANYAKI

Ukai-tei Ginza

The French Belle Époque-style décor fits well with the building, which served as the main house of a wealthy farmer before being relocated from Tokamachi. Kobe beef is used, as well as black-haired cattle bred on a designated farm in Tottori. The speciality dish of abalone steamed in rock salt is also good. Other options make the best of the seasons: spring vegetables, autumn *matsutake* and truffles in winter.

■ Opening hours, last orders
Lunch = 12:00-14:00 (L.O.)
Sat., Sun. and Public Holidays
12:00-15:00 (L.O.)
Dinner = 17:00-23:00 L.O.21:00

■ Annual and weekly closing
Closed 31 December-4 January

■ Price
Lunch = set ¥ 6,830-9,450
à la carte ¥ 14,000-43,000
Dinner = set ¥ 16,800-24,150
à la carte ¥ 14,000-43,000
Service charge = 10%

TEL. 03-3544-5252
Jiji-Tsushin Building,
5-15-8 Ginza, Chuo-ku, Tokyo

www.ukai.co.jp/ginza

Ukai-tei Omotesando

Opened in Omotesando-dori in 2007, but its interior dates back about 150 years. Its construction centres around a merchant's house from Kanazawa; it was moved and reassembled here. For the cooking, black-haired cattle, known as '*ukai-gyu*', come from a designated farm in Tottori and abalone steamed in rock salt is a speciality. After dinner, you will be invited to take dessert in the salon. Terrace seating is available.

■ Opening hours, last orders
Lunch = 12:00-14:30 (L.O.)
Dinner = 17:30-23:00 L.O.21:00
Sat., Sun. and Public Holidays
11:30-23:00 L.O.21:00

■ Annual and weekly closing
Closed 1 January

■ Price

Lunch = set		¥ 6,830-12,600
	à la carte	¥ 14,000-43,000
Dinner = set		¥ 12,600-24,150
	à la carte	14,000-43,000

Service charge = 10%

TEL. 03–5467–5252
Omotesando Gyre 5F,
5-10-1 Jingumae, Shibuya-ku,
Tokyo

www.omotesando-ukaitei.jp

JAPANESE SUSHI

Umi
海味

High quality fresh ingredients are what draws one to Umi. Rare fish come from Kyushu and Hokkaido and, with sushi and appetisers, up to 30 different types can be sampled. Rice is prepared slightly harder and saltier than usual and the mellow-flavoured vinegar is a blend of two red vinegars: one aged for three years with a bouquet of sake lees and another, thinner variety. This lively restaurant runs like clockwork.

■ Opening hours, last orders
Dinner = 18:00-23:00 (L.O.)

■ Annual and weekly closing
Closed mid-August, late December-early January, Sunday and Public Holidays

■ Price
Dinner = set ¥ 20,000

TEL. 03-3401-3368
3-2-8 Minamiaoyama, Minato-ku, Tokyo

Uotoku
うを徳

Uotoku has a history dating back to the beginning of the Meiji Era, when a fish dealer in Hatchobori moved his business to Kagurazaka and changed the name to Uotoku. The *ebi-shinjo* deserves a mention: the shrimps are carefully minced with a knife to maintain their firm texture before being deep-fried. *Tai-no matsukawa-zukuri* uses a method passed down from the founder, parboiling the fish with its skin. Service is excellent.

■ Opening hours, last orders
Lunch = 11:30-14:30
Dinner = 17:00-22:30

■ Annual and weekly closing
Closed mid-August and late December-early January

■ Price
Lunch = set ¥ 10,500-15,750
Dinner = set ¥ 21,000-26,250
Service charge = 10%

TEL. 03–3269–0360
3-1 Kagurazaka, Shinjuku-ku, Tokyo

www.uotoku.com

Usukifugu Yamadaya
臼杵ふぐ山田屋

13

This is a *fugu* restaurant on Ushizaka in Nishiazabu which opened as a branch of a *ryotei* in Usuki, Oita in 2006. In season, *tora fugu* is delivered daily from Oita. Thick slices of *fugu* are served with homemade *ponzu* dipping sauce made from soy sauce and juicy citrus *kabosu* fruit harvested in Oita. A speciality is a sushi of the local Usuki dish *o-han* -yellow rice coloured with gardenia fruit- topped with grilled *shirako*.

■ Opening hours, last orders
Dinner = 18:00-24:00 L.O.22:30

■ Annual and weekly closing
Closed Golden week, mid-August, late December-early January, Sunday and Public Holidays

■ Price
Dinner = set ¥ 21,000-31,500
à la carte ¥ 12,000-22,000
Service charge = 10%

TEL. 03-3499-5501
Fleg Nishi-Azabu Vierge B1F,
4-11-14 Nishiazabu, Minato-ku,
Tokyo

www.usuki.info/yamadaya

JAPANESE

Waketokuyama
分とく山

Waketokuyama provides cuisine in touch with the times. The head chef offers a variety of creative dishes, sourcing up to as many as 100 different ingredients nationwide. The speciality is *awabi-no-isoyaki*: lightly baked in its shell, the steamed Sanriku abalone is covered with a sauce of puréed offal, *kudzu* and topped with seaweed. Besides the counter and table seating, the annexe has a private room overlooking a garden.

■ Opening hours, last orders
Dinner = 17:00-23:00 L.O.21:00

■ Annual and weekly closing
Closed late December-early January and Sunday

■ Price
Dinner = set ¥ 15,750
Service charge = 10%

TEL. 03–5789–3838
5-1-5 Minamiazabu, Minato-ku, Tokyo

JAPANESE

Yamaji
山路

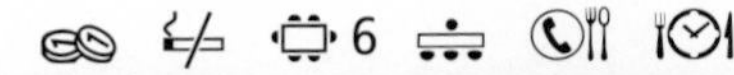

6

The speciality here is sea bream, fresh from the owner-chef's hometown, Ehime. All the fish is used: the body for *sashimi*; the head is salt-grilled or used for *tsukeyaki* or steamed with sake and kelp; lean parts are used for soup. Another specialty is *tai-chazuke* with aged black sesame sauce. Only a set menu is served but adjustments can be made. At lunch there are also rice bowl dishes; try the grilled beef or salmon belly.

■ Opening hours, last orders
Lunch = 12:00-14:00 L.O.13:00
Dinner = 17:30-23:00 L.O.22:00

■ Annual and weekly closing
Closed mid-August, late December-early January, Sunday and Public Holidays

■ Price
Lunch = set ¥ 2,625-15,750
Dinner = set ¥ 18,900-26,250

TEL. 03–5565–3639
Ginza 7 Building B1F,
7-14-14 Ginza, Chuo-ku, Tokyo

Yamanochaya
山の茶屋

   30 

An *unagi* restaurant in the grounds of Sanno Hie Shrine; the entrance is opposite the rear gate of Hibiya High School. *Kabayaki* is the speciality: *unagi* from areas such as Shizuoka and Kagoshima are broiled without seasoning, steamed slowly, then broiled over *bincho* charcoal with a sweet sauce. We recommend *horigotatsu*-style sunken seating in the annexe. Prices are high but lunch and Saturday evening menus are more reasonable.

■ Opening hours, last orders
Lunch = 11:30-13:00 (L.O.)
Dinner = 17:00-19:00 (L.O.)

■ Annual and weekly closing
Closed mid-August, late December-early January, Sunday and Public Holidays

■ Price
Lunch = set ¥ 9,450-16,170
Dinner = set ¥ 13,650-18,270
Service charge = 10%

TEL. 03-3581-0585
2-10-6 Nagatacho, Chiyoda-ku, Tokyo

JAPANESE

Yamasaki
山さき

It's on the 2nd floor of a building in front of Bishamonten Zenkokuji Temple, but hard to spot. From October-May, the owner-chef offers *negima nabe*. She dips *setoro* in soup; it goes well with scallion and seaweed, watercress and parsley. Also recommended are scallops, clams and pen shells, offered in February and March. Summer staples include *ainame; moryo nabe* uses chicken or Shamo gamecock. Prices are modest considering the quality.

■ Opening hours, last orders
Dinner = 18:00-22:00 L.O.20:00

■ Annual and weekly closing
Closed mid-August, late December-early January, Sunday and Public Holidays

■ Price
Dinner = set ¥ 7,350-15,750
Service charge = 5%

TEL. 03–3267–2310
Fukuya Building 2F,
4-2 Kagurazaka, Shinjuku-ku,
Tokyo

Yokota
よこ田

Tsuneo Yokota goes to Tsukiji with his son, in search of ingredients for his *omakase* set menu. The light-tasting oil is a mix of sesame and corn oils, and the chef varies the amount of batter used. All pieces come with *tentsuyu*, salt, lemon juice and curry powder - the chef will advise you which to use for each ingredient. *Tempura* with curry powder is a new concept and, according to the chef, best with flathead fish and *anago*.

■ Opening hours, last orders
Dinner = 17:30-20:30 (L.O.)

■ Annual and weekly closing
Closed Golden week, mid-August, late December-early January and Wednesday

■ Price
Dinner = set ¥ 10,500

TEL. 03-3408-4238
Patio Azabu-Juban II 3F,
3-11-3 Motoazabu, Minato-ku,
Tokyo

JAPANESE TEMPURA

Yokoyama
よこやま

Tadashi Yokoyama trained at a *tempura* restaurant in Kyoto before gaining more experience at its Tokyo branch. Ingredients include tiger prawns, *megochi*, white asparagus, sweetfish in spring and pike conger in summer. No dipping sauce is served, just salt and lemon juice. Seasoned grated radish is for refreshing the palate. *Tencha*, a speciality, is a must to finish with. Please refrain from using strong perfume or cologne.

■ Opening hours, last orders
Dinner = 17:30-22:00 L.O.20:00

■ Annual and weekly closing
Closed mid-August, late December-early January, Wednesday, Sunday and Public Holidays

■ Price
Dinner = set ¥ 13,125

TEL. 03-3631-3927
2-7-10 Kotobashi, Sumida-ku, Tokyo

FUSION

Yonemura
よねむら

Having started his career specialising in French cuisine, Masayasu Yonemura is "not concerned about the categories of cuisine, I have established my own style by responding to my customers' requests; always searching for new ideas" and serves 'Yonemura-style' dishes, rich in creativity. A small toasted rice ball placed on a spoon and topped with a layer of sautéed foie gras and another of roasted duck breast are two examples.

■ Opening hours, last orders
Lunch = 12:00-15:30 L.O.14:00
Dinner = 17:30-23:00 L.O.21:00

■ Annual and weekly closing
Closed mid-August, late December-early January and Monday

■ Price
Lunch = set ¥ 6,000-10,000
Dinner = set ¥ 12,500-14,500

TEL. 03–5537–6699
Kojun Building 4F,
6-8-7 Ginza, Chuo-ku, Tokyo

Yoneyama
よねやま

Spring dishes include giant clams seasoned with a little soy sauce and sake; abalone, moistened in hot bonito soup stock then sliced and served with strained liver sauce, is a summer speciality. *Sashimi* of *tai* is the chef's pick. The typical winter dish is *matsuba* crab mixed with sweet white *miso*. A *fugu* set menu is also available until February. The owner-chef speaks mostly through the diligent efforts of his cooking.

■ Opening hours, last orders
Dinner = 18:00-21:30 (L.O.)

■ Annual and weekly closing
Closed mid-August, late December-early January and Sunday

■ Price
Dinner = set ¥ 10,500-15,750

TEL. 03-3341-3117
15 Arakicho, Shinjuku-ku, Tokyo

JAPANESE IZAKAYA

Yorozuya Okagesan
萬屋 おかげさん

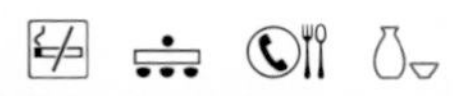

The warmth and dedication of the owner-chef has added to the popularity of this restaurant, whose theme is 'seasonal vegetables and local sake'. Order the assortment of *sashimi* first; everything is carefully prepared, including straw-smoked young tuna and *kinmedai* dusted with *karasumi*. The salted rice ball is a popular item to end with. The sake menu resembles a wine list. If you don't speak Japanese, go with someone who does.

■ Opening hours, last orders
Dinner = 18:00-23:00 L.O.20:00

■ Annual and weekly closing
Closed Golden week, mid-August, late December-early January, Sunday, Monday and Public Holidays

■ Price
Dinner = set ¥ 5,250
à la carte ¥ 5,500-6,000
Seat charge=¥ 420/person

TEL. 03–3355–8100
Matsumoto Building B1F,
2-10 Yotsuya, Shinjuku-ku, Tokyo

www.okagesan.net

JAPANESE YAKITORI

Yoshicho
よし鳥

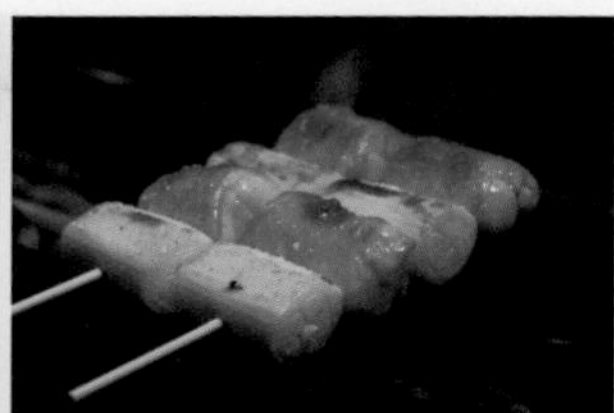

Yoshicho, well-known for its *negima*, specialises in Aomori *shamorokku* gamecock cuisine. All *yakitori* - served as a set 5 or 7-skewer meal, including one vegetable item - are seasoned with salt and grilled over Kishu *bincho* charcoal. Start with some snacks and sake before ordering the set menu. Depending on the size of your appetite, you can either order more skewers or complete the meal with chicken *zosui* or *ontama soborodon*.

■ Opening hours, last orders
Dinner = 17:00-23:30 L.O.22:30

■ Annual and weekly closing
Closed mid-August, late December-early January, Sunday and Public Holidays

■ Price
Dinner = Set ¥ 1,500-2,100
à la carte ¥ 4,000-6,000

TEL. 03–5793–5050
Il Viare Gotanda Building 2F,
1-12-9 Higashigotanda,
Shinagawa-ku, Tokyo

www.yoshichou.info

JAPANESE

Yoshifuku
与志福

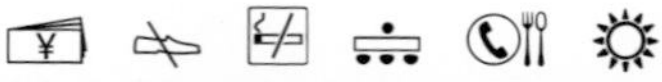

The young owner-chef, Kenji Takahashi, opened this restaurant in his hometown in 2008, having trained in Kyoto. His set menus include original ideas such as the seared and marinated *hamo* and spring onion salad with sesame flavoured dressing. There are two *omakase* set menus; both of which include *sashimi*. There are also dedicated *hamo* and crab menus available. Particular effort goes into the making of stocks and soups.

■ Opening hours, last orders
Dinner = 18:00-20:00 (L.O.)

■ Annual and weekly closing
Closed mid-August, late December-early January and Wednesday

■ Price
Dinner = set ¥ 10,500-15,750
Service charge = 5%

TEL. 03–6905–7767
New Island Higashikitazawa 2F,
3-1-10 Kitazawa, Setagaya-ku,
Tokyo

JAPANESE SUKIYAKI

Yoshihashi
よしはし

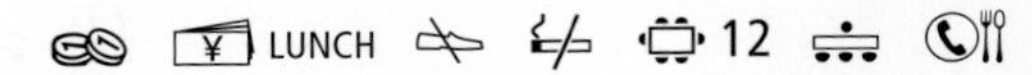

The high-quality marbled beef is chosen not because of the origin but by its quality. Thickly cut meat is coated with comparatively dense *sukiyaki* sauce and pan-roasted to the preferred tenderness. To create an egg dipping sauce, the egg white is beaten quickly with chopsticks into a meringue-like foam, while the yolk is left whole. Three *sukiyaki* set menus are available. Visitors are advised not to wear strong perfume.

■ Opening hours, last orders
Lunch = 11:30-15:00 L.O.13:30
Dinner = 17:30-22:30 L.O.20:30

■ Annual and weekly closing
Closed mid-August, late December-early January, Sunday and Public Holidays

■ Prices
Lunch = set ¥ 2,100-3,700
Dinner = set ¥ 12,000-17,000
à la carte¥ 10,000-20,000
Private room fee = less than 4 persons ¥ 5,000/hour
Service charge = 15% (dinner)

TEL.03-3401-3129
1-5-25 Motoakasaka, Minato-ku, Tokyo

JAPANESE TEMPURA

Yotaro
与太呂

This speciality sea bream and *tempura* restaurant is run by owner-chef Motohiro Kawaguchi and his son. The *tai* comes from ports throughout Japan, as regional variations complement different dishes: wild *tai* with a firm texture is used for *sashimi*, while *tai* with a more tender texture is used for *tai-meshi*. Thinly battered *tempura* is lightly fried, enclosing the flavour of fish and the natural fragrance of seasonal vegetables.

■ Opening hours, last orders
Dinner = 18:00-22:00 (L.O.)

■ Annual and weekly closing
Closed Golden week, mid-August, late December-early January and Sunday

■ Price
Dinner = set ¥ 13,650

TEL. 03–3405–5866
4-11-4 Roppongi, Minato-ku, Tokyo

www.roppongi-yotaro.com

JAPANESE

Yotsuya Uemura NEW
四谷 うえ村

Using Kyoto cuisine as a starting point, the chef aims to create his own original expressions. He is partial to tuna and, for *sashimi*, he uses fish from different areas depending on the season. He also specialises in eggplant cuisine, the grilled and steamed eggplant with sea urchin is one of his recommended dishes. In midsummer, there is also an *unagi* rice dish made with natural *unagi* from Lake Hamanako and Lake Shinjiko.

■ Opening hours, last orders
Dinner=18:00-21:30 (L.O.)

■ Annual and weekly closing
Closed Golden week, mid-August, late December-early January, Sunday and Public Holidays

■ Price
Dinner = set ¥ 7,350-15,750
Service charge = 10%

TEL. 03-5363-1046
8-1 Arakicho, Shinjuku-ku, Tokyo

SPANISH CONTEMPORARY

Zurriola NEW

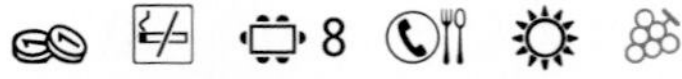

The name of the restaurant comes from the San Sebastian coast, where the chef once lived, and his dishes link Japanese and Spanish perceptions of how food should be. The *omakase* consists of several appetisers followed by plentiful fish and meat dishes. Cooked over charcoal, the flounder offers two different textures and tastes: the fillet, saturated with juices from the bones, and the gelatinous meat at the base of the fin.

■ Opening hours, last orders
Lunch = 11:30-13:30 (L.O.)
Dinner = 18:00-21:30 (L.O.)

■ Annual and weekly closing
Closed mid-August, late December-early January and Monday

■ Price
Lunch = set ¥ 4,800
Dinner = set ¥ 11,000
Service charge = 10%
Private room fee = ¥ 6,000-20,000

TEL. 03-5730-0240
3-2-7 Azabujuban, Minato-ku, Tokyo

www.zurriola.jp

HOTELS

HOTELS BY ORDER OF COMFORT

NEW : new entry in the guide

ANA Intercontinental

Opened in 1986, at the same time as Akasaka Ark Hills. Rooms are on the 7-35th floors; the front lobby is on the 2nd. Standard rooms are between 28 - 32m^2 and have a comfortable, chic feel. Those staying on the Club Intercontinental Floor have access to the lounge, which is the biggest in Japan. The three sides of the triangular-shaped hotel provide views of the Imperial Palace Outer Garden, Tokyo Tower and Roppongi Hills.

■ Price
= ¥ 38,850-51,450
= ¥ 38,850-51,450
Suite = ¥ 78,750-252,000
= ¥ 2,300
Service charge = 10%
Rooms = 801
Suites = 43
Restaurants = 7

TEL. 03–3505–1111
FAX. 03–3505–1155
1-12-33 Akasaka, Minato-ku, Tokyo

www.anaintercontinental-tokyo.jp

Century Southern Tower

This hotel occupies the 19-35th floors of the Odakyu Southern Tower; the lobby is on the 20th floor. Although next to a busy railway, rooms are soundproofed. Those on the eastern side boast views of Shinjuku Gyoen; rooms on the west look onto the Shinjuku skyscraper and Yoyogi Park. Despite cutting out services such as bell and room service, it caters for its guests through vending machines and a small convenience shop.

■ Price
🚹 = ¥ 18,480-57,750
🚹🚹 = ¥ 27,720-63,525
☕ = ¥ 2,194

Rooms = 375
Restaurants = 3

TEL. 03–5354–0111
FAX. 03–5354–0100
2-2-1 Yoyogi, Shibuya-ku, Tokyo
www.southerntower.co.jp

Cerulean Tower Tokyu

♿ ⪡ P 🚭 ⛹ 🏊 🚲

All the rooms feature soothing décor with Japanese design elements and views across the capital. The 33-37th are executive floors; guests here have access to the exclusive salon. French cuisine can be enjoyed on the top floor; the jazz club hosts live music (except on Sundays and public holidays). Those interested in traditional Japanese performing arts can take in a *Noh* or *Kyogen* performance at the Cerulean Tower *Noh* Theatre.

■ Price
🚹 = ¥ 33,000-79,000
🚹🚹 = ¥ 43,500-81,500
Suite = ¥ 100,000-485,000
☕ = ¥ 3,003

Rooms = 402
Suites = 9
Restaurants = 8

TEL. 03-3476-3000
FAX. 03-3476-3001
26-1 Sakuragaokacho,
Shibuya-ku, Tokyo

www.ceruleantower-hotel.com

Claska

Rooms comes in three different types: 'Japanese Modern', with elegant furniture collected from all over Asia; 'Tatami', furnished with low beds and natural wood, and 'Weekly Residence', which feature a conceptual design and are geared to those on long stays. There are also distinctive 'DIY' rooms that were personally created by the designer. The hotel has a multi-purpose studio for exhibitions, photo shoots and events.

■ Price
🚹 = ¥ 9,450-12,600
🚹🚹 = ¥ 19,950-89,250
☕ = ¥ 900
Service charge = 10%

Rooms = 18
Restaurants = 1

TEL. 03–3719–8121
FAX. 03–3719–8122
1-3-18 Chuocho, Meguro-ku, Tokyo

www.claska.com

Conrad

The front desk is found on the 28th floor of the Tokyo Shiodome Building, along with the main lobby, bar & lounge. Mizuki Spa and fitness centre with a 25m indoor pool has floor-to-ceiling windows and offers various relaxation facilities and treatments. Rooms are spacious and divided into two types: 'City', facing the Shiodome area, and 'Garden', opposite Hamarikyu Gardens. The hotel is conveniently located and fashionable.

■ Price
🚹 = ¥ 71,000-86,000
🚹🚹 = ¥ 76,000-91,000
Suite = ¥ 89,000-622,000
☕ = ¥ 2,800

Rooms = 222
Suites = 68
Restaurants = 4

TEL. 03–6388–8000
FAX. 03–6388–8001
1-9-1 Higashishinbashi, Minato-ku, Tokyo

www.conradtokyo.co.jp

Four Seasons Chinzan-so

Chinzan-so was built by Aritomo Yamagata, a military leader and politician of the Meiji Era, in the scenic surroundings of Mejirodai; this smart and tranquil hotel opened in the garden in 1992. As well as streams flowing along gentle natural slopes and abundant greenery, the gardens are dotted with 3-storey pagodas and stone lanterns reminiscent of those at Hannyaji Temple. Guests can use the hot spring baths, pool and spa.

■ Price
† = ¥ 45,150-65,100
†† = ¥ 45,150-65,100
Suite = ¥ 72,450-577,500
☕ = ¥ 2,970
Service charge = 10%

Rooms = 259
Suites = 24
Restaurants = 4

TEL. 03-3943-2222
FAX. 03-3943-2300
2-10-8 Sekiguchi, Bunkyo-ku, Tokyo

www.fourseasons-tokyo.com

Four Seasons Marunouchi

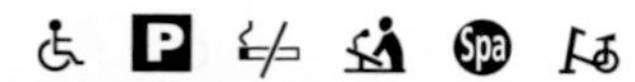

All its exterior walls are glass, providing cityscape views. The vibe is one of urban sophistication: rooms, in tones of beige and grey, have a contemporary, elegant feel. Staff numbers are high in relation to the hotel's size and they provide attentive service. A greetings service is also available and can be arranged for guests arriving at Narita Airport or Tokyo Station. Facilities include a spa and fitness centre.

■ Price
† = ¥ 49,350-59,850
†† = ¥ 49,350-59,850
Suite = ¥ 84,000-525,000
☕ = ¥ 2,900
Service charge = 10%

Rooms = 48
Suites = 9
Restaurants = 1

TEL. 03–5222–7222
FAX. 03–5222–1255
Pacific Century Place Building,
1-11-1 Marunouchi, Chiyoda-ku,
Tokyo

www.fourseasons.com/jp/marunouchi

Gracery Tamachi NEW

♿ 🚭

Gracery Tamachi opened in 2008 as a brand of the Washington Hotel. Guest rooms have a functional yet stylish feel with calm colours. Appliances like trouser presses and mobile phone chargers, and services like the night time laundry service make it suitable for business use. With a homely atmosphere created by low furniture, the 'Ladies' Guest Rooms' are popular. Choose between a buffet-style breakfast or room service.

■ Price
† = ¥ 13,500-14,500
†† = ¥ 19,500-23,000
☕ = ¥ 1,500
Rooms = 216
Restaurants = 1

TEL. 03-6699-1000
FAX. 03-6699-1155
3-8-1 Shibaura Minato-ku, Tokyo
www.gracery-tamachi.com

Grand Hyatt

This modern hotel marks a clear departure from competitors in terms of design, comfort and size. A contemporary ambience is created with materials unique to Japan, such as the stone pool in the Nagomi Spa & Fitness club. A wide variety of cosmopolitan restaurants attract many guests beyond those staying in the hotel. Along with its stylish interior, it offers extensive amenities, such as state-of-the-art telecommunications.

■ Price
🚹 = ¥ 50,820-73,920
🚹🚹 = ¥ 56,595-79,695
Suite = ¥ 102,795-801,570
☕ = ¥ 2,860

Rooms = 361
Suites = 28
Restaurants = 7

TEL. 03–4333–1234
FAX. 03–4333–8123
6-10-3 Roppongi, Minato-ku, Tokyo

www.tokyo.grand.hyatt.jp

Grand Pacific Le Daiba

A 30-storey hotel connected directly to Daiba Station. Each room has a different panoramic view: the Rainbow Bridge, central Tokyo, Tokyo Bay or Haneda Airport. Standard rooms range from 30 to 50m² and are decorated in an 18C European style; renovated in 2011, they come in chic brown tones and have large bathrooms with a marble finish. As the front desk is often crowded, a flexible check-out service is also available.

■ Price
† = ¥ 33,000-61,000
†† = ¥ 39,000-67,000
Suite = ¥ 96,000-500,000
☕ = ¥ 1,850

Rooms = 860
Suites = 24
Restaurants = 10

TEL. 03–5500–6711
FAX. 03–5500–4507
2-6-1 Daiba, Minato-ku, Tokyo

www.grandpacific.jp

Hilton

This 38-storey hotel, with its distinctive S-shaped wave, is set in Nishishinjuku. The 808 rooms take on a simple, modern style with Japanese touches. The 12 Gallery suites feature fine art by one of 12 young artists and are available for small meetings. The 32-38th floors are Executive floors and offer a higher level of comfort for business and leisure guests. There is a fitness centre, and its gym is open around the clock.

■ Price
🚹 = ¥ 23,900-49,900
🚹🚹 = ¥ 27,400-53,400
Suite = ¥ 31,900-191,400
☕ = ¥ 2,600

Rooms = 684
Suites = 124
Restaurants = 6

TEL. 03–3344–5111
FAX. 03–3342–6094
6-6-2 Nishishinjuku, Shinjuku-ku, Tokyo

www.hilton.co.jp/tokyo

Hyatt Regency

Bedrooms are divided into Regency Club rooms and Standard rooms and are further classified according to their view; choose from a cityscape of high-rises or an outlook across Shinjuku Chuo Park. The Regency Club rooms, renovated in 2009, have a check in/out service in the executive lounge. There is also restaurant Cuisine[s] Michel Troisgros, recommended in this guide. A complimentary shuttle bus runs from Shinjuku Station.

■ Price
single = ¥ 35,700-57,750
double = ¥ 38,850-60,900
Suite = ¥ 73,500-262,500
breakfast = ¥ 1,900
Service charge = 10%

Rooms = 726
Suites = 18
Restaurants = 6

TEL. 03-3348-1234
FAX. 03-3344-5575
2-7-2 Nishishinjuku, Shinjuku-ku, Tokyo

www.hyattregencytokyo.com

Imperial

This hotel has been hosting overseas dignitaries since 1890 and its history reflects the ebb and flow of Japan's modernisation. The Wright building, designed by American architect Frank Lloyd Wright and opened in 1923, was replaced by the Main Building in 1970. Dining and bar options include the Old Imperial Bar and Les Saisons. The suite on the 14th floor of the Main Building incorporates elements of Wright's design.

■ Price
🚹 = ¥ 37,800-105,000
🚹🚹 = ¥ 43,050-110,250
Suite = ¥ 84,000-262,500
☕ = ¥ 2,700
Service charge = 10%

Rooms = 875
Suites = 56
Restaurants = 13

TEL. 03–3504–1111
FAX. 03–3581–9146
1-1-1 Uchisaiwaicho, Chiyoda-ku, Tokyo

www.imperialhotel.co.jp

Intercontinental Tokyo Bay

All rooms offer commanding views: of the Rainbow Bridge and Ferris wheel in Odaiba or of the Sumida-gawa river threading among high-rise buildings. Guests staying on the Club Floors (20th to top) can check in and out at a dedicated desk. The restaurants are on the 3rd floor which connects to Takeshiba Station. Combining functionality with the feel of a resort, this hotel is popular with businesspeople and holidaymakers.

■ Price
single = ¥ 41,780-71,810
double = ¥ 41,980-72,010
Suite = ¥ 115,700-346,900
breakfast = ¥ 1,848

Rooms = 331
Suites = 8
Restaurants = 5

TEL. 03–5404–2222
FAX. 03–5404–2111
1-16-2 Kaigan, Minato-ku, Tokyo
www.interconti-tokyo.com

Keio Plaza

Rooms are spread over two buildings: the 47-storey Main Tower, which opened in 1971, and the South Tower, dating from 1980. More than half the rooms have been upgraded as part of a renovation programme. Contemporary décor and comprehensive facilities create strong comfort levels in the completed Plaza Premier rooms. For overseas guests keen to experience tradition, there are older Japanese rooms with *hinoki* bathtubs.

■ Price
🚹 = ¥ 29,075-55,640
🚹🚹 = ¥ 32,740-59,305
Suite = ¥ 107,415-415,800
☕ = ¥ 2,514

Rooms = 1409
Suites = 27
Restaurants = 13

TEL. 03–3344–0111
FAX. 03–3345–8269
2-2-1 Nishishinjuku, Shinjuku-ku, Tokyo

www.keioplaza.co.jp

Mandarin Oriental

The Japanese-inspired decoration adds to the air of elegance and tranquillity of this hotel. Rooms use bamboo and other natural materials, while the fabrics carry a nature motif. The west side offers views of the gardens of the Imperial Palace; to the east you can see Odaiba in Tokyo Bay and the Sumida-gawa River. The luxurious spa also offers breathtaking views. Try Cantonese cooking at Sense and French cuisine in Signature.

■ Price
🚹 = ¥ 73,500-85,050
🚹🚹 = ¥ 73,500-85,050
Suite = ¥ 141,750-997,500
☕ = ¥ 2,800
Service charge = 10%

Rooms = 157
Suites = 21
Restaurants = 6

TEL. 03-3270-8800
FAX. 03-3270-8828
2-1-1 Nihonbashimuromachi,
Chou-ku, Tokyo

www.mandarinoriental.co.jp/tokyo

Marunouchi

Located in front of Tokyo Station's Marunouchi North exit, this hotel is convenient for both businesspeople and tourists. Rooms on the east side overlook the busy, red-bricked station; those on the west face the Marunouchi business district – but both sides are quiet. Single rooms are not especially large, but their coved or arched ceilings add a feeling of space. This is a distinguished hotel with all modern conveniences.

■ Price
single = ¥ 23,300-52,175
double = ¥ 31,385-52,375
Suite = ¥ 115,900
breakfast = ¥ 1,900

Rooms = 204
Suites = 1
Restaurants = 3

TEL. 03–3217–1111
FAX. 03–3217–1115
1-6-3 Marunouchi, Chiyoda-ku, Tokyo

www.marunouchi-hotel.co.jp

Meguro Gajoen

Meguro Gajoen, well-known as a wedding venue, opened in 1931. The house that lies within the property, known as Hyakudan Kaidan, is a registered cultural property and served as inspiration for the film 'Spirited Away'. Rooms provide a tranquil space, in contrast to the lavishly decorated public areas. The Western rooms include Ryukyu tatami in the corner; those on the west overlook the Meguro-gawa River and the cherry blossom.

■ Price
single = ¥ 70,000-116,000
double = ¥ 70,000-116,000
breakfast = ¥ 2,400

Rooms = 23
Restaurants = 4

TEL. 03–3491–4111
FAX. 03–5434–3931
1-8-1 Shimomeguro, Meguro-ku, Tokyo

www.megurogajoen.co.jp

Metropolitan Marunouchi

Connecting directly to Tokyo Station, Sapia Tower opened in 2007 and has a private elevator that takes you to the front lobby on the 27th floor. Guests can admire Tokyo Bay or look out in the Makuhari direction or the mountains of Chiba; at night there is modern metropolitan scenery like Tokyo Tower and Shinjuku to enjoy. The staff at the front desk can make arrangements for JR tickets, including for the limited express.

■ Price
single = ¥ 18,680-25,610
double = ¥ 30,230-40,825
tea = ¥ 2,300

Rooms = 343
Restaurants = 1

TEL. 03–3211–2233
FAX. 03–3211–2244
1-7-12 Marunouchi, Chiyoda-ku, Tokyo

www.hm-marunouchi.jp

Mitsui Garden Ginza

The lobby is situated on the 16th floor overlooking Tsukiji market. The hotel has a large number of compact rooms, in stylish brown and simple white tones. Guests choosing the View Bath Double or Twin rooms can luxuriate in the bathtub against the backdrop of Tokyo at night. For an even higher level of comfort, book a 25th or Executive floor room. Mitsui Garden Ginza impresses with its functional yet contemporary design.

■ Price
single = ¥ 18,900-44,100
double = ¥ 25,200-44,100
breakfast = ¥ 2,100
Rooms = 361
Restaurants = 1

TEL. 03–3543–1131
FAX. 03–3543–5531
8-13-1 Ginza, Chou-ku, Tokyo
www.gardenhotels.co.jp

New Otani (The Main)

This hotel consists of the Main Building and the Garden Tower - this guide covers just the Main Building, which underwent a major renovation in 2007. Rooms feature a simple décor which includes elements of Japanese design. For greater comfort levels, try a well-equipped deluxe room with contemporary design; a concierge service at the exclusive lounge is also available. There is an art museum, tennis courts and a golf range.

■ Price
(single) = ¥ 31,500-73,500
(double) = ¥ 39,900-73,500
Suite = ¥ 126,000-273,000
(breakfast) = ¥ 1,890
Service charge = 10%

Rooms = 614
Suites = 29
Restaurants = 29

TEL. 03–3265–1111
FAX. 03–3221–2619
4-1 Kioicho, Chiyoda-ku, Tokyo

www.newotani.co.jp/tokyo

Nikko

Nikko describes itself as 'the balcony of Tokyo' as every room has one. The lobby on the 2nd floor, with its atrium and high columns, offers views of Rainbow Bridge. Designed with the theme of 'Tokyo Resort', all the rooms - completely renovated in 2009 - are in contemporary, chic tones. For greater comfort levels, there are suites with their own gardens. This is an urban resort hotel with a relaxing, leisurely feel.

■ Price
Single = ¥ 36,000-62,000
Double = ¥ 42,000-68,000
Suite = ¥ 150,000-400,000
Breakfast = ¥ 2,310

Rooms = 435
Suites = 17
Restaurants = 8

TEL. 03–5500–5500
FAX. 03–5500–2525
1-9-1 Daiba, Minato-ku, Tokyo

www.hnt.co.jp

Niwa

Opened in 2009, Niwa is next to the Nihon University College of Economics. It was founded as a Japanese-style inn but changed into a more modern lodging hotel over the course of three generations. The bedrooms are decorated with Japanese paper and sliding screens; the carpet is designed to resemble *tatami*. There is also a lounge and a workout room on the 3rd floor. A 24-hour business centre is available on the 1st floor.

■ Price
single = ¥ 18,900-36,750
double = ¥ 23,100-40,950
breakfast = ¥ 2,310
Service charge = 10%

Rooms = 238
Restaurants = 2

TEL. 03–3293–0028
FAX. 03–3295–3328
1-1-16 Misakicho, Chiyoda-ku, Tokyo

www.hotelniwa.jp

Okura

The Hotel Okura opened in 1962 and its regal atmosphere has changed little since. Visitors are drawn into the lobby by the all-wood décor and the glow of lantern-like lights suspended from the ceiling. Rooms vary in size, style and the view on offer, but all are comfortable and well-equipped. The wine, dining & cigar bar, Baron Okura, has an impressive wine list. This is a hotel with a proud tradition and impeccable service.

■ Price
single = ¥ 36,750-63,000
double = ¥ 42,000-66,150
Suite = ¥ 94,500-577,500
breakfast = ¥ 1,890
Service charge = 10%

Rooms = 712
Suites = 89
Restaurants = 8

TEL. 03–3582–0111
FAX. 03–3582–3707
2-10-4 Toranomon, Minato-ku, Tokyo

www.hotelokura.co.jp/tokyo

Park

This hotel, whose interior boasts a modern design, occupies the top floors of the Shiodome Media Tower. The large bedroom windows face Tokyo Tower, Tokyo Bay or Tokyo Station, but those on the Tokyo Tower side enjoy more far-reaching scenery. All rooms, except the suites, have bath and shower modules. The hotel is directly linked to the Shiodome subway station, making it convenient for sightseeing as well as for business use.

■ Price
🚹 = ¥ 21,000-37,800
🚹🚹 = ¥ 26,250-37,800
Suite = ¥ 105,000
☕ = ¥ 2,310
Service charge = 10%

Rooms = 272
Suites = 1
Restaurants = 2

TEL. 03–6252–1111
FAX. 03–6252–1001
Shiodome Media Tower 25F,
1-7-1 Higashishinbashi,
Minato-ku, Tokyo

www.parkhoteltokyo.com

Park Hyatt

This hotel occupies the 39th to 52nd floors of the high-rise Shinjuku Park Tower, offering panoramic views of the city from the bedrooms - on a clear day Mt. Fuji can be seen from the west. The Club on The Park Spa and Fitness Centre also offers the same spectacular views. Drawings by contemporary artists are on display throughout the hotel, which was used as the setting for Sofia Coppola's film, 'Lost in Translation'.

■ Price
† = ¥ 69,300-87,780
†† = ¥ 69,300-87,780
Suite = ¥ 167,475-924,000
☕ = ¥ 3,300

Rooms = 154
Suites = 23
Restaurants = 4

TEL. 03–5322–1234
FAX. 03–5322–1288
3-7-1-2 Nishishinjuku, Shinjuku-ku, Tokyo

www.tokyo.park.hyatt.jp

Royal Park

Close to Tokyo City Air Terminal, this hotel offers regular services to and from Narita and Haneda Airports. Bedrooms are on the 6th to 18th floors and have chic modern interiors, as well as panoramic views and extras such as a computer. The private salon, swimming pool, fitness club and meeting rooms are free of charge for those on the Executive Floors. Stroll in the beautiful 5th floor garden with its own tea house.

■ Price
= ¥ 27,300-53,550
= ¥ 35,700-57,750
Suite = ¥ 89,250-262,500
= ¥ 1,365
Service charge = 10%

Rooms = 395
Suites = 11
Restaurants = 6

TEL. 03–3667–1111
FAX. 03–3667–1115
2-1-1 Nihonbashikakigaracho,
Chuo-ku, Tokyo

www.rph.co.jp

Royal Park Shiodome Tower

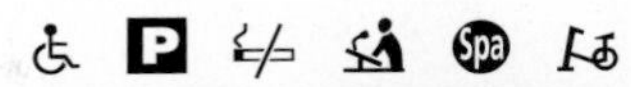

Rooms are varied, ranging from singles to Tower suites, and their décor is modern and simple. Rooms are equipped with personal computers and a Cyber-Concierge; the latter answers queries relating to hotel facilities and delivery services. All rooms have an air cleaning & humidifying system; ask for a view of Hamarikyu Gardens, Tokyo Tower or the Imperial Palace. The hotel also has a coin laundry for those on longer stays.

■ Price
† = ¥ 23,100-69,300
†† = ¥ 23,100-69,300
Suite = ¥ 103,950
☕ = ¥ 1,501

Rooms = 456
Suites = 2
Restaurants = 3

TEL. 03–6253–1111
FAX. 03–6253–1115
1-6-3 Higashishinbashi,
Minato-ku, Tokyo

www.rps-tower.co.jp

Ryumeikan NEW
龍名館

The Gofukubashi branch of an inn from the late Meiji period, Ryumeikan was reborn as a hotel in 2009; the original sign hangs in the hall. So all customers can enjoy the view, the front desk and lobby are on the top floor. Rooms, in traditional Edo purple, retain vestiges of the past and are popular with families and foreign guests for their inn-like feel. Breakfast is a Japanese-style buffet of mostly vegetables and seafood.

■ Price
🚹 = ¥ 16,500-21,000
🚹🚹 = ¥ 28,000-45,000
Suite = ¥ 72,000
☕ = ¥ 2,500

Rooms = 134
Suites = 1
Restaurants = 2

TEL. 03-3271-0971
FAX. 03-3271-0977
1-3-22 Yaesu, Chuo-ku, Tokyo
www.ryumeikan-tokyo.jp

Seiyo Ginza

This 12-storey hotel exudes an air of serenity and comfort. The hotel's aim is to offer high-level hotel services in the ambience of a private residence; in line with this, a tail-coated butler is assigned to each room. Seiyo Ginza was the first hotel in Tokyo to offer this service which, along with a concierge, is available 24 hours a day. Bedrooms are designed in an 18C European style and have spacious bathrooms.

■ Price
† = ¥ 63,525-78,540
†† = ¥ 63,525-78,540
Suite = ¥ 92,400-219,450
☕ = ¥ 2,772

Rooms = 51
Suites = 26
Restaurants = 4

TEL. 03–3535–1111
FAX. 03–3535–1110
1-11-2 Ginza, Chuo-ku, Tokyo

www.seiyo-ginza.co.jp

Shangri-La

Opened in 2009 inside the Marunouchi Trust Tower Main and occupying floors 27-37. The west side overlooks the Imperial Palace; the east side, Tokyo Bay. Rooms feature an elegant oriental design. The CHI spa - where the treatments are based on Chinese and Himalayan healing therapy - was the first of its kind in Japan. The lavish facilities and hospitality usher you off into a mystical and graceful land in the heart of the city.

■ Price
🚹 = ¥ 73,500-98,700
🚹🚹 = ¥ 73,500-105,000
Suite = ¥ 262,500-1,050,000
☕ = ¥ 2,900
Service charge = 10%

Rooms = 194
Suites = 6
Restaurants = 2

TEL. 03–6739–7888
FAX. 03–6739–7889
Marunouchi Trust Tower Main,
1-8-3 Marunouchi, Chiyoda-ku,
Tokyo

www.shangri-la.com/jp

Sheraton Miyako

First opened in 1979 and renamed in 2007. Bedrooms are divided into three types: the bright, standard rooms which are enjoying continued popularity; the premium floors, featuring a tranquil colour scheme; and 'Floor Seven' which fuses Japanese tradition with a modern Western theme. All guest rooms have 'Sweet Sleeper' beds with comfortable mattresses, Egyptian cotton sheets and three types of pillows to choose from.

■ Price
† = ¥ 28,350-44,100
†† = ¥ 31,500-74,550
Suite = ¥ 294,000
☕ = ¥ 2,415
Service charge = 10%

Rooms = 493
Suites = 2
Restaurants = 3

TEL. 03–3447–3111
FAX. 03–3447–3133
1-1-50 Shirokanedai, Minato-ku, Tokyo

www.miyakohotels.ne.jp/tokyo

The Agnes

Based on a warm beige colour scheme, the hotel's accommodation is comfortable and relaxing and most rooms have a balcony. Pleasant staff take care of each guest's needs. The hotel is particularly appreciated by those seeking a peaceful environment. For longer-term guests, there are apartments equipped with a refrigerator, microwave, washing machine, dryer and so on. In the tearoom, enjoy sweets from patisserie Le Coin Vert.

■ Price
single = ¥ 22,000-35,000
double = ¥ 27,000-40,000
Suite = ¥ 50,000-80,000
breakfast = ¥ 2,100

Rooms = 51
Suites = 5
Restaurants = 1

TEL. 03-3267-5505
FAX. 03-3267-5513
2-20-1 Kagurazaka, Shinjuku-ku, Tokyo

www.agneshotel.com

The Capitol Tokyu NEW

Having opened in 1963 as the first foreign-operated hotel in Japan, it was reborn in 2010 as The Capitol Tokyu. Although located in the centre of the city, it is surrounded by the verdant scenery of the Hie Jinja Shrine, and the quiet atmosphere will make you forget the hustle and bustle of the city. Guest rooms, with 6m-wide windows, feature creative and stylish interiors that incorporate *shoji* and other Japanese elements.

■ Price
🚹 = ¥ 60,000-92,000
🚹🚹 = ¥ 65,000-97,000
Suite = ¥ 170,000-650,000
☕ = ¥ 3,003

Rooms = 238
Suites = 13
Restaurants = 3

TEL. 03-3503-0109
FAX. 03-3503-0309
2-10-3 Nagatacho, Chiyoda-ku, Tokyo

www.capitolhoteltokyu.com

The Peninsula

In an enviable position opposite the Imperial Palace Outer Garden and Hibiya Park. The front desk is behind the eye-catching bamboo. Rooms are a 'fusion of Peninsula standard and Japanese culture'; doors made of horse chestnut, vermillion-lacquered counters and cypress ajiro woven ceilings create a warm feel. The telephone, TV and lights can be operated from the bathtub. You'll find a Cantonese restaurant on the 2nd floor.

■ Price
🚹 = ¥ 69,300-92,400
🚹🚹 = ¥ 69,300-92,400
Suite = ¥ 138,000-2,310,000
☕ = ¥ 2,800

Rooms = 267
Suites = 47
Restaurants = 4

TEL. 03–6270–2888
FAX. 03–6270–2000
1-8-1 Yurakucho, Chiyoda-ku, Tokyo

www.peninsula.com/tokyo/jp

The Prince Park Tower

Amid the greenery of Shiba Park is a hotel which stresses the importance of comfort through its relaxation facilities. Its 33 storeys are divided into sections: the Park Floors on the 3rd-18th, the Superior Floors on the 2nd and 19-28th, and Premium Floors on the 29-31st. Personal butler services are available for those staying in any of the comfortable Royal Suites, decorated in British, French, Italian and Japanese styles.

■ Price
单 = ¥ 34,000-70,000
双 = ¥ 34,000-70,000
Suite = ¥ 104,000-980,000
Breakfast = ¥ 3,000

Rooms = 639
Suites = 34
Restaurants = 9

TEL. 03–5400–1111
FAX. 03–5400–1110
4-8-1 Shibakoen, Minato-ku, Tokyo

www.princehotels.co.jp/parktower

The Ritz-Carlton

This hotel is in the 53-storey Midtown Tower that soars 248m above the Tokyo Midtown complex. All 248 rooms have a floor space of at least 52m², elegant décor and, along with Japanese-inspired art deco furniture, boast large-screen TVs, including one in their sleek bathrooms. On the 46th floor is a 20m pool, a well-equipped fitness centre and spa. Stunning views take in Mt. Fuji and Tokyo Tower.

■ Price
🚹 = ¥ 73,500-92,400
🚹🚹 = ¥ 78,750-102,900
Suite = ¥ 126,000-2,100,000
☕ = ¥ 2,850
Service charge = 10%

Rooms = 212
Suites = 36
Restaurants = 7

TEL. 03–3423–8000
FAX. 03–3423–8001
Tokyo Midtown, 9-7-1 Akasaka, Minato-ku, Tokyo

www.ritzcarlton.com/ja/tokyo

The Strings by Intercontinental

Connected by the Skyway pedestrian overpass, this hotel is a two-minute walk from Shinagawa Station's Konan exit and occupies the 26th to the top floor. Rooms are stylishly decorated in shades of brown and beige and have large windows; bathrooms feature wood and marble floors. Rooms come in a variety of sizes and facilities include a 24-hour business centre and a fitness centre with the same spectacular views as the bedrooms.

■ Price
single = ¥ 31,000-57,000
double = ¥ 38,000-64,000
Suite = ¥ 162,000-237,000
breakfast = ¥ 2,656
Rooms = 199
Suites = 6
Restaurants = 2

TEL. 03–5783–1111
FAX. 03–5783–1112
Shinagawa East One Tower,
2-16-1 Konan, Minato-ku, Tokyo
www.intercontinental-strings.jp

Villa Fontaine Shiodome

 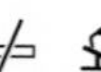

Founded in 2004 as a business hotel and occupying floors 2-10 of the 27-storey Shiodome Sumitomo Building. Calm, stylish colour schemes are used in the bedrooms, which feature spacious bathrooms and plenty of amenities. Computers are available in the first floor business centre; guests staying in the Premier rooms can borrow computers from the front desk. There is no restaurant, but breakfast is included in the room price.

■ Price
🚹 = ¥ 10,000-16,000
🚹🚹 = ¥ 14,000-18,000
Rooms = 497

TEL. 03-3569-2220
FAX. 03-3569-2111
1-9-2 Higashishinbashi, Minato-ku, Tokyo
www.hvf.jp/shiodome

Westin

This 22-storey building is part of Yebisu Garden Place. Its décor was inspired by early 19C French style and the use of marble fits well with Japanese design elements like prints and folding screens. Choose from two types: Deluxe or Executive Club - those in the latter check in at the exclusive lounge on the 17th floor. Chinese and Japanese restaurants are on the 2nd; *teppanyaki* and French are on the top floor.

■ Price
= ¥ 65,100-76,650
= ¥ 65,100-76,650
Suite = ¥ 157,500-525,000
= ¥ 2,600

Rooms = 418
Suites = 20
Restaurants = 5

TEL. 03–5423–7000
FAX. 03–5423–7600
1-4-1 Mita, Meguro-ku, Tokyo

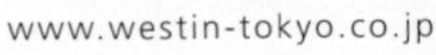
www.westin-tokyo.co.jp

YOKOHAMA

RESTAURANTS & HOTELS

RESTAURANTS

STARRED RESTAURANTS

All the restaurants within the Tokyo Yokohama Shonan Guide have one, two or three Michelin Stars and are our way of highlighting restaurants that offer particularly good food.

When awarding stars there are a number of factors we consider: the quality and freshness of the ingredients, the technical skill and flair that goes into their preparation, the clarity of the flavours, the value for money and, ultimately, the taste. Of equal importance is the ability to produce excellent food not once but time and time again. Our inspectors make as many visits as necessary so that you can be sure of this quality and consistency.

A two or three star restaurant has to offer something very special in its cooking that separates it from the rest. Three stars – our highest award – are given to the very best. Cuisines in any style of restaurant and of any nationality are eligible for a star. The decoration, service and comfort levels have no bearing on the award.

Excellent cuisine, worth a detour.

Skillfully and carefully crafted dishes of outstanding quality.

Restaurant		Comfort	Cuisine	Page
Chiso Kimura		X	Japanese	380
Masagosaryo		XX	Japanese	383
Sugai	↗	X	Japanese	387

A very good restaurant in its category.

A place offering cuisine prepared to a consistently high standard.

Restaurant		Comfort	Cuisine	Page
Aichiya		XXX	Japanese	376
Azabu Nodaiwa		XX	Japanese Unagi	377
Chatsubo	NEW	XX	Japanese	378
Chez Naka		XX	French	379
Fukunishi	NEW	X	Japanese Tempura	381
Furaikyo		X	Japanese Soba	382
Mizuki		X	Japanese	384
Ota Nawanoren		XX	Japanese Sukiyaki	385
Rinkaen		XXX	Japanese	386
Sushi Hachizaemon		X	Japanese Sushi	388
Sushi Hamada		X	Japanese Sushi	389
Tenhama		XX	Japanese Tempura	390
Tenshichi		X	Japanese Tempura	391
Ukai-tei Azamino		XXXX	Japanese Teppanyaki	392

NEW : new entry in the guide
↗ : restaurant promoted from 1 to 2 stars or 2 to 3 stars

RESTAURANTS BY AREA

NEW : new entry in the guide
☺ : restaurant promoted from 1 to 2 stars or 2 to 3 stars

RESTAURANTS BY CUISINE TYPE

NEW : new entry in the guide
☺ : restaurant promoted from 1 to 2 stars or 2 to 3 stars

RESTAURANTS SERVING LUNCH AND/ OR DINNER FOR ¥ 5,000 AND LESS

Azabu Nodaiwa	✿	XX	lunch & dinner	377
Chez Naka	✿	XX	lunch & dinner (weekday)	379
Chiso Kimura	✿✿	X	lunch	380
Fukunishi	NEW ✿	X	lunch & dinner	381
Furaikyo	✿	X	lunch & dinner	382
Rinkaen	✿	XXX	lunch	386
Tenshichi	✿	X	lunch	391

NEW : new entry in the guide

RESTAURANTS OPEN ON SUNDAY

Restaurant		Stars	Comfort	Cuisine	Page
Aichiya		✿	XXX	Japanese	376
Chatsubo	NEW	✿	XX	Japanese	378
Chez Naka		✿	XX	French	379
Chiso Kimura		✿✿	X	Japanese	380
Fukunishi	NEW	✿	X	Japanese Tempura	381
Furaikyo		✿	X	Japanese Soba	382
Masagosaryo		✿✿	XX	Japanese	383
Rinkaen		✿	XXX	Japanese	386
Sugai	↗	✿✿	X	Japanese	387
Sushi Hachizaemon		✿	X	Japanese Sushi	388
Ukai-tei Azamino		✿	XXXX	Japanese Teppanyaki	392

NEW : new entry in the guide
↗ : restaurant promoted from 1 to 2 stars or 2 to 3 stars

JAPANESE

Aichiya
あいちや

Head west from Yokohama Station and you will come upon this elegant establishment with a serene, timeless atmosphere – one of the few *ryotei* still found in Yokohama. The chef has been showcasing his skills here for over 20 years; his creed is 'everything starts with the ingredients', which are from a Tsukiji wholesaler. He includes one feature dish in the set menus, avoids quirkiness and serves orthodox Japanese cuisine.

■ Opening hours, last orders
Lunch = 11:30-14:00 (L.O.)
Dinner = 17:00-20:00 (L.O.)

■ Annual and weekly closing
Closed late December-early January

■ Price
Lunch = menu ¥ 5,250-16,800
Dinner = menu ¥ 8,400-18,900
Service charge = 20% (lunch 10%)

TEL. 045-311-2528
2-17-6 Minamisaiwai, Nishi-ku, Yokohama

www.aichiya.jp/honten

Azabu Nodaiwa
麻布 野田岩

20

Akio Kanemoto's restaurant shares the same name as his brother's in Tokyo; he prepares the *unagi* earnestly each day so as not to tarnish his brother's name. Rare natural *unagi* is served from April to November and his sauce is slightly lighter than his brother's. The popular set menu is the sweet *unagi* made with *ume*, a rare find in *unagi* restaurants; the rich sourness and natural sweetness is the result of much trial and error.

■ Opening hours, last orders
Lunch = 11:30-14:00 (L.O.)
Dinner = 17:00-20:30 (L.O.)

■ Annual and weekly closing
Closed mid-August, late December-early January and Sunday

■ Prices

Lunch =	set	¥ 8,190-11,550
	à la carte	¥ 2,520-10,000
Dinner =	set	¥ 8,190-11,550
	à la carte	¥ 2,520-10,000

Service charge = 10%

TEL. 045–320–3224
2-13-9 Kitasaiwai, Nishi-ku, Yokohama
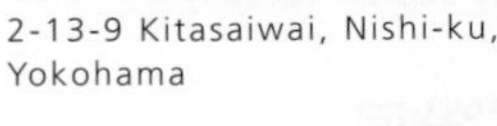

JAPANESE

Chatsubo NEW
茶つぼ

Originally from Zama City, the owner-chef studied cooking in Kyoto before opening his own restaurant. The focus is on orthodox Japanese cuisine, but there are also many novel items: grilled *nodoguro* is steeped in sweet soy sauce and served with vinegared *mozuku*, and tempura covered in *ankake* sauce. The *goritsukudani* and *awa-fu* are rare finds in Yokohama. The store curtain becomes visible about 100m up Shiokumizaka.

■ Opening hours, last orders
Lunch = Wed.-Sun. except 2nd Wed.
12:00-13:00 (L.O.)
Dinner = 18:00-20:00 (L.O.)

■ Annual and weekly closing
Closed 25 December-5 January,
Monday and 2nd Tuesday

■ Prices
Lunch = set ¥ 5,250
Dinner = set ¥ 8,400-10,500
Service charge = 10%

TEL. 045-633-3348
3-147-7 Motomachi, Naka-ku,
Yokohama

www.geocities.jp/hakusyaku2004/tyatubo/tyatubo

FRENCH

Chez Naka

The spotless interior of this small restaurant on Kanjo Route 3, with its antique furnishings, radiates warmth. Food is traditionally prepared and every effort is made to ensure that flavours are just right – pineapple purée is added to the sauce to give the duck a refreshing taste; portions are kept to a reasonable size. The chef provides courteous service; credit cards can only be used for meals totalling 10,000 yen or more.

■ Opening hours, last orders
Lunch = 11:30-14:00 (L.O.)
Dinner = 18:00-21:00 (L.O.)

■ Annual and weekly closing
Closed late August-early September, late December-early January, and Wednesday except Public Holidays

■ Prices

Lunch =	set	¥ 2,500-10,500
	à la carte	¥ 8,500-9,500
Dinner =	set Mon.-Fri.	¥ 4,200-10,500
	set Sat.,Sun	¥ 5,800-10,500
	à la carte	¥ 8,500-9,500

Service charge = 10% (dinner)

TEL. 045–891–6701
1-21-16 Koyamadai, Sakae-ku, Yokohama
http://cheznaka.easy-magic.com

JAPANESE

Chiso Kimura
馳走 きむら

The monthly set menus are the draw here. The owner-chef goes to the market each day to pick out ingredients and exercises creativity with their textures and tastes. As he handles everything himself, be prepared to wait; his politeness will also leave an impression. With garnishing that includes flowers, the colours are also appealing. Care has been taken with the serving dishes and interior to highlight the seasons.

■ Opening hours, last orders
Lunch = 11:30-15:00 L.O.14:00
except Saturday
Dinner = 18:00-22:00 L.O.20:00

■ Annual and weekly closing
Closed Golden week, mid-August, late December-early January, Monday and 3rd Tuesday

■ Prices
Lunch = set ¥ 2,800-9,000
Dinner = set ¥ 6,000-9,000

TEL. 045-901-2606
5-14-1 Utsukushigaoka, Aoba-ku, Yokohama

Fukunishi NEW
ふく西

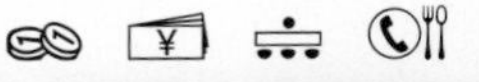

The owner-chef - whose hobby is pottery - visits Tsukiji and fishing ports in Sajima and Nagai to buy seafood. Having trained at a *tempura* restaurant in Tokyo that also has a branch in Kansai, he takes the best from both the *Edomae* and Kansai traditions. For example, he uses his own blend of sesame-based oil, but his *tempura* sauce is sweet. We recommend the *tendon*, which features fragrant *sakuraebi* complemented by sweet sauce.

■ Opening hours, last orders
Lunch = 11:30-14:00 (L.O.)
Dinner = 17:00-21:00 (L.O.)

■ Annual and weekly closing
Closed 1-4 January, mid-August and Thursday

■ Prices
Lunch = set ¥ 1,500-7,000
Dinner = set ¥ 2,800-12,000

TEL. 045-621-2924
2-37 Hongocho, Naka-ku,
Yokohama

www.tenpura-fukunishi.com

Furaikyo
風來蕎

After originally aspiring to be a film director, the owner-chef decided to change course and direct a *soba* restaurant instead. *Seiro soba* is ground with a millstone and cut into thin noodles that are supple and sweet. Smooth, deep-tasting hand-ground *soba* is only served on Saturdays and holidays; the sharp sauce goes well with *sobayu* and has the aroma of bonito. *Oboro dofu* and *nama-yuba* are from the owner's parents' tofu shop.

■ Opening hours, last orders
Lunch = 11:30-15:00 (L.O.)
Dinner = 18:00-20:30 (L.O.)

■ Annual and weekly closing
Closed early January, mid-August, Wednesday and 3rd Tuesday of each month

■ Prices

Lunch = set		¥ 3,500
	à la carte	¥ 2,000-5,000
Dinner = set		¥ 3,500-5,000
	à la carte	¥ 2,000-5,000

TEL. 045–904–8345
4-19-19 Utsukushigaoka, Aoba-ku, Yokohama

www.soba-furaikyo.com

JAPANESE

Masagosaryo
真砂茶寮

Built in the style of a tea-ceremony house but surrounded by modern buildings. The owner-chef serves two types of cuisine: *Kaiseki ryori* is artfully arranged, evokes the seasons and draws out natural flavours without excess seasoning; *Enseki* ryori is for family milestone celebrations. The sea bream *shiogamayaki* served on a large plate with *sekihan* is particularly popular. Lunch bookings must be made at least a day in advance.

■ Opening hours, last orders
Lunch = 11:30-14:30
Dinner = 17:30-23:00

■ Annual and weekly closing
Closed mid-August and late December-early January

■ Prices
Lunch = set ¥ 5,800-15,000
Dinner = set ¥ 7,800-15,000
Service charge = 10%

TEL. 045–663–6692
2-16 Masagocho, Naka-ku, Yokohama

www.masago.jp

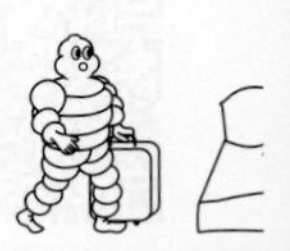

JAPANESE

Mizuki
瑞木

Light spills out from the latticework at the front of this restaurant; there's a Japanese cypress counter inside and a friendly atmosphere courtesy of the owner-chef's personality. The highlight is seafood caught off the Miura Peninsula; the owner-chef goes to the port himself to check the quality. There are also creative dishes like lightly grilled *shime saba* and duck *kuwayaki* with *sansho*. *Takikomi-gohan* concludes the meal.

■ Opening hours, last orders
Dinner = 17:30-23:00 L.O.22:30

■ Annual and weekly closing
Closed mid-August, late December-early January and Sunday

■ Prices
Dinner = set ¥ 6,300-10,500
Service charge = 5% (private room 10%)

TEL. 045–663–8483
5-63 Sumiyoshicho, Naka-ku, Yokohama

www.geocities.jp/kannai_wasyoku_mizuki

JAPANESE SUKIYAKI

Ota Nawanoren
太田なわのれん

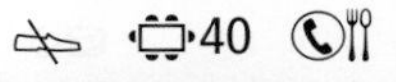

Using a shallow iron pan, the founder came up with beef dishes that were steamed instead of grilled and opened the first *gyunabe* restaurant in 1868. Today, customers are treated to *kaiseki* style cuisine centred around *gyunabe*. The *butsugiri gyunabe* speciality features cubed pieces of beef boiled in Edo *amamiso;* the tokusen beef requires reservations at least the day before. With only 4 tables in a *tatami* room, book early.

■ Opening hours, last orders
Lunch = Sat., Sun. and Public Holidays
12:00-15:00 L.O.14:00
Dinner = 17:00-22:00 L.O.21:00
Sat., Sun. and Public Holidays
17:00-21:00 L.O.20:00

■ Annual and weekly closing
Closed mid-August, late December-early January, Monday and 3rd Sunday

■ Prices
Lunch = set ¥ 7,870-15,750
à la carte ¥ 10,000-14,000
Dinner = set ¥ 9,450-15,750
à la carte ¥ 10,000-14,000
Service charge = 10%

TEL. 045-261-0636
1-15 Sueyoshicho, Naka-ku, Yokohama

www.ohtanawanoren.jp

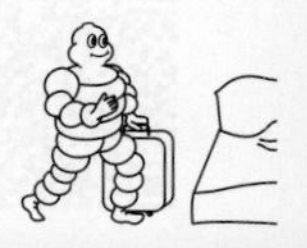

JAPANESE

Rinkaen
隣花苑

This Ashikaga era country house was relocated by Sankeien founder Sankei Hara; enjoy home-style, straightforward cooking, in a nostalgic setting. First comes several small dishes including seasonal vegetables with sesame dressing and *nuta*. Sankei *soba*, included in every set menu, is famous as the dish served by Sankei at tea gatherings. Ask for the room facing the garden but check in advance about a possible room charge.

■ Opening hours, last orders
12:00-21:00 L.O.18:00

■ Annual and weekly closing
Closed late December-early January, August and Wednesday

■ Prices
Lunch = set ¥ 3,675-18,900
Dinner = set ¥ 10,500-18,900
Private room fee = ¥ 5,250-10,500/h
Service charge = 10%

TEL. 045–621–0318
52-1 Honmokusannotani, Naka-ku, Yokohama

www.rinkaen.jp

JAPANESE

Sugai
菅井

Enjoy traditional Japanese cuisine such as the generous appetiser and the tuna *tsukuri* with young green onions, plus a range of dishes with that little bit extra. Just one monthly-changing set menu is offered. *Nabe ryori* is served all year, with *shabu-shabu* loaded with *kinome*. The aroma on the counter grill whets the appetite and at the end comes *takikomi-gohan*. This is a *kaiseki*-style restaurant, but comfortably relaxed.

■ Opening hours, last orders
Lunch = 12:00-15:00 L.O.12:00
Dinner = 18:00-22:30 L.O.20:30

■ Annual and weekly closing
Closed late December-early January and Wednesday

■ Prices
Lunch = set ¥ 5,250
Dinner = set ¥ 10,500
Service charge = 10% (dinner)

TEL. 045-664-2885
5-69 Otamachi, Naka-ku, Yokohama

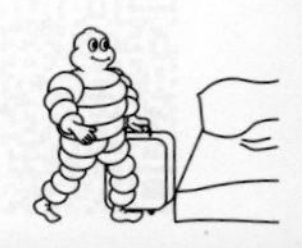

JAPANESE SUSHI

Sushi Hachizaemon
すし 八左ェ門

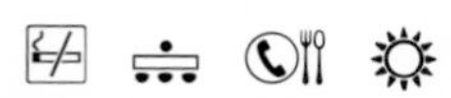

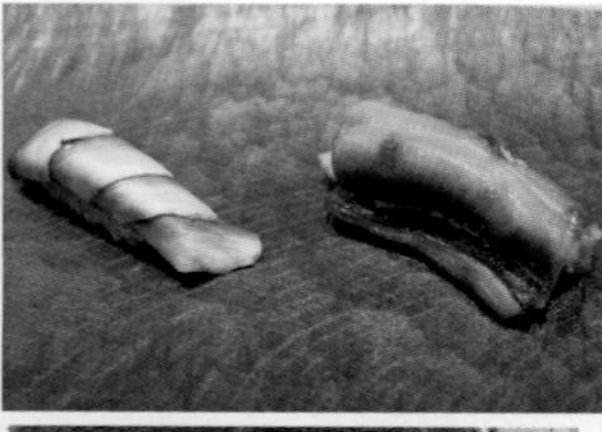

An out-of-the-way restaurant run by the owner-chef alone, on the 3rd floor of an ivy-clad commercial building unadorned by signs; he has the spirit of a true artisan and is very friendly. Because the items are specially selected to go with the rice flavoured with matured red vinegar, there is not a wide selection, but this is one of the things he is particular about. Just leave it all up to him and enjoy the day's specialities.

■ Opening hours, last orders
Dinner = 18:00-22:00

■ Annual and weekly closing
Closed Golden week, mid-August, late December-early January and Monday

■ Prices
Dinner = set ¥ 15,000
Service charge = 5%

TEL. 045-433-3154
Nisshin Building Shinkoyasu 3F,
1-8-3 Shinkoyasu, Kanagawa-ku,
Yokohama

Sushi Hamada
鮨 はま田

The owner-chef's restaurant is in Kannai, but he is more committed to *Edomae* sushi than most and, while valuing traditional techniques, he does also try new ideas. Focusing on hand-rolled sushi means the selection of seafood is not especially large; he goes to Tsukiji himself to gather ingredients. Rice is cooked in batches so that it can be served freshly made and is marked by the taste of self-blended vinegar.

■ Opening hours, last orders
Dinner = 17:30-22:00 L.O.20:30

■ Annual and weekly closing
Closed Golden week, mid-August, late December-early January, Sunday and Public Holidays

■ Prices
Dinner = set ¥ 15,750-21,000

TEL. 045–211–2187
2-21-2 Otamachi, Naka-ku, Yokohama

Tenhama
天濱

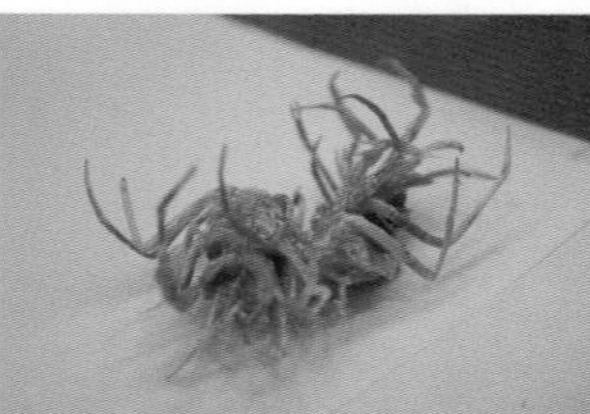

The owner-chef has been honing his skills for over 30 years. He and his wife run the place alone, so proceed into the *tatami* room and announce the reservation name. First comes the fried head and legs, then the body of a lobster straight from the tank, followed by white-fleshed fish, vegetables, *anago* with green tea salt and grated radish, and honey-braised Japanese apricots. The *tencha* is garnished with lime and *wasabi*.

■ Opening hours, last orders
Dinner = 17:30-21:30 L.O.20:30

■ Annual and weekly closing
Closed mid-August, late December-early January, Sunday and Public Holidays

■ Prices
Dinner = set ¥ 13,650

TEL. 045-662-6660
4-48 Otamachi, Naka-ku, Yokohama

JAPANESE TEMPURA

Tenshichi
天七

Yokohama Port may be near but it is still unusual to see a chef in what looks like a sailor's cap. His oil is a mix of refined sugar and roasted sesame oil. Whiting backbone comes with curry salt, and the *anago*, with green tea salt, is served with radish and lemon; low-salt *umeboshi* and fruit *tempura* provide variety and we recommend the *tendon*. The restaurant relocated in 2011; its back counter can be used as a private room.

■ Opening hours, last orders
Lunch = 11:30-15:00
Dinner = 17:00-23:00

■ Annual and weekly closing
Closed mid-August, late December-early January and Sunday

■ Prices
Lunch = set ¥ 3,500
Dinner = set ¥ 8,000-12,000
Service charge = 10%

TEL. 045–681–3376
5-64 Sumiyoshicho, Naka-ku, Yokohama

JAPANESE TEPPANYAKI

Ukai-tei Azamino

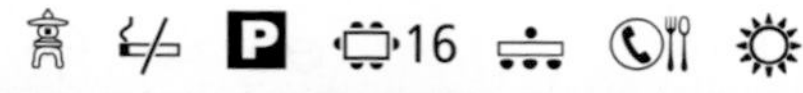

16

Found in an elegant hillside building, this restaurant is enveloped in a resort-like atmosphere and has the feel of an undersea world. French techniques have been incorporated to create an original style. Specialities are rock salt steamed abalone and Ukai beef. At the end comes *somen*, garlic rice with a burnt soy sauce aroma and other eclectic dishes. The private room, for parties of 4 or more, is ideal for special occasions.

■ Opening hours, last orders
Lunch = 12:00-15:00 (L.O.)
Dinner = 15:00-23:00 L.O.21:00

■ Annual and weekly closing
Closed 31 December-4 January

■ Prices
Lunch = set ¥ 6,830-8,400
à la carte ¥ 12,000-15,000
Dinner = set ¥ 10,500-18,900
à la carte ¥ 12,000-15,000
Service charge = 10%

TEL. 045–910–5252
2-14-3 Azaminominami, Aoba-ku, Yokohama

www.ukai.co.jp/azamino

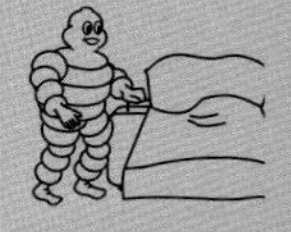

HOTELS

Grand Intercontinental

The building resembles a wind-filled yacht sail and the inside, including the spacious lobby, has a relaxing air. Bedrooms feature light-toned interiors and wicker furniture for a resort-like feel. The Harbour Suite, found at the nose of the V-shaped building, has a bathroom overlooking the harbour. The simple, modern rooms - in black, grey and white – are also suited for business use. Have breakfast facing the ocean.

■ Prices
= ¥ 50,000-120,000
= ¥ 52,000-120,000
Suite = ¥ 120,000-580,000
= ¥ 3,234

Rooms = 555
Suites = 39
Restaurants = 6

TEL. 045–223–2222
FAX. 045-221-0650
1-1-1 Minatomirai, Nishi-ku, Yokohama

www.interconti.co.jp/yokohama

New Grand

Located in front of Yamashita Park, this hotel has been welcoming celebrities from all over the world since 1927. It consists of a main building and a 17-storey tower added in 1991. For an exotic feel, we recommend the Deluxe Twin or larger rooms in the main building. The atmosphere is reminiscent of bygone days, especially in the elegant bar. The impeccable service is just what one would expect from such an established hotel.

■ Prices
🚹 = ¥ 13,860-43,890
🚹🚹 = ¥ 38,115-49,665
Suite = ¥ 92,400-346,500
☕ = ¥ 2,888

Rooms = 237
Suites = 12
Restaurants = 4

TEL. 045–681–1841
FAX. 045-681-1895
10 Yamashitacho, Naka-ku,
Yokohama

www.hotel-newgrand.co.jp

Pan Pacific Yokohama Bay Tokyu

Your eyes will be drawn to the painting stretching from the pillars to the ceiling. The rooms feature simple interiors and bathrooms have shower booths; reserve a room with a balcony, where the salty breeze makes you forget the everyday. The Pacific Floors (23-25) offer extra services such as an exclusive butler and breakfast in the lounge. Other facilities include a salon and Japanese, Western and Chinese restaurants.

■ Prices
🚹 = ¥ 42,000-105,000
🚹🚹 = ¥ 42,000-105,000
Suite = ¥ 125,000-710,000
☕ = ¥ 3,003

Rooms = 454
Suites = 26
Restaurants = 4

TEL. 045–682–2222
FAX. 045-682-2223
2-3-7 Minatomirai, Nishi-ku, Yokohama

http://pphy.co.jp

Richmond

Offering comfort and convenience, this 201-room hotel was opened in 2003 on Bashamichi, which connects Minatomirai-odori with Kannai Station and is within walking distance from China Town and Minatomirai. Situated near JR and subway stations, it is also convenient for business use. The rooms are spacious: single rooms are 18m²; twins 28m². All have new air purifiers, large flat-screen TVs and negative ion hair dryers.

■ Prices
🚹 = ¥ 7,800-27,000
🚹🚹 = ¥ 12,600-43,800
☕ = ¥ 1,000

Rooms = 201
Restaurants = 2

TEL. 045-228-6655
FAX. 045-228-6355
5-59 Sumiyoshicho, Naka-ku, Yokohama

www.richmondhotel.jp/yokohama

Rose

Located near Choyo-mon – this is the largest hotel in China Town. Guest rooms are spacious, with even the smallest being 26.5m^2; beds range from semi-double to king sizes. The Deluxe floor features a tranquil atmosphere, having been created by renowned Hong Kong designer, John Chan. It is close to the popular tourist spots and within walking distance of Yamashita Park, Minatomirai and Yokohama Park, home of Yokohama Stadium.

■ Prices
single = ¥ 27,000-41,000
double = ¥ 32,000-41,000
Suite = ¥ 80,000-90,000
breakfast = ¥ 2,651

Rooms = 174
Suites = 4
Restaurants = 2

TEL. 045–681–3311
FAX. 045-681-5082
77 Yamashitacho, Naka-ku, Yokohama

www.rosehotelyokohama.com

Royal Park

Equipped for a variety of needs, this hotel is located in Yokohama Landmark Tower, the symbol of Minatomirai. The front desk is on the 1st floor; bedrooms are on the 52nd floor and above. The rooms are comfortable and decorated in calm hues, with the exception of the 60th floor, with its modern décor and vivid colours. The large windows provide superb vistas. Breakfast is served on the top floor, 277 metres above ground.

■ Prices
🚹 = ¥ 34,650-60,900
🚹🚹 = ¥ 39,900-66,150
Suite = ¥ 105,000-525,000
☕ = ¥ 2,940
Service = 10%

Rooms = 583
Suites = 20
Restaurants = 6

TEL. 045–221–1111
FAX. 045-224-5153
2-2-1-3 Minatomirai, Nishi-ku, Yokohama

www.yrph.com

Sheraton Yokohama Bay

  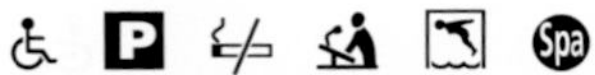  

Just 3 minutes from the West Exit of Yokohama Station, this hotel is also close to department stores. Its lobby is lit by a 'wind'-themed chandelier and the wooden furniture of the elegant guest rooms provides a natural feel, with black veneer adding a modern touch. The express video check-out is a convenient facility. Tower floors (26th and 27th) offer higher levels of service. The fitness room has a pool and sauna.

■ Prices
🚹 = ¥ 26,000-53,000
🚹🚹 = ¥ 36,000-65,000
Suite = ¥ 150,000-250,000
☕ = ¥ 2,800

Rooms = 396
Suites = 2
Restaurants = 5

TEL. 045–411–1111
FAX. 045-411-1343
1-3-23 Kitasaiwai, Nishi-ku,
Yokohama

www.yokohamabay-sheraton.co.jp

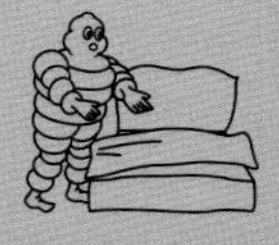

SHONAN

RESTAURANTS
RYOKANS
& HOTELS

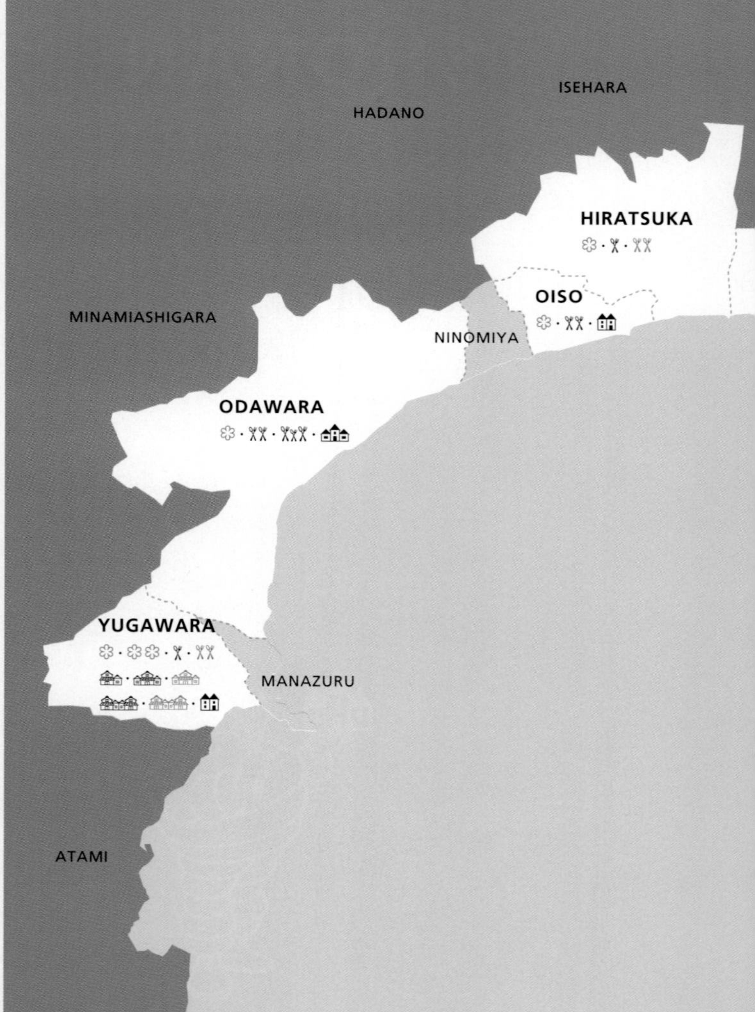
SHONAN AREA
ATSUGI
ISEHARA
HADANO
HIRATSUKA
OISO
MINAMIASHIGARA
NINOMIYA
ODAWARA
YUGAWARA
MANAZURU
ATAMI

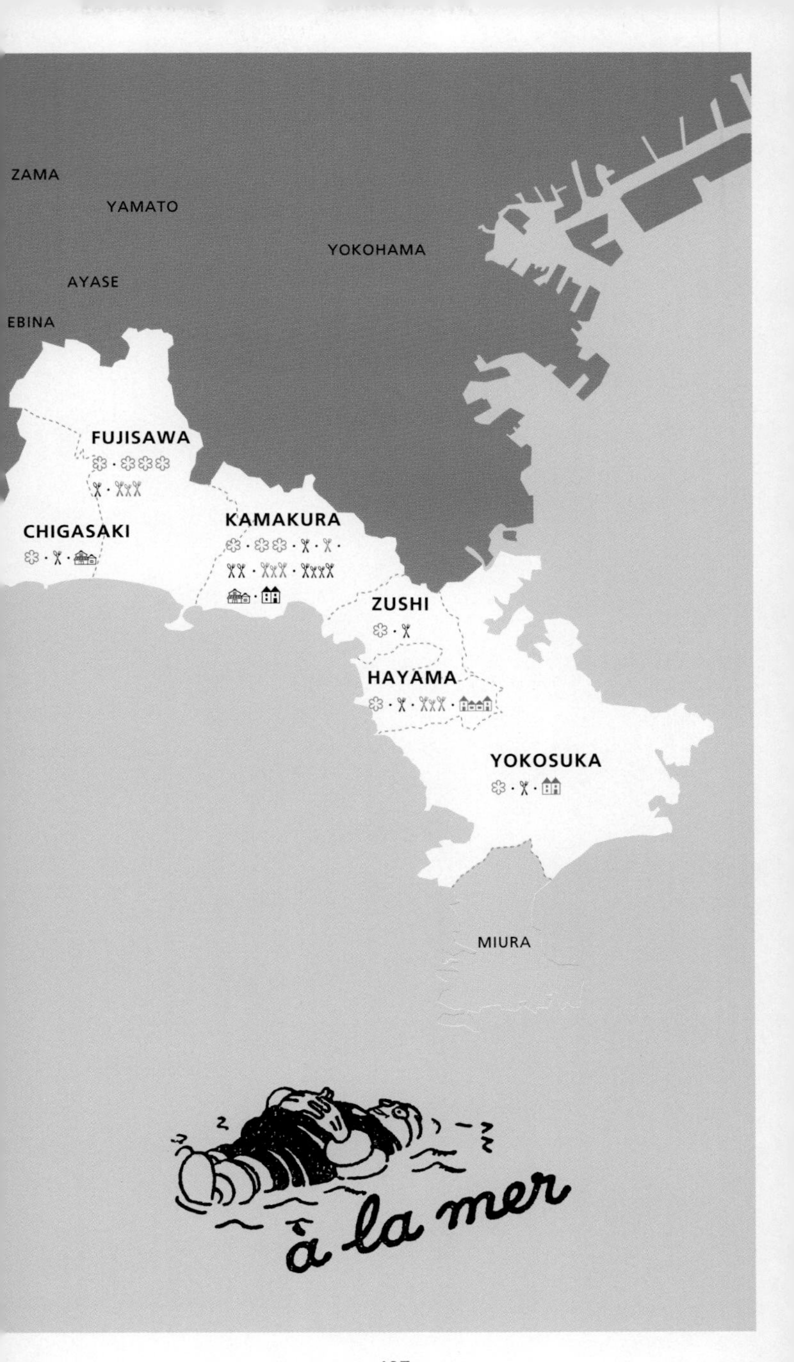
ZAMA
YAMATO
YOKOHAMA
AYASE
EBINA
FUJISAWA
CHIGASAKI
KAMAKURA
ZUSHI
HAYAMA
YOKOSUKA
MIURA
à la mer

RESTAURANTS

STARRED RESTAURANTS

All the restaurants within the Tokyo Yokohama Shonan Guide have one, two or three Michelin Stars and are our way of highlighting restaurants that offer particularly good food.

When awarding stars there are a number of factors we consider: the quality and freshness of the ingredients, the technical skill and flair that goes into their preparation, the clarity of the flavours, the value for money and, ultimately, the taste. Of equal importance is the ability to produce excellent food not once but time and time again. Our inspectors make as many visits as necessary so that you can be sure of this quality and consistency.

A two or three star restaurant has to offer something very special in its cooking that separates it from the rest. Three stars – our highest award – are given to the very best. Cuisines in any style of restaurant and of any nationality are eligible for a star. The decoration, service and comfort levels have no bearing on the award.

Exceptional cuisine, worth a special journey.

One always eats here extremely well, sometimes superbly. Distinctive dishes are precisely executed, using superlative ingredients.

Koan		XXX	Japanese	428

Excellent cuisine, worth a detour.

Skillfully and carefully crafted dishes of outstanding quality.

En	⤴	X	Japanese	419
Sekiyo (ryokan)		🏠	Japanese	455

A very good restaurant in its category.

A place offering cuisine prepared to a consistently high standard.

Bonzo		X	Japanese Soba	418
Gentoan	NEW	XX	Japanese	420
Hachinoki Kitakamakura		XX	Japanese Shojin	421
Hamura		X	Japanese Tempura	422
Herlequin Bis		XX	French	423
Hikagechaya		XXX	Japanese	424
Izumi		X	Japanese Sushi	425
Kamakurayama		XXXX	Japanese Beef Specialities	426
Kisei		X	Japanese	427
Kuikiri Hirayama		X	Japanese	429
Kuniyoshi		XX	Japanese Unagi	430
Pleins d'Herbes	NEW	XXX	French	431

NEW : new entry in the guide
⤴ : restaurant promoted from 1 to 2 stars or 2 to 3 stars

Ren	X	Japanese	432
Shirako	X	Japanese	433
Shunsai Sekine	X	Japanese	434
Soba Hirai	X	Japanese Soba	435
Taku-tei	X	Japanese	436
Tamoto	X	Japanese	437
Ten ichibo	XX	Japanese Tempura	438
Teuchisoba Okamura	X	Japanese Soba	439
Tomoei	XX	Japanese Unagi	440
Tsuruya	X	Japanese Unagi	441
Ukyo	XXX	Japanese	442
Unahei	X	Japanese Unagi	443
Yonekura	X	Japanese	444
Yunoki	X	Japanese	445

RESTAURANTS BY AREA

Chigasaki

Restaurant		Stars	Comfort	Cuisine	Page
Yunoki		✿	X	Japanese	445

Fujisawa

Restaurant		Stars	Comfort	Cuisine	Page
Koan		✿✿✿	XXX	Japanese	428
Kuikiri Hirayama		✿	X	Japanese	429
Soba Hirai		✿	X	Japanese Soba	435
Unahei		✿	X	Japanese Unagi	443

Hayama

Restaurant		Stars	Comfort	Cuisine	Page
Hikagechaya		✿	XXX	Japanese	424
Taku-tei		✿	X	Japanese	436

Hiratsuka

Restaurant		Stars	Comfort	Cuisine	Page
Kisei		✿	X	Japanese	427
Ten ichibo		✿	XX	Japanese Tempura	438

Kamakura

Restaurant		Stars	Comfort	Cuisine	Page
Bonzo		✿	X	Japanese Soba	418
En	↗	✿✿	X	Japanese	419
Gentoan	NEW	✿	XX	Japanese	420
Hachinoki Kitakamakura		✿	XX	Japanese Shojin	421
Izumi		✿	X	Japanese Sushi	425
Kamakurayama		✿	XXXX	Japanese Beef Specialities	426
Pleins d'Herbes	NEW	✿	XXX	French	431
Ren		✿	X	Japanese	432
Tamoto		✿	X	Japanese	437
Tsuruya		✿	X	Japanese Unagi	441
Yonekura		✿	X	Japanese	444

Odawara

Restaurant		Stars	Comfort	Cuisine	Page
Tomoei		✿	XX	Japanese Unagi	440
Ukyo		✿	XXX	Japanese	442

NEW : new entry in the guide
↗ : restaurant promoted from 1 to 2 stars or 2 to 3 stars

RESTAURANTS BY CUISINE TYPE

JAPANESE

En	⤴	✿✿	X	Kamakura	419
Gentoan	NEW	✿	XX	Kamakura	420
Hikagechaya		✿	XXX	Hayama	424
Kisei		✿	X	Hiratsuka	427
Koan		✿✿✿	XXX	Fujisawa	428
Kuikiri Hirayama		✿	X	Fujisawa	429
Ren		✿	X	Kamakura	432
Sekiyo (ryokan)		✿✿	ryokan	Yugawara	455
Shirako		✿	X	Yugawara	433
Shunsai Sekine		✿	X	Yugawara	434
Taku-tei		✿	X	Hayama	436
Tamoto		✿	X	Kamakura	437
Ukyo		✿	XXX	Odawara	442
Yonekura		✿	X	Kamakura	444
Yunoki		✿	X	Chigasaki	445

JAPANESE BEEF SPECIALITIES

Kamakurayama	✿	XXXX	Kamakura	426

JAPANESE SHOJIN

Hachinoki Kitakamakura	✿	XX	Kamakura	421

JAPANESE SOBA

Bonzo	✿	X	Kamakura	418
Soba Hirai	✿	X	Fujisawa	435
Teuchisoba Okamura	✿	X	Zushi	439

JAPANESE SUSHI

Izumi	✿	X	Kamakura	425

NEW : new entry in the guide
⤴ : restaurant promoted from 1 to 2 stars or 2 to 3 stars

JAPANESE TEMPURA

Hamura	✿	X	Yokosuka	422
Ten ichibo	✿	XX	Hiratsuka	438

JAPANESE UNAGI

Kuniyoshi	✿	XX	Oiso	430
Tomoei	✿	XX	Odawara	440
Tsuruya	✿	X	Kamakura	441
Unahei	✿	X	Fujisawa	443

FRENCH

Herlequin Bis	✿	XX	Yugawara	423
Pleins d'Herbes	NEW ✿	XXX	Kamakura	431

RESTAURANTS SERVING LUNCH AND/ OR DINNER FOR ¥ 5,000 AND LESS

Restaurant		Stars	Comfort	Meals	Page
Bonzo		✿	X	lunch & dinner	418
En	↗	✿✿	X	lunch	419
Gentoan	NEW	✿	XX	lunch	420
Hachinoki Kitakamakura		✿	XX	lunch	421
Hamura		✿	X	lunch & dinner	422
Herlequin Bis		✿	XX	lunch	423
Hikagechaya		✿	XXX	lunch & dinner	424
Kisei		✿	X	dinner	427
Kuikiri Hirayama		✿	X	dinner	429
Kuniyoshi		✿	XX	lunch	430
Pleins d'Herbes	NEW	✿	XXX	lunch	431
Ren		✿	X	lunch & dinner	432
Shirako		✿	X	lunch & dinner	433
Shunsai Sekine		✿	X	dinner	434
Soba Hirai		✿	X	lunch & dinner	435
Taku-tei		✿	X	lunch	436
Tamoto		✿	X	lunch	437
Teuchisoba Okamura		✿	X	lunch & dinner	439
Tomoei		✿	XX	lunch & dinner	440
Tsuruya		✿	X	lunch & dinner	441
Ukyo		✿	XXX	lunch & dinner	442
Unahei		✿	X	lunch & dinner	443

NEW : new entry in the guide
↗ : restaurant promoted from 1 to 2 stars or 2 to 3 stars

Bonzo
梵蔵

The thin *juwari* noodles prepared by this young owner-chef are smooth and firm. First, try the *juwari* as-is to enjoy the fragrance, then add salt to savour the sweetness and finally, dip it in the seasoned sauce; last comes rich *sobayu*. Drinking snacks are also good, like *ayu-miso*, *goma-dofu* and *tamago-yaki*. If there are a few in your party, we also recommend the *kamoyaki*. Reservations are only accepted for dinner.

■ Opening hours, last orders
11:30-21:00 L.O.20:30

■ Annual and weekly closing
Closed early January, mid-August and Thursday except Public Holidays

■ Prices

Lunch =	à la carte	¥ 1,200-3,500
Dinner =	set	¥ 5,000
	à la carte	¥ 1,200-3,500

TEL. 0467-73-7315
3-17-33 Zaimokuza, Kamakura City

http://kamakurabonzo.blog102.fc2.com

En
円

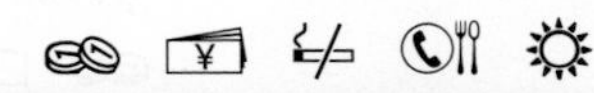

From a window seat on the second floor, one can enjoy the view of the Byakurochi pond in front of Engaku-ji Temple. The simple arrangements accentuate the inherent appeal of the seasonal ingredients, and unusual combinations bring out their flavours; try the hiryuzu and eggplant *takiawase* with bamboo shoots and also good is the grilled trout with *kinome* vinegar. Dinner requires reservations at least a day in advance.

■ Opening hours, last orders
Lunch = 11:30-14:00 (L.O.)
Dinner = 17:00-19:00 (L.O.)

■ Annual and weekly closing
Closed mid-August, late December-early January and Monday

■ Prices
Lunch = set ¥ 3,675-8,400
Dinner = set ¥ 5,250-10,500

TEL.0467-23-6232
2F, 501 Yamanouchi, Kamakura City
www.kitakamakura-en.com

Gentoan NEW
幻董庵

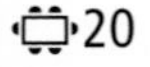

Found within a 2-storey 80-year-old house with antiques, this restaurant sits on a small hill in a residential area. The owner-chef uses traditional techniques but adds his own touches, making use of the flavour of the stock. Set menus are comprised of 7-8 items and conclude with sushi, *chazuke* or other specialities prepared with rice cooked in a pot. Enjoy the meal while listening to the sounds of birds at the foot of the mountain.

■ Opening hours, last orders
Lunch = 11:30-14:30 (L.O.)
Dinner = 18:00-21:00 (L.O.)

■ Annual and weekly closing
Closed late December-early January and Monday except Public Holidays

■ Prices
Lunch = set ¥ 3,675-8,400
Dinner = set ¥ 7,350-18,900
Private room fee = ¥ 5,250 (lunch)
Service charge = 10% (dinner)

TEL. 0467-43-5695
823 Yamanouchi, Kamakura City

Hachinoki Kitakamakura
鉢の木 北鎌倉

20

Opened in 1979 as somewhere to enjoy Buddhist cuisine in a *kaiseki* format, it uses only vegetables, including soybeans and seaweed. The turnip in winter, *kintoki* carrot and deep-fried tofu *takiawase* are brilliantly coloured; their flavours enhanced by stock. The speciality is the *Enmei Fukusa*: 7 kinds of fruits and vegetables fried in *yuba*. During hydrangea season, pure white tofu is garnished with vegetable-coloured gelatine.

■ Opening hours, last orders
Lunch = 11:30-14:30 (L.O.)
Sat. and Sun. 11:00-15:00 (L.O.)
Dinner = 17:00-19:00 (L.O.)

■ Annual and weekly closing
Closed late December-early January and Wednesday

■ Prices
Lunch = set ¥ 2,625-7,350
Dinner = set ¥ 5,250-10,500
Private room fee = 10%
Service charge = 10%

TEL.0467–23–3722
350 Yamanouchi, Kamakura City
www.hachinoki.co.jp

Hamura
葉むら

Kunio Sekizawa has run his own restaurant for nearly 30 years. Without doubt, it is the consistent craftsman-like way he does things that has earned him the support of his regulars. Despite being in Sagami Bay, most of the seafood comes from Tsukiji; he goes twice a week and selects it himself. The frying oil is a blend of two types of sesame oil and cottonseed oil. The *kakiage* features plenty of *kobashira* and *koebi*.

■ Opening hours, last orders
Lunch = 12:00-14:00 (L.O.)
Dinner = 17:30-20:00 (L.O.)
Sat., Sun. and Public Holidays
17:00-20:00 (L.O.)

■ Annual and weekly closing
Closed mid-August, late December-early January and Monday except Public Holidays

■ Prices

Lunch = set	¥ 2,100-8,400
Dinner = set	¥ 2,100-8,400

TEL. 046-855-5222
4293 Akiya, Yokosuka City

www.tempura-hamura.sakura.ne.jp

FRENCH YUGAWARA

Herlequin Bis
エルルカン ビス

Surrounded by beautiful scenery, this restaurant is like a hideaway. Fusing traditional French cuisine with Japanese theory and techniques, the chef serves mild, simple dishes. With the emphasis on creativity, the crystal water sauce he uses is an original blend that accentuates the flavour of the vegetables and shellfish. He also has experience with pastry making; a typical dessert is coconut-flavoured Brazilian pudding.

■ Opening hours, last orders
Lunch = 11:30-14:00 (L.O.)
Dinner = 17:30-20:30 (L.O.)
Sat., Sun. and Public Holidays
18:00-20:30 (L.O.)

■ Annual and weekly closing
Closed Wednesday

■ Prices
Lunch = set ¥ 3,675-5,250
à la carte ¥ 6,000-10,000
Dinner = set ¥ 5,775-12,600
à la carte ¥ 6,000-10,000
Service charge = 10%

TEL. 0465-62-3633
744-49 Miyakami, Yugawaramachi, Ashigarashimo-gun

www.herlequin.com

Hikagechaya
日影茶屋

60

Founded as a *chaya* in the Edo period, this historic restaurant was also a *ryokan* for a time and has been the setting for several novels. It's 3,300m^2 and the Japanese house, which is registered as a cultural asset, has table seating and an annexe with a *tatami* room. Specialities are dishes using local fish and vegetables. Filefish is served with liver as *sashimi* or sometimes deep-fried; Miura vegetables are served as *nimono*.

■ Opening hours, last orders
Lunch = 11:30-14:30
Dinner = 17:00-21:00

■ Annual and weekly closing
Closed late December-early January and Wednesday except Public Holidays

■ Prices
Lunch = set ¥ 3,360-15,750
à la carte ¥ 5,000-15,000
Dinner = set ¥ 3,360-15,750
à la carte ¥ 5,000-15,000
Private room fee = ¥ 2,100-8,400
Service charge = 10%

TEL. 046-875-0014
16 Horiuchi, Hayamamachi, Miura-gun

Izumi
以ず美

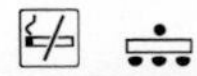

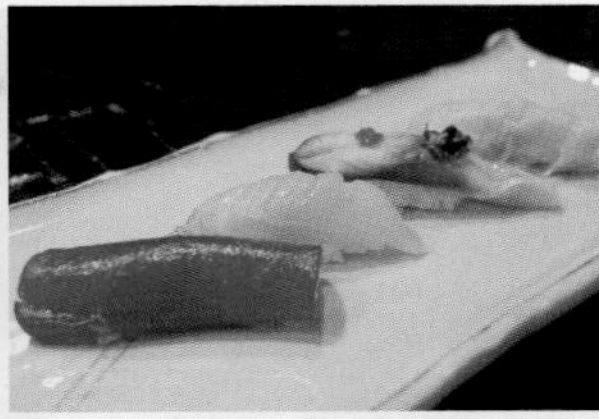

The *uni* is eaten with salt to bring out its refined sweetness. The sushi rice has a mild taste and several types of vinegar are used with the various items; bamboo shoot rice balls are aromatic; squid is cut in a wave-like shape. Enjoy chatting with the owner over his *Edomae* sushi made in the traditional way, but with a twist. For weekend lunches, it is best to arrive by noon. Every detail speaks of the owner-chef's taste.

■ Opening hours, last orders
Lunch = Sat. and Sun. 12:00-14:00
Dinner = 18:00-22:00 L.O.20:00

■ Annual and weekly closing
Closed late January-early February and Wednesday

■ Prices
Lunch = set ¥ 15,000-20,000
Dinner = set ¥ 15,000-20,000

TEL.0467–22–3737
2-17-18 Hase, Kamakura City

Kamakurayama
鎌倉山

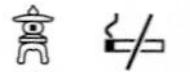

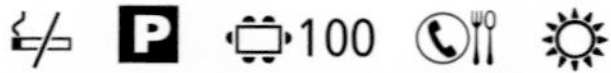

Founded in 1970, this restaurant has an elegant atmosphere that fuses Japanese and Western sensibilities; its tables are decorated with orchids. Well-aged meat, selected for its marbling and taste, is cooked tender. It is then sliced in front of the customer, revealing its beautiful red colour. There are two types of sauce: consommé based and soy sauce with garlic. Dessert is served in the courtyard when the weather allows.

■ Opening hours, last orders
Lunch = 11:30-15:00 L.O.14:00
Dinner = 17:00-22:00 L.O.20:00

■ Annual and weekly closing
Closed late December-early January

■ Prices
Lunch = set ¥ 5,250-16,800
à la carte ¥ 20,000-25,000
Dinner = set ¥ 10,500-36,750
à la carte ¥ 20,000-25,000
Private room fee = ¥ 10,500-31,500
Service charge = 12%

TEL. 0467-31-5454
3-11-1 Kamakurayama,
Kamakura City

www.roastbeef.jp/ho.html

Kisei
樹勢

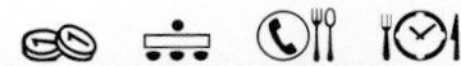

The owner-chef keeps a row of cups behind the counter for his regulars but gives newcomers just as warm a welcome. He trained for 14 years at a kappo restaurant in Tokyo and his hand-written menu features about 30 items; the *chawanmushi*, *fugu kara-age* and steak are particularly popular. When in season, there is also a *tora-fugu* set menu. The couple opened the restaurant in 1997 – the phone number (22-1997) is a coincidence.

■ Opening hours, last orders
Dinner = 17:00-23:00 L.O.22:30

■ Annual and weekly closing
Closed mid-August, late December-early January and Sunday

■ Prices
Dinner = set ¥ 5,250-15,750
à la carte ¥ 3,500-8,000
Seat charge = ¥ 1,050/person
(à la carte only)

TEL. 0463-22-1997
7-2 Akashicho, Hiratsuka City

Koan
幸庵

The owner-chef weaves creativity into traditional cuisine, coming up with new combinations of flavours and textures. He says he became a chef after being inspired by the faces of people enjoying meals. That sentiment can be seen in every detail as there is harmony between the cooking, serving dishes, arrangements and hospitality. In summer, wind chimes create a feeling of coolness; in autumn, leaves are used as decoration.

■ Opening hours, last orders
Lunch = 11:30-15:00 L.O.13:30
Dinner = 17:30-23:00 L.O.20:00

■ Annual and weekly closing
Closed mid-August and late December-early January

■ Prices
Lunch = set ¥ 5,800-18,000
Dinner = set ¥ 8,600-18,000
Private room fee = ¥ 1,000/person (dinner)

TEL. 0466-50-6226
2-8 Kugenumahanazawacho, Fujisawa City

www.kouan.info

Kuikiri Hirayama
喰い切り ひら山

The owner-chef opened his restaurant with the motto 'you are what you cook' and believes 'sake should have no additives and is better warm'; he serves Japanese cuisine and *junmai-shu*. Most of his seafood is from Sagami Bay but he also orders from Tsukiji. First-timers should try the well-priced set menus. His Tokyo training is evident in dishes like abalone *tempura*, and *sumashijiru* with *uni-shinjo* and early ripening mushrooms.

■ Opening hours, last orders
Dinner = 18:00-23:00 L.O.22:00

■ Annual and weekly closing
Closed mid-August and late December-early January

■ Prices
Dinner = set ¥ 3,675-18,900
à la carte ¥ 5,000-8,000
Seat charge = ¥ 525/person
(à la carte only)

TEL. 0466-50-4910
3-22 Kugenumahanazawacho,
Fujisawa City

Kuniyoshi
國よし

Kuniyoshi was founded in 1803 as a tavern before later becoming an *unagi* restaurant and the current third-generation owner-chef carries on the traditions passed down to him. Although somewhat pricey, we recommend the 'Tokusenunagi' which features *unagi* raised for more than two years; in Kanto style, it is split open, steamed and then chargrilled with *kishu-binchotan*. A little sauce is applied to bring out the flavour.

■ Opening hours, last orders
Lunch = 11:30-14:00 (L.O.)
Dinner = 17:00-18:00 (L.O.)
Sat., Sun. and Public Holidays
17:00-19:00 (L.O.)

■ Annual and weekly closing
Closed late December-early January,
Wednesday, 2nd and 4th Thursday

■ Prices
Lunch = set ¥ 8,000-8,500
à la carte ¥ 4,200-7,500
Dinner = set ¥ 8,500-12,000
à la carte ¥ 5,500-7,500
Service charge = 10%

TEL. 0463-61-0423
1085 Oiso, Oisomachi, Naka-gun

www.oiso-kuniyoshi.com

Pleins d'Herbes NEW
プランデルブ

Set in a residential area, this restaurant is operated jointly by a manager and chef who met in Karuizawa. The ingredients, primarily vegetables from Kamakura, are prepared traditionally and, as the name suggests, the kitchen makes good use of herbs and seasonings. Although the set menus change seasonally, *pâté en croûte* and sautéed foie gras with seasonal fruits are available year round. The Shonan pork is also popular.

■ Opening hours, last orders
Lunch = 12:00-14:00 (L.O.)
Dinner = 17:30-20:00 (L.O.)

■ Annual and weekly closing
Closed late August-early September, late December-early January and Tuesday

■ Prices
Lunch = set ¥ 3,500-7,000
Dinner = set ¥ 7,000-9,000
Service charge = 10%

TEL.0467-47-4567
3-32-11 Kajiwara, Kamakura City
www.pdh.jp

Ren
連

The owner-chef has put together a menu of seafood and local vegetables and works on adapting to the times – he does not step out of the bounds of tradition, but does incorporate modern touches, such as a plate of banana peppers. The handmade soba and desserts are prepared by his wife; sake is served in cups made by her father. The menu is reasonably priced and it is easier getting reservations for dinner than it is for lunch.

■ Opening hours, last orders
Lunch = 11:30-15:00 L.O.14:00
Dinner = 17:30-22:00 L.O.20:00

■ Annual and weekly closing
Closed Golden week, mid-August, late December-early January, Monday and 3rd Tuesday

■ Prices
Lunch = set ¥ 2,100-3,990
Dinner = set ¥ 3,990-7,350

TEL.0467–32–6730
155-1 Tokiwa, Kamakura City

Shirako
しらこ

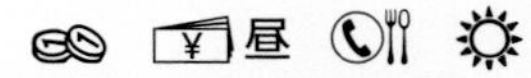

For the simple *kappo* cuisine, seafood comes primarily from nearby Manazuru Port. The lunch sets are popular, but the restaurant really shines at night. In early summer, enjoy lightly boiled sweet Hokkai shrimp; in winter *shabu-shabu*, featuring golden eye snapper caught that day; and not to be missed is the *takikomi-gohan* with raw whitebait or *sakuraebi* in early spring. The husband and wife team create a homely atmosphere.

■ Opening hours, last orders
Lunch = 11:30-13:45 (L.O.)
Dinner = 18:00-21:00 (L.O.)

■ Annual and weekly closing
Closed mid-August, late December-early January and Tuesday except Public Holidays

■ Prices

Lunch =	set	¥ 1,575-3,150
	à la carte	¥ 3,000-5,000
Dinner =	set	¥ 4,200-10,500
	à la carte	¥ 4,000-6,000

TEL. 0465-63-6363
1-5-15 Doi, Yugawaramachi, Ashigarashimo-gun

www.sirako.net

Shunsai Sekine
旬菜 せきね

The owner-chef has been cooking for more than 50 years and opened this *kappo*-style restaurant in 2007. There are set menus, but we recommend trying a selection from the list of over 30 items on the menu. Particularly noteworthy are the 'seasonal vegetable *Takiawase*', the carefully kneaded 'Warabi Dofu' and 'rainbow salad' with seven vegetables. There are also creative dishes like escargot-style *sazae* and seasonal fruit soup.

■ Opening hours, last orders
Dinner = 17:00-21:00

■ Annual and weekly closing
Closed 1 January, Tuesday and Wednesday

■ Prices
Dinner = set ¥ 5,000-7,000
à la carte ¥ 4,500-7,000
Seat charge = ¥ 800/person
(à la carte only)

TEL. 0465-62-5397
1-10-18 Doi, Yugawaramachi, Ashigarashimo-gun

Soba Hirai
蕎麦 ひら井

Among the *soba* shops at Fujisawa Honmachi Station is one run by two brothers; the younger one is in charge of cooking. Not satisfied with just training at a Tokyo restaurant, he also studied buckwheat cultivation in Niseko, Hokkaido. He buys whole, unpolished buckwheat, grinds it himself and uses a 9:1 ratio of buckwheat to flour. The delicate ultrafine soba goes well with the sauce prepared with high-quality *katsuo-bushi*.

■ Opening hours, last orders
Lunch = 11:30-14:30 (L.O.)
Dinner = 17:30-21:00 (L.O.)

■ Annual and weekly closing
Closed early January, mid-August and Tuesday

■ Prices
Lunch = set ¥ 3,000
à la carte ¥ 1,200-3,000
Dinner = set ¥ 3,000
à la carte ¥ 1,200-3,000

TEL. 0466-24-5091
3-2-5 Fujisawa, Fujisawa City

Taku-tei
琢亭

Ingredients come from a vendor the owner-chef has known since his days of training; fresh vegetables are picked that morning and the owner-chef's wife collects them from the farm herself. From a nearby fishing port, the barracuda and hairtail are scored and flash-grilled in order to bring out the flavour between the skin and flesh. The annotated list of sake is handwritten by his wife, who is a licensed master of sake.

■ Opening hours, last orders
Lunch = 12:00-15:00 L.O.13:30
Dinner = 18:00-21:30 L.O.20:00

■ Annual and weekly closing
Closed late December-early January and Monday except Public Holidays

■ Prices
Lunch = set ¥ 3,000-6,800
Dinner = set ¥ 7,350-13,500
Service charge = 5% (dinner)

TEL. 046-807-6157
925-3 Isshiki, Hayamamachi, Miura-gun

Tamoto
田茂戸

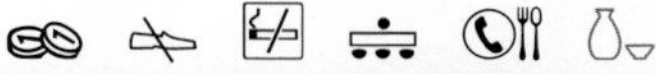

Adhering to the basics of Japanese cuisine, the food occasionally pushes boundaries but is never eccentric. There is much creativity, like pigs' feet and ginger, tapioca *manju* with crabmeat, and duck wrapped in bamboo; the fried greenling and spring cabbage with micro tomatoes is a perfect fit for the elegant plate. The blend of modern exterior, warm bark interior, food, service and price might well turn you into a regular.

■ Opening hours, last orders
Lunch = 11:30-14:30 L.O.13:30
Dinner = 17:00-22:00 L.O.21:00

■ Annual and weekly closing
Closed mid-August, late December-early January, Sunday and Public Holidays

■ Prices
Lunch = set ¥ 3,800-6,800
Dinner = set ¥ 6,800

TEL.0467–24–0283
8-25 Sakanoshita, Kamakura City

JAPANESE TEMPURA HIRATSUKA

Ten ichibo
天一坊

8

The young owner-chef trained at a *kappo* restaurant in Kyoto and follows in his father's footsteps, serving *tempura* and Japanese cuisine. Using mostly local ingredients, the *tempura* is fried in golden sesame oil to a yellowish colour and goes well with both the Izu Oshima natural salt and the salty sauce. The dignified atmosphere makes it suitable for entertaining guests and parties of 8 or more can reserve the entire counter.

■ Opening hours, last orders
Lunch = 11:30-13:30 (L.O.)
Dinner = 17:30-20:30 (L.O.)

■ Annual and weekly closing
Closed late August, 31 December, 1 January, mid-January and Sunday

■ Prices
Lunch = Set ¥ 5,250-6,300
Dinner = Set ¥ 5,250-15,750

TEL. 0463-35-5678
8-3 Ryujogaoka, Hiratsuka City

Teuchisoba Okamura
手打蕎麦 おかむら

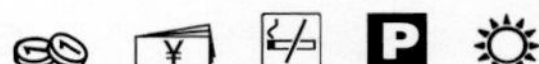  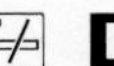 

Inspired by the *soba* of an expert cook, the owner-chef opened his restaurant aged 55. He grinds whole buckwheat with its outer shell and prepares *soba* in a 2:8 ratio of buckwheat to flour. He places importance on balancing texture, aroma and sauce. Aged *kaeshi* sauce is mixed with stock made from *kombu*, dried *shiitake* and thin shaved *katsuo*, and flour is added to the *sobayu*, which contains a large amount of nutritious rutin.

■ Opening hours, last orders
Lunch = 11:30-15:00 L..O.14:30
Dinner = Tue.-Sun. 17:30-20:00
L.O. 19:30

■ Annual and weekly closing
Closed early January, Tuesday and Wednesday except Public Holidays

■ Prices
Lunch = à la carte ¥ 1,500-3,000
Dinner = à la carte ¥ 1,500-3,000

TEL. 046-872-9803
6-1326-74 Sakurayama, Zushi City

www.okamura.zushi.ne.jp

Tomoei
友栄

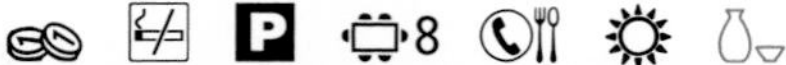

Upon arrival, you'll be greeted by an energetic voice from the kitchen at this lively and welcoming restaurant. First, enjoy some sake with snacks like salted *unagi* liver or grilled *unagi* liver in egg yolk. In winter, try the natural *unagi* grilled in *miso*. End the meal with *unaju* featuring plump *unagi* on rice covered in a lightly sweetened sauce. We also recommend the *shirayaki* eaten with *sanshomiso*, *yuzu* pepper and *wasabi*.

■ Opening hours, last orders
Lunch = 11:00-14:30 (L..O.)
Dinner = 17:00-20:30 (L..O.)
Sun. and Public Holidays
11:00-19:00 (L..O.)

■ Annual and weekly closing
Closed late December-early January, 3rd week of January, late September, Thursday except Public Holidays and Friday except Public Holidays

■ Prices
Lunch = set ¥ 6,300-10,500
à la carte ¥ 3,500-6,000
Dinner = set ¥ 6,300-10,500
à la carte ¥ 3,500-6,000

TEL. 0465-23-1011
157 Kazamatsuri, Odawara City

www15.ocn.ne.jp/~tomoei

Tsuruya
つるや

It opened in 1929 and has welcomed famous literary men of Kamakura like Yasunari Kawabata and Masaaki Tachihara. Preparation begins once an order is taken, so the wait is about 40 minutes. Open the Kamakura-style tiered box to reveal the fatty *unagi*, cooked over a charcoal flame. The moderately sweet sauce, fluffy *unagi* and tasty rice come together in complete harmony. Delivery is available, but it is best right off the grill.

■ Opening hours, last orders
11:30-19:00 (L.O.)

■ Annual and weekly closing
Closed 1 January and Tuesday except Public Holidays

■ Prices
à la carte ¥ 2,310-5,000

TEL.0467-22-0727
3-3-27 Yuigahama, Kamakura City

Ukyo
右京

This elegant *ryotei* stands in a quiet residential area and its *sukiya*-style interior exudes a dignified atmosphere; there is table, counter and private room seating. As expected, the owner-chef serves traditional *kaiseki* cuisine, lightly seasoned, and uses vegetables from Kyoto and local Odawara. For first timers, we recommend the 'Kiyose kaiseki'. In December 2011 he plans to open a Japanese confectionery shop next door.

■ Opening hours, last orders
Lunch = 11:30-14:30 (L.O.)
Dinner = 17:00-22:00 L.O.20:00

■ Annual and weekly closing
Closed late December-early January and Monday except Public Holidays

■ Prices
Lunch = set ¥ 1,890-6,300
Dinner = set ¥ 3,780-13,650
Private room fee = 10%

TEL.0465-23-7878
4-3-29 Honcho, Odawara City
www.ukyo.jp

Unahei
うな平

Since its founding in 1959, the sauce and grilling technique have remained the same. The rice finishes cooking when the tender *unagi* comes off the grill, completing the hot *unaju*; the lightly sweetened sauce creates a balance between the *unagi* and rice. The personalities of the conscientious owner-chef and his cheerful wife are also reasons for the restaurant's popularity. Due to the current *unagi* shortage, prices may vary.

■ Opening hours, last orders
Lunch = 11:30-14:00 L.O.13:30
Dinner = 17:00-20:00 L.O. 19:00

■ Annual and weekly closing
Closed late December-early January, Wednesday, 1st and 3rd Tuesday

■ Prices
Lunch = à la carte ¥ 2,520-3,675
Dinner = à la carte ¥ 2,520-3,675

TEL. 0466-36-7070
2-2-8 Higashikaigan, Tsujido, Fujisawa City

Yonekura
米倉

Near the main gate of Zuisenji Temple; look for the maple tree and bamboo fence. Carefully prepared *hassun* is garnished with a seasonal flower; on certain days in spring comes unforgettable soup with fluffy *shinjo* in *katsuo*-flavoured stock. In winter, set menus are given a twist with stone-cooked meat and seafood steeped in *shuto*. The meal ends with smooth *soba* made by the owner-chef. Creative sweets are another treat.

■ Opening hours, last orders
Lunch = 12:00-14:30
Dinner = 17:30-21:00

■ Annual and weekly closing
Closed late December-early January

■ Prices
Lunch = set ¥ 5,250-15,750
Dinner = set ¥ 6,300-15,750
Service charge = 5% (dinner)

TEL.0467-25-2395
728-20 Nikaido, Kamakura City

Yunoki
柚の木

Opened in 1980, Yunoki serves simple yet savoury dishes. The proprietress changes the menu monthly, and seasonal *haiku* serve as themes for the menus. The *tsukuri* features whatever seafood is caught in Sagami Bay on that particular day. Using creative combinations of familiar ingredients, whatever dish she creates remains in the memory. The meal concludes with carefully prepared *usucha* and the handmade sweets are also popular.

■ Opening hours, last orders
Lunch = 12:00-14:00 L.O.13:00
Dinner = 18:00-21:00 L.O. 19:30

■ Annual and weekly closing
Closed mid-August, late December-early January, Wednesday and 3rd Tuesday

■ Prices
Lunch = set ¥ 5,250-21,000
Dinner = set ¥ 10,500-21,000
Service charge = 10%

TEL. 0467-86-6828
2-14 Asahigaoka, Chigasaki City

RYOKANS

Chigasakikan
茅ヶ崎館

Built in 1899, this inn is a registered cultural property. The paper ceiling and coloured glass of the bathroom were undamaged by the Great Kanto earthquake in 1923 and offer a glimpse into the past. All rooms face the garden, and a pleasant sea breeze blows from the ocean nearby. The annexe is best for families. This was the favourite hotel of film director and writer Yasujiro Ozu and many scripts were conceived in Room 2.

■ Prices
Price per person with dinner:
¥ 11,500-13,500

Set Menu = ¥ 3,675-8,400

■ Rooms = 10

■ Annual and weekly closing
Closed late December-early January

TEL. 0467-82-2003
FAX. 0467-82-3133
3-8-5 Nakakaigan, Chigasaki City

www.chigasakikan.co.jp

Fukazawa
深沢

    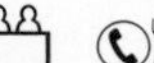

Just 5 minutes from the station, Fukazawa is like a traditional Kyoto inn, in the middle of the downtown area, and the soft sound of *akoto* can be heard as you enter. Both the spacious 'Takinoyu' with its waterfall, and 'Chojunoyu' with its decorative crane and turtles, are recommended. 'Shoten', the open-air bath, can be exclusively reserved. Dinner is served in your room, but breakfast is in the 52-*tatami* 'Hiten' hall.

■ Prices
Price per person with dinner:
¥ 14,850-37,800

Set Menu = ¥ 5,250-20,475

■ Rooms = 10

TEL. 0465-64-0150
FAX. 0465-62-5457
5-4-6 Doi, Yugawaramachi,
Ashigarashimo-gun

www.ryokan-fukazawa.co.jp

Fukiya
ふきや

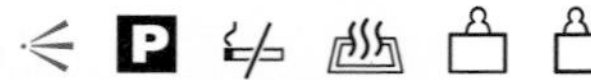

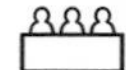

Taking advantage of the south-facing slope, guest rooms offer good views and a tranquil *sukiya*-style design. There are various types, from large rooms facing the garden to compact ones for those travelling alone. Features include uniquely designed ceramic wash bowls and *fusuma* handles, but care is also taken to provide modern comforts. The 7 different styles of bath, including 3 open-air baths, feature clear spring water.

■ Prices
Price per person with dinner:
¥ 28,500-51,400

■ Rooms = 20

TEL. 0465-62-1000
FAX. 0465-63-6594
398 Miyakami, Yugawaramachi,
Ashigarashimo-gun

www.yugawarafukiya.com

Homura
秀邑

Surrounded by the beautiful natural scenery of Okuyugawara, famous for its crimson foliage, this inn styles itself as the ideal holiday home. It has just two guest rooms, roughly 100m^2 each. The view from the large window includes a garden with a green mountain in the background. The high quality hot spring water is gentle on the skin, and there's an open-air bath in one corner of the garden beside the Fujikigawa River.

■ Prices
Price per person with dinner:
¥ 55,000-66,000

■ Rooms = 2

TEL. 0465-63-6641
683-18 Miyakami, Yugawaramachi, Ashigarashimo-gun

www.okuyugawara.jp

Kaihin-so NEW
かいひん荘

The western-style part of this beachfront inn, built in 1924 as a private residence, is a registered cultural property. On the 1st floor is the lobby and salon, and on the 2nd floor are 2 western-style rooms, 'Ran-no-ma' being the most popular. All rooms in the new building are Japanese-style, with alcoves; the 15-*tatami* 'Takenoma' looks out on the garden. A book by former Prime Minister Eisaku Sato is placed at the entrance.

■ Prices
Price per person with dinner:
¥ 18,900-36,750

Set Menu = ¥ 6,000-15,000

■ Rooms = 14

TEL. 0467-22-0960
FAX. 0467-25-6324
4-8-14 Yuigahama, Kamakura City
www.kaihinso.jp

Kamata
加満田

Roughly 16,530m^2 plot of land along the Fujikigawa River is called Kamata Garden; enjoy the scenery all year, from green leaves in spring to fireflies in summer and crimson foliage in autumn. Bath water is drawn from 2 private hot springs; it is heated but not filtered or disinfected. Each guest room is different - some are favourites of artists and writers. Drawings of *kappa* by manga artist Kon Shimizu decorate the walls.

■ Prices
Price per person with dinner:
¥ 23,100-36,750

Set Menu = ¥ 15,000-18,000

■ Rooms = 13

TEL. 0465-62-2151
FAX. 0465-62-9125
784 Miyakami, Yugawaramachi,
Ashigarashimo-gun

www.kamata-oku.com

Sansuiro
山翠楼

Built in the spacious *sukiya*-style, this inn comprises 4 different wings, from Jurakudai with mainly 12-*tatami* guest rooms to Momoyamadai with 2 rooms of a combined size of over 20 *tatami* mats. The Japanese and Western combination rooms face the garden and come with a *tsukimidai*. The'Ozora' open-air bath on the roof is available to men and women at different times. From your room watch the mountain scenery change by the hour.

■ Prices
Price per person with dinner:
¥ 30,600-100,950

Set Menu = ¥ 15,750-21,000

■ Rooms = 57

TEL. 0465-63-1111
FAX. 0465-63-1116
673 Miyakami, Yugawaramachi,
Ashigarashimo-gun

www.sansuirou.co.jp

Sekiyo
石葉

Accented with decorative pieces that will have you smiling, the refined *sukiya* design of the rooms blends with a modern interior, for an atmosphere that soothes and relaxes. 'Iwato' is popular with groups and foreign guests; the two 10-*tatami* rooms have a moon-viewing platform outside, and the flowers on the plum, peach and cherry trees are beautiful to look at. Creative and carefully prepared *kaiseki* cuisine is served.

■ Prices
Price per person with dinner:
¥ 29,025-70,000

Set Menu = ¥ 23,250-29,025

■ Rooms = 9

TEL. 0465-62-3808
FAX. 0465-63-5707
749 Miyakami, Yugawaramachi,
Ashigarashimo-gun

www.sekiyou.com

Tsubaki
海石榴

The exquisite gate is surrounded by green leaves and all guest rooms are named after camellia; most are 12-*tatami* in size. There are also Japanese and Western-style combination rooms and variously sized rooms with open-air baths or wooden decks. Capacity is kept low for a relaxed atmosphere. There is also a comfortable lobby, a bathing area with an open-air bath and sauna, and other facilities like a bar and beauty salon.

■ Prices
Price per person with dinner:
¥ 45,300-144,700

Set Menu = ¥ 21,000-31,500

■ Rooms = 29

TEL. 0465-63-3333
FAX. 0465-63-6640
776 Miyakami, Yugawaramachi,
Ashigarashimo-gun

www.tubaki.net

Yui
結唯

This hidden away inn by Fujikigawa River has just five rooms, each with a 15-*tatami* main room and 6-*tatami* anteroom. The big wall to wall and floor to ceiling window adds to the sense of openness and in early summer you can watch fireflies dancing outside. Both the baths and drainboards in the rooms are made from *hinoki*. The natural, clear hot spring water is soft to the touch. Meals are served in the dining room downstairs.

■ Prices
Price per person with dinner:
¥ 29,925-36,750

■ Rooms = 5

TEL. 0465-63-6643
683-25 Miyakami, Yugawaramach,
Ashigarashimo-gun

www.yui.okuyugawara.jp

HOTELS

Hilton Resort & Spa

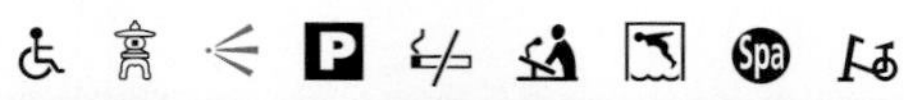

Let the green trees and blue sea and sky refresh you physically and mentally at this hotel, located atop a verdant hill, where every room enjoys a view of the ocean. In addition to western-style rooms, there are Japanese-style rooms, combinations and maisonette-type cottages suitable for families. It also promises fun for all ages with ample recreational and leisure facilities, ranging from tennis courts to karaoke rooms.

■ Prices
🚹 = ¥ 15,000-40,000
🚹🚹 = ¥ 26,000-165,000

Rooms = 172
Restaurants = 1

TEL. 0465-29-1000
FAX. 0465-28-1233
583-1 Nebukawa, Odawara City

www.hiltonodawara.jp

La Cienega

Relax and enjoy the luxury of doing nothing at this resort hotel at the base of the Manazuru peninsula, where all rooms have a view of Sagami Bay. Even the standard rooms have $37m^2$ of floor space and a balcony where you can enjoy tea time while taking in the sea breeze. Although there are no hot springs, beside the outdoor pool is a Jacuzzi and sauna. To preserve the sophisticated atmosphere, children under 13 are not allowed.

■ Prices
🚹 = ¥ 11,000 - 35,000
🚹🚹 = ¥ 22,000 - 70,000
☕ = ¥ 2,079

Rooms = 30
Restaurants = 1

TEL. 0465-62-0100
FAX. 0465-60-1500
69 Yoshihama, Yugawaramachi, Ashigarashimo-gun

www.lacienega.co.jp

Otowanomori
音羽ノ森

This small hotel with a welcoming family-like atmosphere stands on a hill and all rooms have a view of the ocean. The horizon opens before your eyes and, on clear days, you can see Mt. Fuji. The facilities, decorations and even the appearance of the building have a European feel to them, and guest rooms feature elegant colour tones; we recommend the ones with balconies. The sun deck on the side of the mountain has a Jacuzzi.

■ Prices
single = ¥ 26,800 - 47,200
double = ¥ 29,000 - 60,000
Suite = ¥ 100,000 - 110,000
breakfast = ¥ 2,310

Rooms = 18
Suites = 2
Restaurants = 1

TEL. 046-857-0108
FAX. 046-856-7265
5596-1 Akiya, Yokosuka City

www.otowanomori.jp

Park

Standing beside Route 134, all rooms at this 3-storey resort hotel—most of them twins—offer an ocean view, along with elegantly designed furniture and plenty of amenities. The Japanese-style rooms are best for families; there are also Japanese and Western style banquet halls, and chairs can be provided for the *tatami* rooms. Internet access is available in the lobby. Enjoy the warm hospitality only a small hotel can provide.

■ Prices
single = ¥ 17,850-30,450
double = ¥ 25,200-53,550
Suite = ¥ 56,700-69,300
breakfast = ¥ 2,310

Rooms = 44
Suites = 2
Restaurants = 2

TEL. 0467–25–5121
FAX. 0467-25-3778
33-6 Sakanoshita, Kamakura
www.kamakuraparkhotel.co.jp

Prince Kamakura

Standing on a slope of a small hill, all this hotel's rooms overlook Shichirigahama and, on a clear day, Mt. Fuji can be seen from some of them. The décor is simple and rooms have small verandas. Enjoy breakfast on the 2nd floor, gazing out at the horizon. The chapel is popular for weddings, thanks also to the views, and the pool, from July to mid-September, is free for guests. A shuttle bus runs from Shichirigahama Station.

■ Prices
🚹 = ¥ 32,400-48,600
🚹🚹 = ¥ 32,400-48,600
Suite = ¥ 92,400-115,500
☕ = ¥ 2,200

Rooms = 94
Suites = 1
Restaurants = 2

TEL. 0467–32–1111
FAX. 0467-32-9290
1-2-18 Shichirigahamahigashi, Kamakura

www.princehotels.co.jp/kamakura

Prince Oiso

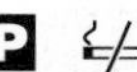  

With a wide range of amenities, from banqueting halls and wedding facilities to a bowling alley, golf course and swimming pools, there is something here for all ages. Guest rooms have a view of either the ocean or the mountains; the standard is Twin Room B, but there are also family rooms. Appropriate for a beachside hotel, the interior is light blue. Wake to the exhilarating scene of the sun rising over the horizon.

■ Prices
🚹 = ¥ 15,000-60,000
🚹🚹 = ¥ 15,000-60,000
Suite = ¥ 81,000-93,000
☕ = ¥ 2,100

Rooms = 474
Suites = 6
Restaurants = 2

TEL. 0463-61-1111
FAX.0463-61-6281
546 Kokufuhongo, Oisomachi,
Naka-gun

www.princehotels.co.jp/oiso

Scapes The Suite

Enjoy the convenience of the city while being on the beach. The concept is "making an escape to beautiful landscapes" and they have created an environment of relaxation without the need to step outside your room – an instant escape into calm. Each room has its own colour scheme, based on the natural colours of Hayama. On the roof is a Jacuzzi that can be reserved and items for hire include mountain bikes and yoga mats.

■ Prices
👥 = ¥ 43,000-67,000
Suite = ¥ 82,000-97,000

Rooms = 3
Suites = 1
Restaurants = 1

TEL. 046-877-5730
FAX.046-877-5731
922-2 Horiuchi, Hayamamachi, Miura-gun

www.scapes.jp

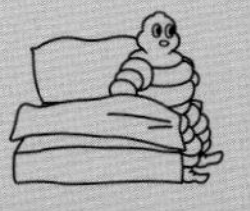

GLOSSARY

Term : Definition

aemono : a salad of cooked vegetables

ainame : greenling

akami : red flesh fish

akaza ebi : Japanese lobster

akazake : a brown-coloured sweet rice wine from Kumamoto

akazu : red vinegar made from sake lees

ajiro : a woven or plaited wicker mat

amamiso : sweet miso

anago : conger eel

A-sai : a Chinese leafy green

awabi : abalone

awa-fu : foxtail millet steamed with wheat starch

awamori : kind of shochu made in Okinawa

ayu : sweetfish

bancha : tea harvested from the second flush of sencha

barachirashi : assorted cubed fish on sushi rice

bincho : high-grade charcoal

bozushi : sushi pressed in a box rather than by hand

chakaiseki : tea ceremony cuisine

chameshi : rice cooked with tea

chanoyu : tea ceremony

chawanmushi : savoury egg custard

chazuke : rice with green tea poured over

chiai : fish flesh that is red with blood

chimaki-zushi : sushi wrapped in bamboo leaves

chirashi-zushi : a bowl of sushi rice with toppings

chirinabe : for fugu hotpot (boiled water with dried kelp where fugu is cooked then eaten with ponzu sauce)

chu-toro : moderately fatty, sweet flesh of tuna

daidai : Asian variety of bitter orange

dashi : soup stock

dashimaki tamago=dashimaki : stock-flavoured thick Japanese omelette roll

dengaku miso : sweet red miso sauce

dou ban jiang : Chinese seasoning made from broad bean chilli paste

ebi-imo : Kyoto yam

ebi-shinjo : shrimp dumplings

edomae : Tokyo-style

enseki ryori : banquet cuisine

eringi : king oyster mushrooms

fugu : puffer fish

fu ru : Chinese fermented tofu

galbi : Korean grilled dish made with marinated beef or pork ribs

goma-dofu : sesame tofu

goritsukudani : sweetened soy glaze

gotenjo : coffered ceiling

gujeolpan : Korean dish of nine different foods arranged on a wooden plate

gyunabe : beef hotpot

haiku : 17-syllable poem

hanasansho : pepper flowers

hamo : pike conger

hamo zukushi : pike conger set meal

harakami : the upper belly of raw tuna

hassun : appetiser plate

hatsu gatsuo : katsuo caught in spring

hegizukuri : thinly sliced sashimi

honesenbei : deep-fried or dried fish bones

hinoki : Japanese cypress

hire : eel's fin

hiryuzu : deep-fried tofu mixed with thinly sliced vegetables

hiyashijiru-gohan : chilled miso soup poured over warm rice

horigotatsu-style : low seating at a covered table placed over a sunken area in the floor

hotate-shinjo : scallop dumplings

ichiyaboshi : fish salted and dried overnight

ikebana : flower arrangement

itamae kappo : traditional cuisine where the chef prepares the fish in front of the customer

itawasa : slices of white fish paste served with horseradish and soy sauce

izakaya : Japanese-style pub

jakomeshi : rice with dried fish-fry

jibuni : traditional Kaga dish featuring duck, bran and vegetables boiled in a broth until thick

junmai-shu : pure rice wine

junsai : watershield

juwari soba : 100% buckwheat noodles

kabayaki : eel broiled and basted with a sweet sauce

kaeshi : ripened soy sauce mixed with sweetened sake and sugar

kaiseki=kaiseki ryori : traditional multi-course Japanese meal

kaki soba : soba with oysters

kamoyaki : grilled duck

kamonasu : a Kyoto variety of eggplant

kanpo : Chinese herbal medicine

kappa : mythical creature that lives in water

kappo : counter style restaurant serving traditional Japanese cuisine

kara-age : soy sauce-marinated fried meat, usually chicken

karasumi : salted and dried grey mullet roe

kasugodai : young Pacific sea bream

katsuo : bonito

katsuo-bushi : dried bonito flakes

kiji-chazuke : chazuke with Japanese pheasant meat

kiku-zukuri : thinly sliced sashimi arranged in the shape of a chrysanthemum

kimono : traditional Japanese clothing

kinmedai : golden-eye snapper

kinome : young pepper leaves

kishu-binchotan : bincho charcoal produced in Wakayama

kobashira : the two round muscles on both sides of the 'tongue' in shellfish

kobujime : fish pressed between two sheets of kelp

koebi : small shrimp

koi-no-arai : carp sashimi served with a vinegar miso sauce

kombu : kelp

konnyaku : solidified jelly made from devil's tongue

koto-negi : a variety of green onion

kudzu : a type of vine

kuroge wagyu : a breed of cattle

kuromitsu : brown sugar syrup

kushikatsu : deep-fried kebab

kuwayaki : meat and vegetables pan-fried in mirin and soy sauce

kuzukiri : kudzu starch noodles

kuzuyose : dessert made from kudzu powder

Kyogen : a form of traditional Japanese theatre

Kyo-ryori : Kyoto cuisine

makiebi : small tiger prawn

manju : steamed yeast bun with filling

Mapo tofu : Sichuan-style bean curd

maruage-dofu : deep-fried tofu

marunuki : whole buckwheat with its outer shell

masu : trout

matcha : powdered green tea

matsubagani : snow crab

matsutake : mushroom

megochi : big-eyed flathead

mirin : a type of sweet sake used in cooking

misansho : pepper made from immature seeds, with a stronger taste

miso : soybean paste

mizore-nabe : hotpot with grated radish

mizudako : North Pacific giant octopus

mizunasu : a juicy eggplant

momiji-oroshi : grated daikon radish and red chilli peppers

mukobone : eel spine

mukozuke : starter dish forming part of the kaiseki

myoga : ginger

nabe ryori : hotpot cuisine

nama-yuba : raw bean curd

name-fu shigureni : wheat gluten and ginger marinated in sweet soy sauce to be eaten with plain rice

nameko : variety of mushroom

nanbanni : sweet and sour sauce

negima : dishes based on spring onions and tuna

nianago : simmered conger eel

nidako : simmered octopus

nigiri : sushi

nigari : bittern

nihamaguri : simmered clams

nikiri : condensed soy sauce

nikogori : jellied fish or meat broth

nitsume : soy syrup

nodoguro : rosy sea perch

Noh : traditional Japanese chanted drama

nuta : salad seasoned with vinegar and miso

oba=shiso : perilla leaf

oboro dofu : very soft tofu served with condiments

oborozuke : dish seasoned with fish flakes

ochazuke-style : cooking style in which green tea is poured over a rice dish

oden : various ingredients stewed in a thin soy soup

ohitashi : boiled greens

ojiya : rice gruel seasoned with miso or soy sauce

okara : bean curd lees

okimari=omakase : set meal

ontama soborodon : rice with hot spring eggs and minced meat

oshizushi : sushi rice and other ingredients pressed in a box or mould

o-toro : the fattier, melt-in-the-mouth flesh of tuna

ponzu : Japanese sauce made primarily of soy sauce and citrus juice

rafute : stewed and glazed pork

ryori : cooking

ryotei : traditional Japanese restaurant

saimaki ebi : young tiger prawns

sakamushi : seafood seasoned with salt and sake then steamed

sakura ebi : stardust shrimps

samgyetang : Korean soup primarily made from chicken and ginseng

samue : monk's working clothes

sansho : pepper

sashimi : sliced raw fish

satsuma age : a fried fish cake

sazae : horned turban shell

sekihan : sticky rice steamed with azuki beans

seiro : basket used for steaming food

setoro : fatty back flesh of tuna

shabu-shabu : sliced meat or vegetable boiled by dipping it in hot kombu broth or water

shamisen : three-stringed Japanese guitar

shiitake : mushroom

shime saba : pickled mackerel

shin-soba : newly harvested buckwheat

shiogamayaki=shioyaki : salt-baked fish or meat

shiraae : salad with mashed tofu dressing

shirako : milt

shirayaki : broiled unseasoned fillet

shiro tora-fugu : white tiger pufferfish

shochu : liquor similar to vodka

Shojin : Buddhist vegetarian (dishes)

shungiku : chrysanthemum garland

shuto : salted and fermented bonito gut

soba : buckwheat noodles

sobayu : hot water in which soba has been boiled

somen : thin, white noodles made from wheat flour

sudachi : citrus fruit

sukiya : tea-ceremony room

sukiyaki : hot pot dish with slices of beef and various vegetables, usually cooked at the table.

sumashijiru : clear soup

surinagashi : pureed soup made from various vegetables

tai : species of reddish-brown Pacific sea bream

tai-meshi : slices of raw sea bream over steaming hot rice

Tai-no matsukawa-zukuri : snapper 'pine bark' sashimi

takiawase : vegetables served with meat, fish or tofu, all simmered separately

takikomi-gohan : a rice dish seasoned with soy sauce and boiled with various ingredients

tamago-yaki : rolled omelette

tatami : straw floor coverings

teishoku : set meal

tempura : fish and vegetables deep-fried in a light batter

tencha : rice in a green tea broth with tempura

tendon : tempura served over a bowl of rice

tentsuyu : tempura dipping sauce

teppanyaki : cuisine prepared on a hot steel plate in the centre of the table

tofu-dengaku : tofu with sweet miso sauce

tonburi : a type of edible seed, sometimes called 'mountain caviar'

tonkatsu : pork cutlet

tora fugu : tiger pufferfish

tsukeyaki : broiling with soy

tsukimidai : a terrace for gazing at the moon

tsukuri : decoratively arranged sashimi

udon : a type of thick wheat-flour noodle

umaki : Japanese style omelette with eel

ume : apricot

unagi : eel

unaju : broiled eel served over rice in a lacquered box

uni : sea urchin

usucha : thin tea

uzaku : eel and vegetables with vinegar sauce

wabi-sabi : a Japanese concept of finding beauty in the transient

wagyu : breed of Japanese cattle

warabimochi : bracken-starch dumpling

waridashi : seasoned stock

warishita : stock mixed with soy sauce, mirin and sugar

wasabi : Japanese horseradish

wasabi-yaki : chicken skewer with wasabi on top

watari-gani : blue crab

yakiniku : grilled meat, originating from Korean barbecue

yakitori : chicken pieces grilled on a skewer

yakuzen : (Chinese) medicinal food

yuba : bean curd skin

yuzu : citrus fruit

zuke-maguro : soy marinated tuna

zarudofu-zaru tofu : tofu on a bamboo basket with dipping sauce on the side

zenmai : Japanese royal fern

zosui : risotto-like rice soup made from pre-cooked rice and water

PICTURE COPYRIGHT

74-Michelin, 75-Aimée Vibert, 76,77-Michelin, 78-Akasaka Tan-tei, 79-Akimoto, 80-Michelin, 81-Ànu Retrouvez-vous, 82-Aragawa, Michelin, 83-Michelin, 84-Argento Aso, Michelin, 85,86,87,88,89,90-Michelin, 91-Basara, Michelin, 92,93-Michelin, 94-Bon Chemin, Michelin, 95-Bulgari Il Ristorante, 96,97-Michelin, 98-China Blue, Michelin, 99-Michelin, 100-Chugoku Hanten Fureika, Michelin, 102-Michelin, 103-Cuisine[s] Michel Troisgros, 104,105,106,107-Michelin, 108-Édition Koji Shimomura, Michelin, 109,110-Michelin, 111-Émun, Michelin, 112,113-Michelin, 114-Faro, 115-Feu, Michelin, 116-Florilège, Michelin, 117,118,119,120-Michelin, 121-Ginza Okuda, Michelin, 122-Michelin, 123-Gordon Ramsay, 124-Gorio, 125-Grill Ukai, 126-Hamadaya, Michelin, 127-Michelin, 128-Hashimoto, Michelin, 129,130-Michelin, 131-Hifumian, 132-Michelin, 133-Hiramatsu, 134,135,136,137,138,139,140-Michelin, 141-Ibuki, Michelin, 142,143,144,145,146-Michelin, 147-Ikku, 148,150,151,152-Michelin, 153-Izumi, 154-Michelin, 155-Joël Robuchon, 156,157-Michelin, 158-Kagura, Michelin, 159-Kamiya Nogizaka, 160,161,162,163,164,165-Michelin, 167-KM, Michelin, 168,169,170,171,172,173,174,175,176,177,178-Michelin, 179-L'Asse, Michelin, 180-La Table de Joël Robuchon, 181-L'Atelier de Joël Robuchon, 182-Michelin, 183-La Tour d'Argent, 184,185,186,187-Michelin, 188-L'Effervescence, 189-Le Jeu de l'Assiette, Michelin, 190-Michelin, 191-L'Embellir, Michelin, 192-Les Créations de Narisawa, 193-Les Enfants Gâtés, Michelin, 194-Les Rosiers Eguzkilore, Michelin, 195-Les Saisons, 196-Lugdunum Bouchon Lyonnais, 197-Maison Paul Bocuse, 198-Michelin, 199-Masa's Kitchen 47,200,201,203,204,205-Michelin, 206-Monnalisa Ebisu, Michelin, 207-Monnalisa Marunouchi, 208-Moranbong, Michelin, 210-Michelin, 211-Muto, 213-Nadaman Honten Sazanka-so, 214-Nagazumi, 215-Nakajima, Michelin, 216-Nico, 217-Nigyo, Michelin, 218-Nodaiwa, 220-Ogasawara Hakushaku-tei, 221,222,223,225-Michelin, 226-Pachon, 227-Michelin, 228-Pierre Gagnaire, 229,230-Michelin, 231-Ranjatai, Michelin, 232-Reikasai, 233-Michelin, 234-Restaurant- I, Michelin, 235-Révérence, Michelin, 236-Ristorante Aso, 237,238,239,240-Michelin, 241-Ryugin, Michelin, 242-Ryuzu, Michelin, 243,244-Michelin, 245-Sangoan, Michelin, 246-Michelin, 247-Sant Pau, 248,249-Michelin, 250-Seiju, Michelin, 251-Seika Kobayashi, Michelin, 252,253,254-Michelin, 255-Sennohana, 256-Sense, 257-Michelin, 258-Shigeyoshi, Michelin, 260-Shofukuro, 261-Michelin, 262-Signature, 263-Michelin, 264-Sukiyabashi Jiro Honten, Michelin,

265-Sukiyabashi Jiro Roppongi, Michelin, 266,267-Michelin, 268-Sushiichi, Michelin, 269,270,271,272,273,274,275,276,277-Michelin, 278-Sushi Yoshitake, Michelin, 279-Suzuki, Michelin, 280-Suzunari, 281,282,283-Michelin, 285-Tateru Yoshino Ginza, Michelin, 286-Tateru Yoshino Shiba, Michelin, 287-Tateru Yoshino Shiodome, 288-Tatsumura, Michelin, 289-Tenmo, 290,291-Michelin, 292-Toriki, Michelin, 293,294,295,296-Michelin, 297-Tsukiji Yamamoto, Michelin, 298-Uchitsu, 299,300-Michelin, 301-Ukai-tei Ginza, 302-Ukai-tei Omotesando, 303,304,305,306,307,308,309,310,311-Michelin, 312-Yonemura, Michelin, 313,314,315,316-Michelin, 318-Yotaro, Michelin, 319-Michelin, 320-Zurriola, Michelin, 326-ANA Intercontinental, 327-Century Southern Tower, 328-Cerulean Tower Tokyu, 329-Michelin, 330-Conrad, Michelin, 331-Four Seasons Chinzan-so, 332-Four Seasons Marunouchi, 333-Gracery Tamachi, 334-Grand Hyatt, 335-Grand Pacific Le Daiba, 336-Hilton, 337-Hyatt Regency, 338-Imperial, 339-Intercontinental Tokyo Bay, 340-Keio Plaza, 341-Mandarin Oriental, 342-Marunouchi, 343-Meguro Gajoen, 344-Metropolitan Marunouchi, 345-Mitsui Garden Ginza, 346-New Otani, 347-Nikko, 348-Niwa, 349-Okura, 350-Park , 351-Park Hyatt, 352-Royal Park, 353-Royal Park Shiodome Tower, 354-Ryumeikan, 355-Seiyo Ginza, 356-Shangri-La, Michelin, 357-Sheraton Miyako, 358-The Agnes, 359-The Capitol Tokyu, 360-The Peninsula, 361-The Prince Park Tower , 362-The Ritz-Carlton, 363-The Strings by Intercontinental, 364-Villa Fontaine Shiodome, 365-Westin , 376,377,378,379,380, 381,382-Michelin, 383-Masagosaryo, Michelin, 384-Mizuki, Michelin, 385,386,387,388,389,390-Michelin, 391-Tenshichi, Michelin, 392-Ukai-tei Azamino, 396-Grand Intercontinental, 397-New Grand, 398-Pan Pacific Yokohama Bay Tokyu, 399-Richmond, 400-Rose, 352-Royal Park, 402-Sheraton Yokohama Bay , 418-Bonzo, Michelin, 419-En, Michelin, 421-Hachinoki Kitakamakura, 422-Michelin, 423-Herlequin Bis, Michelin, 424,425-Michelin, 426-Kamakurayama, Michelin, 427,428,429,430-Michelin, 431-Pleins d'Herbes, Michelin, 432,433,434,435,436,437,438-Michelin, 440-Tomoei, 441-Michelin, 442-Ukyo, Michelin, 443,444,445-Michelin, 448-Chigasakikan, 449-Fukazawa, 450-Fukiya, 451-Homura, 452-Kaihin-so, 453-Kamata, 454-Sansuiro, 455-Sekiyo, 456-Tsubaki, 457-Yui, 460-Hilton Resort& Spa, 461-La Cienega, 462-Otowanomori, 463-Park, 464-Prince Kamakura, 465-Prince Oiso, 466-Scapes The Suite, Michelin

Manufacture française des pneumatiques Michelin
Société en commandite par actions au capital de 504 000 004 EUR
Place des Carmes-Déchaux – 63000 Clermont-Ferrand (France)
R.C.S. Clermont-Fd B 855 200 507

Dépot légal Octobre 2011

Made in Japan

Published in 2011

E-mail: nmt.michelinguide@jp.michelin.com
Scan-and-read mobile barcodes : Navitime Japan Co., Ltd
Valid until 31st December 2012
Only applicable with certain phones

Publication design: Kan Akita & Akita Design Kan Inc. Tokyo, (Japan)
Printing and Binding: Toppan, Tokyo (Japan)